What a Coach Can Teach a Teacher

Studies in the
Postmodern Theory of Education

Shirley Steinberg
General Editor

Vol. 293

PETER LANG
New York • Washington, D.C./Baltimore • Bern
Frankfurt • Berlin • Brussels • Vienna • Oxford

JEFFREY M.R. DUNCAN-ANDRADE

What a Coach Can Teach a Teacher

Lessons Urban Schools Can Learn from a Successful Sports Program

PETER LANG
New York • Washington, D.C./Baltimore • Bern
Frankfurt • Berlin • Brussels • Vienna • Oxford

Library of Congress Cataloging-in-Publication Data

Duncan-Andrade, Jeffrey M. R.
What a coach can teach a teacher: lessons urban schools can learn from
a successful sports program / Jeffrey M.R. Duncan-Andrade.
p. cm. — (Counterpoints: vol. 293)
Includes bibliographical references and index.
1. Education, Urban—United States. 2. Critical pedagogy—United States.
3. Urban youth—United States. 4. Sports—Study and teaching—
United States. 5. Coaching (Athletics)—Philosophy. I. Title.
LC5131.D86   371.009173'2—dc22   2009011347
ISBN 978-0-8204-7905-7
ISSN 1058-1634

Bibliographic information published by **Die Deutsche Nationalbibliothek**.
Die Deutsche Nationalbibliothek lists this publication in the "Deutsche
Nationalbibliografie"; detailed bibliographic data is available
on the Internet at http://dnb.d-nb.de/.

Mixed Sources
Product group from well-managed
forests, controlled sources and
recycled wood or fiber
www.fsc.org   Cert no. SCS-COC-002464
©1996 Forest Stewardship Council

Cover art by Refa One

© 2010 Peter Lang Publishing, Inc., New York
29 Broadway, 18th floor, New York, NY 10006
www.peterlang.com

Printed in the United States of America

To Vien (BBB) & Mom and Dad.

To the Lady Wildcats.

To my students here and gone.

You have all shaped my life more than you can know.

I am humbled and grateful.

-JDA

TABLE of CONTENTS

CHAPTER ONE

MISSING THE MARK IN URBAN SCHOOLS

INTRODUCTION

Little research has been done by urban educators to document effective practices in urban schools. This book hopes to work on reducing that gap in the literature on improving urban schools by providing insight into effective program building and educational practices. The position put forth in this book is that across the country, there are numerous urban educators that are consistently successful in schools where mediocrity (and often times failure) are the norm. It perplexes me that the educational reseach community has not put forth a more committed effort to systematically identify these educators and commit to a national reseach agenda that positions them as a guiding force in the field. These educators often work in isolation of one another and their expertise is rarely tapped, even at the local level. This is a massive strategic error on the part of the educational research community. These are people with answers to questions that most educational researchers just theorize about. I can hardly imagine any other applied research field that knew its most perplexing questions were being answered every day, in real time practice, and yet made such a marginal commitment to researching that practice.

In my previous work (Duncan-Andrade & Morrell, 2008), my colleagues and I have made it clear that we do not believe this happens by accident. So, I will not engage here in a larger discussion about why this is happening in our field. Instead, this book presents one possible corrective direction for educational research. I am not a believer in panaceas, but I do believe that our field can, and must, do better for the children it continues to fail to serve. With this goal on my mind, this text stands as an argument for, and commitment to, the extension of urban teacher research that focuses on function, rather than disfunction.

This book presents my first effort at reseaching my own practice, so it leaves bare methodological flaws that a research community, with its own set of flaws (see Tuhiwai-Smith, 1999), will rightly identify. We should welcome these critiques of teacher research from our colleagues. Our ability to respond to them is important if practioner-research is to take its rightful place as an influential voice in our field.

The goal of my work presented here, and elsewhere, has not been to advocate for a singular approach to educational research, or to push us toward a model of absolute empiricism. I have been teaching in urban schools for far too long to believe in that approach to educational research. What my experience as an urban educator and athletic coach has taught me is that educational research can do a better job of offering us insight into frameworks of effective practices. These insights will always be unique to the practitioner and the context, and this is the limitation *and* the strength of teacher driven research. It is a limitation because we cannot simply take the conclusions of the research and map them onto another classroom and expect that we will get similar results. Rather, our field must become more sophisticated at taking these insights from the field and helping other educators make sense of them in their contexts. However, it has been my experience, that educators are most interested in hearing from other educators whose research is about what works, why it works, and *how* it works. When research is done by practitioners themselves, what is lost in objectivity, is made up for in a depth of understanding about the details of effectiveness in our field—and, in teaching, the devil is always in the details.

URBAN EDUCATION—SHOULDN'T WE CONSIDER THIS A NATIONAL CRISIS?

As an urban educator for the last eighteen years, I have witnessed countless students highly committed to and invested in their personal interests outside the classroom (labeled here as *youth popular culture*[1]). Many of these students do not make the same commitments and investments in school. Instead, they frequently find themselves disenfranchised from the institutional and cultural norms of school. The more they find their social and cultural realities misaligned with the dominant culture of the school, the more likely they are to drop out—literally or figuratively. We all know that this result is most prominent among the country's most economically impoverished youth, particularly urban youth of color, even though they may be the group that can least afford to struggle in school.

The impact of academic and social disenfranchisement on students of color has led researchers like Conquergood (1992) to point out the ensuing trap that is laid for urban youth by the definitions of urban life that are embraced by the political, legal, and social power structures.

> Urban youth [particularly black and Chicano youth] are always already inscribed by stigmatizing images of gangs and the so-called inner city that produces this social pathology. Before they tattoo their bodies with gang insignia, they are branded by the official discourse of the media, legal system, social welfare, and public policy institutions as dangerous Others, the menace from the margins. Gangs are constructed in public discourse as the cause, effect, and aberrant response to urban decay and disintegration (4).

Given this social positioning of many urban youth into the margins of society, and consequently the outskirts of academia, their skepticism toward the institution of schooling and its connectedness to upward mobility are understandable. In contrast to the notions of some educational theorists (Ogbu and Davis, 2003; Payne, 2005; Thernstrom, 2004) their lack of success seems to hold more of a causal relationship to low societal expectations and limited socioeconomic and sociopolitical opportunity than to a lack of personal motivation or willingness to assimilate. What we find on the surface of the work of these theorists and mainstream political rhetoric, such as "No Child Left Behind," is the promise that schooling offers urban and poor youth a pathway to rewrite society's negative imagery. On the underbelly of this meritocratic rhetoric lies the cold reality that schools have historically kept youth of color "in their place." The central role that schools play in the process of social reproduction is well documented (Kozol, 1991; MacLeod, 1987; Valenzuela, 1999). The structural inequities between public schools serving poor youth and wealthy youth is not debated. Everyone knows they exist, and everyone knows that they lead to disparate outcomes.

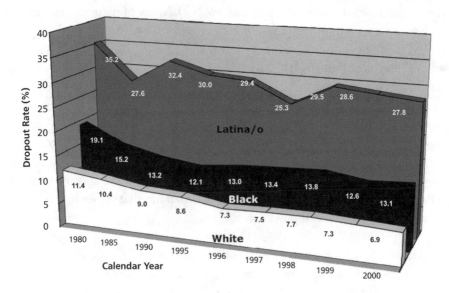

Fig 1.1 Dropout Rates of 16-24 year olds, 1980-2000

Since the 1980s there has been a declared national commitment to improve the quality of education received by urban students. In spite of these nearly thirty years of attempts at reform, the numbers of black and Chicana/o students finding success in U.S. schools has changed very little (Darling-Hammond, 1998b; Pearl, 1995). Dropout rates for black students (13.1%) are nearly double that of white students (6.9%) and Latin@ students (27.8%) have a dropout rate nearly four times that of white students (U. S. Bureau of the Census, 2001).

The conditions facing urban schools do not get much worse than those in California. At the turn of the 21st century, one report stated California's gross domestic product (GDP) would make it the 5th wealthiest country in the world if it were its own nation-state (Sacramento Business Journals Inc, 2001). Yet, *Education Week*'s annual report on schools has California ranked just 43rd nationally in K-12 equitable per pupil spending (Education Week, 2006). Two years later, *Education Week*'s 2008 "Quality Counts" report gave California an overall grade of "F" (51.4) on K-12 education spending (Education Week, 2008). At the same time that the state's school children attend inadequately resourced educational institutions, the California prison industry is the nation's largest, it remains the largest growth industry in the state, and it is often the only state budget item to receive funding increases. To wit, the average annual state expenditure for a California K-12 student is $7,081 (Education Week, 2008) while the average cost of housing one inmate in the California Department of Corrections (CDC) exceeds $35,587 (California Department of Corrections, 2008). These dubious investment policies happen at a time when Federal education policy has raised the requirements, costs and obstacles to becoming a teacher. By comparison, California prison guards need a minimum of a high school equivalency diploma and have the cost of their training covered by the state. Equally as troubling is the fact that the state's average prison guard salary is $45,288 (California Department of Corrections, 2007) while the average starting teacher's salary is only $35,760 (American Federation of Teachers, 2007).

Like the rest of the nation, California's lack of investment in education is felt in schools statewide. Many wealthier communities have responded by passing bond measures and making significant private investments in their schools. For low-income urban schools these "options" are virtually unavailable. These schools are also the ones most likely to exclusively serve poor and non-white children. While the California Department of Corrections does not disaggregate its data by income bracket, it is not difficult to connect the dots between racially and economically isolated black and Mexican/Latin/South American communities, dysfunctional urban schools, high dropout rates and the over-representation of blacks and Latinas/os in the CDC (see Wald & Losen, 2003).

If there is any doubt about which communities are most gravely impacted by an inadequate school system, one need only look at the achievement data from California's urban districts. Take, for example, UC Accord's "Indicators Project" which tracked public high school achievement data across the state over four-year periods as an indicator of the opportunity to learn given to students across the state. The following data for black and Mexican/Latin/South American students

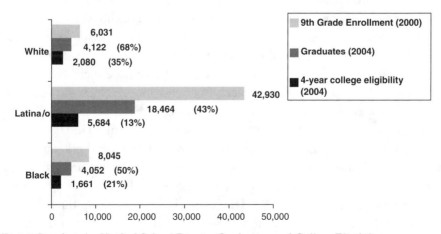

Fig1.2 Los Angeles Unified School District Graduation and College Eligibility

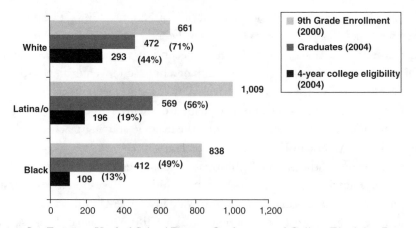

Fig 1.3 San Francisco Unified School District Graduation and College Eligibility Rates

in the state's two best-known cities (Los Angeles and San Francisco) is a trend that has held for decades in almost every urban center in the state.

The charts above track the total number of freshmen that entered these two districts in the year 2000. Over the next four years, these two districts lost over 50% of their black and Latin@ students, and less than a 1/5th of them were even eligible to apply for admission to a four-year college or university.

There are many ways to interpret the persistence of educational statistics like these, and the reforms that have failed to improve them. One is to presume that the problem is so complex that educational theorists have been unable to crack it, despite ever increasing government attention to the problem. Another possible conclusion is that the reform policies necessary to significantly impact these trends of failure for urban youth are so drastic that their implementation lacks the political support necessary for them to take effect. Possibly a combination of these two conclusions is the most likely. Who knows? What we do know is that the urban education ship is sinking, and students and communities are placing less and less faith in the promise of schooling as the ultimate social equalizer.

The detrimental effects of these bleak urban educational achievement patterns are obvious when comparing the national data for college degrees to prison inmate populations—the Dow Jones of institutional success and failure in U.S. society. The graph below reveals a growing trend equivalent to a social crisis for black and Mexican/Latin/South American students, both of whom are alarmingly over-represented in prisons and under-represented in colleges and universities.

Although there is no national data set available for tracking the trajectory of students from urban schools, it does not take a rocket scientist to figure out the trends. Virtually every low-performing urban school in the country has a

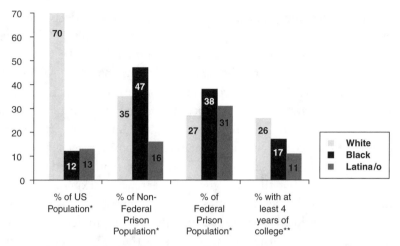

Fig 1.4 2000 Prison and College Participation Rates

student body that is predominantly black and/or Mexican/Latin/South American. Optimists might believe that the school achievement gap and disproportionate incarceration rates are being reduced, but the numbers suggest otherwise. Over the last 20 years incarceration percentages have increased for black Americans (+1%), giving them a rate four times their presence in the nation's population. The incarceration rate for Mexicans and Latin/South Americans (+9%) has more than doubled. The gap in incarceration rates between black/brown and white inmates has grown even wider due to the fact that there has been a 10% decrease in the number of white inmates. And, researchers have begun making direct links between these incarceration trends and educational attainment (Lochner & Moretti, 2004; NAACP, 2007).

In this same time span, the gap in college attendance has widened by 5% between white students and people of Mexican/Latin/South American descent. The one decrease in the college attendance gap in the last 20 years of "reform" has been a 1% closure between whites and blacks. At this rate of "closure" it will be another 200 years before black students attend college at the same rate as white students, and Mexican/Latin/South Americans will never attend college on pace with either group.

TOWARD EFFECTIVE URBAN EDUCATION

This social and educational marginalization of poor and working class students is substantiated in countless studies into the various aspects of schooling. This research has linked the problems facing urban schools to deeper structural problems like under-qualified teachers (Akom, 2003; Delpit, 1995; Oakes & Lipton, 2001), teacher shortages (Darling-Hammond, 1998a; Kozol, 1991; Oakes & Lipton, 2001), and funding inequalities (Anyon, 1997; Kozol, 2005). Such studies have laid important groundwork for the documentation of inequities in our education system. As academic achievement in urban schools remains intolerably low, the need to highlight, examine, and understand effective practices and strategies becomes more urgent. These examinations of success challenge the rhetoric of failing schools and districts that claim to be doing the best that they can with what they are given. Research that exposes the level of inequity (educational, social, political, and economic) in this country and throughout the world must continue and should be ramped up. However, exposés of suffering can lead to hopelessness if they ignore the examples of successful individual and collective action that resist and change such conditions. So, while we continue to expose the "savage inequalities" in urban schools and communities, we must also look at existing effective pedagogies so that we can understand what works, why it works, and help others to be similarly successful.

The field of urban education lacks sufficient studies of pedagogy that increases engagement, achievement, and student transformative agency (see Solorzano & Delgado-Bernal (2001) and Hidalgo & Duncan-Andrade (2009) for discussions of transformational student resistance). This book begins to fill that gap by drawing on social theory of youth popular culture and critical pedagogical theory as tools for developing more effective educational practices with urban youth. This book has three ultimate goals: (1) to provide K-12 educators, teacher educators, school leaders, and youth service providers examples of success when critical pedagogy is blended with youth culture; (2) to provide the educational research community a study of the application of these two rich theoretical frameworks (critical pedagogy and social theory) in the hope that evidence for the effectiveness of this approach will mount; and (3) to tell a counter-narrative about what is possible within urban schools and communities, even given the massive structural inequalities.

This book is a story about what can and should be happening in urban schools. It provides a counter-narrative to the normalized urban school failure by documenting and examining a process that produced success in a school and community where success is too infrequent. This book suggests that we can dramatically increase the number of urban youth that find themselves connected to their school, socially empowered, and academically successful, and it provides practice-based tools for achieving that outcome.

BOOK OUTLINE

The book is broken into two sections. Section One provides examples of the ways in which I have used social and cultural theory to deepen my understanding of how to shape my pedagogy to make it critical (Duncan-Andrade & Morrell, 2008) and culturally relevant (Ladson-Billings, 1994). I debated on whether I should include this section in the book. Social theory can bog down practitioners, especially when our sole preoccupation is with practice. At the risk of this possibility, I chose to include it anyway. I want the educators, and aspiring educators, that read this book to understand the level of theorizing that goes on in my head during my planning and my reflections on teaching. In previous work (Duncan-Andrade & Morrell, 2008) I have explained the process through which I use theory reflexively in greater detail. The short of it is that my approach to planning pedagogy follows a cycle that has five basic steps: 1) identify a problem/need area in my pedagogy, 2) study theory and research that speaks to that problem/need area, 3) develop pedagogical practices grounded in theory, 4) study my practical application of theory, and 5) revise the theory based on my practice.

For the first five years of my career, I rarely intellectualized my work in this way. However, my mid-career return to graduate school taught me one of the most valuable pedagogical lessons I have learned—the value of theorizing and intellectualizing our work as educators. I recognize that many of you reading this book will not return to graduate school to have this experience with theory nor do I think that is necessary. Teachers can self-create conditions similar to those that facilitate this process in graduate school (access to theory and an intellectual community). Some of you might get access to theory through the growing interest in critical inquiry groups, or critical friends/peer groups, in school professional development (see Duncan-Andrade (2004, 2007) for examples of how we have used inquiry groups to facilitate theory-practice with urban teachers in Los Angeles).

Section Two turns to a discussion of the pedagogical approach that developed from integrating the social theoretical framework in Section One with core principles of critical pedagogy taken from my high school English classroom (see Duncan-Andrade & Morrell, 2008 for more discussion on critical pedagogy and my classroom teaching). The first chapter in section two introduces the city, district and school where I did the work. The remainder of this section of the book discusses how the principles of critical pedagogy were applied in a high school girls' basketball program, which will be referred to as the Lady Wildcat Basketball Program (LWBP). What are reported are reflections on a study of one of the most academically and athletically successful sports program in Townville[2] during that period. The chapters are broken up into four distinctive time periods (seasons) during a 12-month cycle. The structures and principles used during each of these seasons are discussed in the context of three elements of critical pedagogy (organic intellectualism, criticla praxis, and counter-hegemony). The relevance of the structures and principles used in the LWBP for the classroom will be immediately obvious in many cases. To crystalize this relationship, each chapter ends with a section called "What a Coach Can Teach a Teacher," where explicit connections are made to the practices that lead urban classrooms and school programs to consistent academic and social success.

Section 1: Theory-Social theory, sports, and youth popular culture

Chapter 2 opens the theoretical section of the book with a heavy dose of social theory to provide a detailed analysis of sports as an element of popular culture. The chapter uses three sociological frameworks (functionalist theory, conflict theory, and critical theory) to explore the multiple interpretations of the influence of sports over popular culture in contemporary society.

Chapter 3 expands the discussion of the societal significance of sports by exploring its impact on youth culture. The chapter draws heavily from the framework of critical theory to discuss the notable impact sport has on youth culture.

Chapter 4 brings the theoretical section to a close, developing an argument for the use of youth popular culture as a strategy for improving academic achievement in urban schools. This argument begins with a critique of the multicultural education movement as having missed the mark because of overly simplified notions of culture. This part of the argument is particularly poignant in that it challenges traditional notions of culture being linked primarily to race, ultimately calling for a more dynamic definition of culture. While lauding the value of a multi-racial perspective in the curriculum for moving us beyond deficit theories, this critique calls for educators to pursue a deeper understanding of the multiple representations of culture in the lives of young people.

Section 2: Moving from theory to practice

Chapter 5 provides a detailed description of Townville High School, the Townville School District and the surrounding community. Using achievement data, the school and district are compared to other schools and districts around the state. Included are insights into pertinent school demographics, Academic Performance Index (API) rating, college admission rate, and description of the physical conditions at the school. The setting also includes some sociopolitical analysis of the city of Townville to help explain apparent discord between the demographics of the neighborhood and the school. The chapter concludes with brief profiles of the four focal students (Ada, Mika, Nancy and Erika) on which the remaining chapters place their focus.

The rest of the chapters in section two focus heavily on the program's impact on those four students. This discussion begins in Chapter 6 by giving a general overview of the program by discussing the program's use of the three tenets of critical pedagogy (organic intellectualism, critical praxis, and counter-hegemony) in three programmatic areas (academic support and advising, athletic development, and critical social/psychological development).

Chapter 7 discusses the summer season, covering the months of June, July and August. It begins with a discussion of the impact of the summer travel component on participants. The chapter discusses the use of summer time as a way to intensify notions of community consciousness among participants. The dialogues and activities used to build this into the program culture are discussed and analyzed. The chapter also reports on the importance of on-going academic development as a central component of the summer activities. This development included specialized assignments and counseling for students going into their senior year to prepare them for the college application process. Chapter 7 concludes with a discussion of individual meetings that took place with students regarding their desired role in the program for the upcoming year, the expectation of the coaches, and pre-semester academic counseling.

Chapter 8 covers the brief, but very important, first six weeks of school. This period was critical to getting students off on the right foot, and for setting expectations for all elements of the program for the remainder of the school year. This chapter tracks two activities, on-going athletic development and immediate academic support. Specifically, this chapter discusses the value added by having students engaged in a comprehensive program from the first day of school, rather than waiting for the traditional basketball season to begin in the winter. The importance of engaging students in rigorous and meaningful activity from the very first day of school is explained as a vital element for getting students to commit to the program's intensive tutorial component. This early academic intervention proved to be particularly helpful in setting a positive tone for the school year and for acclimating newcomers to the social, athletic and academic expectations of participation in the program.

Chapter 9 covers the most intense period of the program. It begins with a discussion of the ways that students came to understand and define what it meant to belong to a team. The chapter explains the use of individual goal setting sessions. In these sessions, participants established athletic, personal and academic goals for themselves and for the team. These goals became the student's roadmap that would be reviewed and, if necessary, revised during the season and throughout the remainder of the school year. This chapter also discusses the variety of methods used to expose students to the intellectual nature of sports. These methods included consistent exposure to philosophical texts (*Tao Te Ching, Hagakure, The Art of War*) and regular discussions of the similarities between successful academic performance and academic excellence. The chapter goes on to reveal how this approach provided solid grounding for the program's emphasis on academics over athletics. Finally, this chapter discusses the value of these multi-layers in developing a counter-culture to the failure that was so rampant at Townville High School.

Chapter 10 highlights the Spring, the period immediately following the end of the basketball season where emotional and physical let downs were serious concerns. The chapter emphasizes that educators committed to a comprehensive, year-round model of social and academic support, will find it critically important to help students finish the school year with the same intensity and support that they had at the outset. The program's emphasis in this period transitioned from broader team goals to more individualized goals, particularly in the students' development as athletes and community members. Special attention was paid to the development of mentorship skills through student-led community based "mini-camps."

Chapter 11 provides a final message to educators, one that synthesizes key elements of the LWBP in the language of pedagogy. The chapter also considers ways the program could have increased its effectiveness with students and parents, and discusses implications of the program for educators, administrators, and policy makers. The chapter concludes with updates on each of the students that are mentioned in the book.

NOTES

1   The definition of youth popular culture that will be used in this chapter is meant as a reference to the popular cultural activities in which youth engage themselves heavily. Examples of these cultural activities are sports, music, film, media (television, videos, popular magazines), style, dress, and language.

2   Townville is a pseudonym for a major city in Northern California where this study took place.

Section One:
Theory-Social Theory, Sports, and Youth Popular Culture

CRITIQUING CRITICS OF SPORT IN SOCIETY: TOWARD A CRITICAL THEORY OF SPORT AND PEDAGOGY IN URBAN SCHOOLS

"…sports is an element of American life so pervasive that virtually no individual is untouched by it …[The] United States is a nation made up of sports fans … [and] sports participants." (Report on American Attitudes Toward Sports, 1984)

From mainstream films like *We Are Marshall*, *Any Given Sunday*, *Remember the Titans*, and *The Hurricane* to overwhelming coverage by mass media outlets, sport has a unique place in U.S. society. The only cultural activity to have an entire section dedicated to it in every major newspaper and on major television network newscasts, sport occupies an influential space in the cultural landscape. Coakley (1990) notes that sport has become such a pervasive part of our society that "in most major North American papers there is more coverage given to sports than any other single topic of interest, including business or politics. The sports section is the most widely read section of the paper, and according to some reasonable estimates it accounts for about 30% of the total circulation for any big city newspaper" (282).

So what is the role of this widespread cultural phenomenon in the larger society? Coakley (1990) points out that there are effectively three schools of thought regarding sport and its place in the U.S. social fabric: functionalist theory, conflict theory and critical theory. Functionalists argue that sport is a valuable social institution benefiting society as well as individual members of society (Luschen, 1967; Kleiber, 1980; Elias, 1986; Zhan, 1999). They believe that sport, in its essence, is a source of inspiration on both personal and social levels. Conflict theorists (Entine, 2000; Edwards, 1973; Edwards, 1983a; Edwards, 1983b; Wiggins, 1994; Hoberman, 1997; Shulman, 2001) perceive sport to be a cultural form distorted by capitalism. Using a Marxist style critique, conflict theorists argue that sport is the opiate of the masses, used to reproduce social and economic inequalities. Critical theorists (Boyd, 1997; Edwards, 1994; Eitzen, 1999; George, 1998; Mahiri, 1994; Mahiri, 1998) interpret sport in ways similar to conflict theorists and often make analyses that overlap with arguments made in conflict theory. However, what separates critical theorists is their belief that sport can influence society in one of two ways; it can be used to alter the status quo or it can reproduce it. This makes critical theory the most promising theoretical approach to understanding the potential of sport to be used in urban schools as a tool to combat forms of inequity.

FUNCTIONALISM: REPRODUCTION IS GOOD PRODUCTION

A structural-functional analysis of sport is most often used to discuss how sport as a social institution helps to satisfy the needs of society. Functionalists believe that there are four key elements to the effectiveness of any social system: 1) the management of social tensions through pattern maintenance, 2) consistent social integration, 3) goal attainment, and 4) social adaptation (Morrow & Torres, 1995).

Pattern maintenance

Pattern maintenance is achieved through a series of systematic methods where people in a given society are taught the rules through social institutions (i.e. families, schools, churches) (Parsons, 1951). This means teaching people what they have to do and how they have to do it. This also means teaching these same people to abide by a set of rules that may sometimes, even frequently, be in direct conflict with their personal interests.

Institutions like sport play a dual role in this process of socialization. At one level, sport helps to teach the values of following the rules, competing for the benefit of the team, respect for authority, and countless other social values. At the same time, sport acts as an outlet for frustrations that emerge as a result of these rules in the larger society. The fact that conflict can result from having to sacrifice self-interest to abide by the rules, sport can become a release for this tension. The physical nature of sport acts as an outlet for pent social frustrations, even though the structures of sport are often simply reinforcing the very rules that have caused the frustration in the first place—ironic, but still effective. Other institutions, such as religion and education, fill similar socially reproductive roles for members of society (see Bourdieu, 1973; Bowles & Gintis, 1976; Gramsci, 1971; MacLeod, 1999).

Social integration

To maintain social order, a system must provide a variety of social apparatuses to bring people into situations where they can establish social networks. These networks are essential to the individual's commitment to the larger goals of the social order and are assisted, again, by institutions such as religion, education and sport. Sporting events provide an opportunity for large social gatherings to take place, and cohesive social networks often develop out of shared sporting interests. This can happen on multiple levels. On an international level, events such as the soccer World Cup and the Olympics can generate large-scale social cohesion through international athletic pride emerging out of the promise of a World Championship or a gold medal.

Goal attainment

The concept of goal attainment is an essential part of functionalist theory. This entails creating institutions that teach people what they can expect to achieve and how they can expect to achieve it. Teams and individual athletes set goals of winning championships. The winning and losing that takes place in pursuit of these goals acts to instruct society on the proper process of goal attainment. To lose a contest and still claim oneself as a champion means nothing in the world of sport because the appropriate process has not been followed. In the institution of sport, the "real" victor emerges through the process of following the rules and competing fairly to achieve victory. This process of defining the winner and the loser through a set of closely defined rules and conducts is used to maintain the "equilibrium" of a society (Morrow 1995: 44). Sport acts as a key institution for establishing acceptable goals and normalizing a set of rules to attain those goals.

Social adaptation

Finally, functionalists argue that social systems must prepare for what Durkheim (1933) calls "the case of change or perish" (272). Durkheim believed that all societies would need to change to survive and that these changes would come in one of two forms of social solidarity: "mechanical" and "organic." He believed that more advanced societies would move toward organic social solidarity, based largely upon equitable divisions of labor and the concern for individual dignity and social justice (Lukes, 1973). However, what has actually manifested in most modern societies are forms of Durkheim's mechanical social system, which is rooted in inequitable distribution of labor, repressive legal structures, and the prevalence of penal law to forcibly maintain social order.

Amidst his theorizing, Durkheim was practical enough to realize that because social environments are inherently complex, and complex things are inherently unstable, then social environments could prove to be unstable. However, he hoped that as societies advanced they would place equality of opportunity at a premium, combating the effects of *anomie*. He believed this would happen when societies committed to social norms of collectivism as a means of redressing inequalities. Aided by an allowance for human interests and open discussion, Durkheim's organic solidarity system would be flexible and prepared to handle "changes in the external social and physical environments...without disrupting the consensus and solidarity on which the social order depends" (Coakley, 1990: 22).

As most modern social systems cling to the principles of mechanical solidarity and continue to be marred by anomie, institutions such as sport play a vital role in normalizing social inequality. By teaching the concept of overcoming adversity as a social value, functionalists argue that sport helps society to accept setbacks as a normal part of life (Boyd, 1997; Coakley, 1990; Edwards, 1973). Rather than creating a sense of panic when things don't go as expected, sports teach us that someone must lose and that it is important to accept losing gracefully. Sport also offers the hope that yesterday's loser can become tomorrow's victorious underdog through the principles of industriousness and humility.

CONFLICT THEORY: CAPITALISM, COMMERCIALISM AND COERCION

Conflict theorists are less concerned with the social system and its needs than are functionalists. Instead, conflict theorists focus their analysis on who has power and how it is being used. This leads them to pay more attention to the way in which change emerges in society and the role inequality plays in that process. Conflict theorists's heavy focus on Marxian critiques of class relations and modes of production leads to a heavy concentration on the coercion and manipulation of workers. Under that argument, sport acts as a popular form of entertainment intended to subdue potentially volatile, oppressed populations. This school of thought argues that "sport in capitalist societies ultimately promotes the interests of those in power because it serves to keep workers emotionally involved in an activity unlikely to lead to reform-oriented changes in society" (Coakley, 1990: 27). Thus, conflict theorists tie sport both to consumption and consumerism (equipment, apparel, tickets) and to elements of social control (emphasis on dominance, obedience, discipline, etc).

Coakley (1990) delineates five areas on which conflict theorists focus to develop their argument that sport is a tool of social oppressiveness:

1. The **alienation** of people from their labor in capitalist societies.
2. The **coercion** and control of people in capitalist societies by those who possess the economic resources and power.
3. The development of **commercialism**.
4. The growth of **nationalism**.
5. The perpetuation of **racism and sexism** (27).

Alienation

The process of social, economic, and political alienation often begins with inadequate schooling for this nation's poorest children (Anyon, 1997; Kozol, 2005; MacLeod, 1987; Valenzuela, 1999). In such schools we find "the education system mirrors the growing contradictions of the larger society" (Bowles 1976: 5). The economic reality awaiting under-served and mis-educated students (Darling-Hammond, 1998; Woodson, 1933) is one where "the job prospects for workers who lack skills in reading, writing, performing arithmetic calculations, and operating a computer are very slim indeed" (William Julius Wilson in Anyon, 1997: ix). This combination of limited institutional resources and economic isolation has been compared to colonialism (Tabb, 1970), political and economic warfare (Gans, 1995; Hacker, 1992), and apartheid (Akom, 1999; Kozol, 2005).

Marx (1867) predicted that groups subjected to this sort of economic and educational isolation would be consistently exploited for their labor. In the context of sports, some conflict theorists interpret professional athletes as workers alienated from the greater means of their production (Coakley, 1990;

see Waquant, 2000). Under this argument, although a few athletes reap significant economic gains from their labor, these opportunities are few and far between and most often result in the forfeiting of control over their own bodies (28). Edwards (1991) argues that sport can act as a dangling carrot for poor youth of color, particularly black males, who see few other viable options for socioeconomic mobility. He notes the long odds against becoming a professional athlete in a major revenue sport, stating that "even if you make your high school varsity basketball team, you are more likely to rob a bank and get away with it (three times), than you are to make it to the NBA."

Coercion

Conflict theorists see sport as a tool of coercion and social control. They argue that those who possess economic resources and power, use sport as a mechanism for social and economic reproduction. This argument has been carried by conflict theorists in two distinct directions, one of which results in the blaming of the victim and the other of which results in a criticism of dominant society. Hoberman (1997) argues that sport has been used as a propagandistic tool to smooth over race problems in the United States. He suggests that this deliberate effort on the part of the owners and controllers of U.S. sports organizations is "elaborated most effectively and ingeniously in advertisements" (xxiii). The imaging of the athletic black male results in the continuous tracking of black Americans into a pipe dream of professional athletic stardom. For Hoberman, this often results in over-investment by the black community in a social track that offers mostly dead ends. Sadly, the majority of Hoberman's work rests upon the premise that the black community takes too much pride in their athletic accomplishments, leading to an almost pathological behavior cycle which prevents them from investing in a more "wise ethnocentrism" (3).

Waquant's (2000) work also takes a critical perspective on sport, and he also argues that sport is used as a coercive tool that takes advantage of athletes, particularly poor athletes of color. However, unlike Hoberman, Waquant's work draws heavily from the voices of the athletes themselves. Waquant's critical inquiry places much of the responsibility for this coercion on the controllers of the sport themselves:

> Fighters are unanimous in holding the view that the game is rife with "crooked managers" ("It's like a ton of them, they out to make a quick buck") and they take as axiomatic that promoters and matchmakers

are "fleshpeddlers" who will not hesitate to dispatch them to "fight King Kong for a dime" so long as it is in their pecuniary interest (2).

While still using the conflict theory framework, Waquant's (2000) work forces us to question more deeply why marginalized groups continue to encourage participation in an activity that they outwardly recognize results in their being taken advantage. According to Waquant (2000), they do it because sport provides them with avenues for self-expression and physical and mental discipline that are absent in virtually every other institution in their lives

In both Hoberman's and Waquant's, like those of other conflict theorists, the athlete experiences a distorted version of themselves such that their goals in life and their relationships with others become defined through the context of sport. They occupy that crucial societal role so that the attention of the sporting public, fan and participant, can be diverted away from larger social, economic and political issues in the society at large. In short, conflict theorists argue that sport pacifies society's most disenfranchised groups by redirecting public attention away from issues of social justice and onto the status of one's favorite sports team.

Commercialism

As sport becomes more and more a part of mainstream commercialism, conflict theorists interrogate the role of sport in the perpetuation of financial profiteering and the use of sport as advertisement for products. There is little doubt that sport is used as a major marketing tool for corporations around the world. Marqusee (2000) sees this trend as increasingly problematic because of a lack of critical perspective on the part of consumers. In his article, "World Games: The U.S. Tries to Colonize Sport," Marqusee tells the story of a "poverty stricken" Sri Lankan child outside the gates of a cricket match. The boy is wearing a tattered tee shirt that was hand decorated with the capital lettering of "NIKE" and a big black swoosh drawn in with a black marker. Marqusse sees this act as evidence of the wide impact of sport commercialism:

> In adorning himself with the swoosh, this sports enthusiast had become part of a vast web that links sweatshop laborers in South and East Asia, kids in the ghettos of North America, the corporate barons of the clothing and footwear industries, the media moguls, and marketing gurus, and not least, sports administrators, sports promoters, and professional sports men and women (39).

Marqusse goes on to say that this child is essentially the outcome of the "media-corporate-sport nexus," a conglomerate that leverages sport to perpetuate social, economic, and political inequalities globally.

Shulman and Bowen (2001) agree that the role of sport has become increasingly more about profiteering and corporate self-promotion. In an examination of U.S. intercollegiate sports, they note the massive increase in media representation for sports over the past 40 years. Comparing television guides from 1955, 1979 and 1993, Shulman and Bowen reveal that the number of televised sporting events available on the third Saturday of November has gone from 3.0 hours to 15.5 hours, to 43 hours respectively (19). Each hour of programming means advertising time and because sports are taking up some much time on the airwaves, companies are seeking to link themselves tightly with these events in hopes of becoming the "official corporate sponsor." To lock in a home audience and thereby guarantee lucrative corporate advertising revenue, "producers have worked hard to make their presentations [of the event] better, in a sense, than reality. Viewers, enjoying the warmth of their living rooms, have become so dependent on features like instant replay that they feel cheated when they attend live games and must actually pay attention to every play" (19). This increasingly tight relationship between sport and the mass media has led to a love affair between major corporations and the sporting world. Using every inch of advertising space, most every household name in U.S. production has found some way to put its stamp on sport. This powerful relationship is intriguing to conflict theorists as they seek to understand the ways in which this partnership has influenced interests in "consumption and a dependence on materialistic criteria to evaluate the achievements of self and others" (Coakley, 1990).

Nationalism

Conflict theorists also see sport as a potential mechanism to promote superficial and dangerous notions of nationalistic and cultural superiority. Investigating events such as professional sports, the Olympics and the World Cup, they examine whether or not sport can act as a lynch pin for commandeering public support for military, political and social policies. Eitzen (1999) notes that sport embodies much of the contradiction we see in our daily lives, and for that reason it can both unite and divide along lines of nationalism. He points out that as we become more globalized, we find nations and regions sharply divided along longstanding lines of ethnic and religious enclaves. On the other hand, we also find global forces at work to increase "tolerance, cooperation, compromise, acceptance of differences and inclusion" in the hopes of reducing exclusion and inequality (Eitzen, 1999: 11–12). The role sport plays in the shaping of these two distinctly different paths for nation states and the world is particularly intriguing to conflict theorists.

On the one hand, sport can produce intense feelings of a confined identity and of disgust over difference. Fans find themselves imbedded in the belief that their team's way is the only way. In the 1980s we see a prime example of this attitude manifesting itself in the National Basketball Association (NBA) league championship series. A predominantly white Boston Celtics team and a predominantly black Los Angeles Lakers team presented a clash of the "old school" versus the "new school" in U.S. culture. The Celtics played a traditional style of half-court basketball often associated with the more conservative roots of the game. They were portrayed as representatives of a perceived dying U.S. cultural commitment to hard work and doing things the "right way." The young, brash and talented Lakers team represented everything that stood in opposition to those cultural characteristics. They played an up-tempo full court style of fast-paced basketball, often associated with "playground" basketball—a perceived unorganized heap of chaos that had no real order or tradition to it. Their in-your-face, hit you quick, hard, and often style was dubbed "Showtime" and described in the media as the polar opposite of the Celtic's style.

In the case of the Celtics and the Lakers, Boyd (1997) argues that sport acted as a national battleground over dominant style and culture—the textbook versus the playground. Translated into issues of our national character, these two teams were effectively playing out a war that was already taking place on the battlefield of our national political landscape. This war of political positioning manifested in arguments such as those over school bussing in the 1970s and the case of Charles Stuart—a white man who murdered his wife for insurance money and blamed an "anonymous black man." Associating a predominantly white team with a "textbook" style of play, clearly meant to be tied with schooling and the classroom, implied that this "intelligent" style was somehow linked to whiteness. In contrast, the predominantly black team's association with a "playground" style of play had obvious undertones of a lack of structure and rules, things often coded onto the urban inner city (117–118).

In this case, sport provided a cultural dividing line, a place for sports fans to choose sides as to which cultural values they would most support. Furthermore, the framing of those cultural values inside of notions of race and cultural superiority created a case of sport being used as a tool for nationalistic division.

We see similar battles of "us against them" each time the World Cup of soccer airs. Eitzen (1999) reports that on multiple occasions, tensions arising from World Cup soccer matches have resulted in full-scale war between nations. He cites the example of the 1970 match between El Salvador and Honduras where a clash between fans concluded with "bombing raids, troop movements and, eventually, 2,000 dead." He goes on to note that the sporting event itself does not create the conflict, but it does provide a staging ground for the two parties to meet under potentially hostile circumstances and this can in fact act as a catalyst for war (14–15).

Racism and sexism

Conflict theorists also argue that sport plays a significant role in the perpetuation and justification of racial and gender stereotypes. Much of this focus has lent itself to analysis of the ways in which sport can act as a pipe dream for young students of color, particularly black males. Edwards (1993b) argued in his early work that the negative social construction of black athletes frequently leads teachers to have low expectations of them, and that students often reciprocate these feelings with similarly low expectations. Ultimately, this leads to a self-fulfilling prophecy that produces academic marginalization and failure (Edwards, 1983b). Similar criticisms of sport can be found from scholars like Hoberman (1997) whose work argues that a "cultural over-investment" in sport has systematically destroyed the black community. Hoberman sees sport as a classic bait and switch game being run on black communities nationwide. He argues that black families have exchanged schoolbooks for playbooks in the hopes that the promise of a professional sports career will bring fame and lucrative earnings, an investment that rarely pans out.

Like their scholarly colleagues examining race, conflict theorists examining the role of gender in sport are interested in the ways sport perpetuates discriminatory notions of masculinity and femininity. Winlock, in her article "Running the Invisible Race," argues that even after the passing of Title IX in 1972, female athletes that fit into the stereotypical female role would be given better opportunities. She writes that "the world of sports taught me to be 'nice,' by offering dazzling rewards to the 'coachable' woman athlete, the one who didn't rock the boat. …Instead of angry women…they get hard-working, nice girls" (27). Coakley (1990) is largely in agreement with Winlock in his analysis of gender roles in modern sport. He argues that in the case of women, sport has been used to reinforce socially debilitating stereotypical notions of women.

In fact, sport has been used to make the case that differences between men and women are "natural" and that women are "naturally inferior" to men, who "by nature" should have power over women. In other words, sport has been used to reproduce a system of patriarchy, that is, power and authority rest in the hands of men, especially in their relationships with women (179).

The root of this problem, according to Coakley, lies in the fact that men still have control of the reigns when it comes to sport. Despite significant increases in participation among females, success in sport continues to be measured on a scale where the accomplishments of male athletes set the standard. The outcome of this is the reinforcement through sport of larger socio-cultural ideologies that normalize men in positions of power and women in positions of inferiority.

CRITICAL THEORY: ATHLETES AS VICTORS AND VICTIMS

Critical theorists "recognize that the existence of sport in society must be explained in terms of something more than simply the needs of the social system" (Coakley, 1990: 31). They emphasize that individuals and groups have the power of agency, which allows them to develop social and cultural institutions that promote social change as well as social reproduction. The use of critical theory to analyze cultural institutions such as sport may hold the most potential for seeing sport as a socially empowering cultural act. Through this lens of analysis, sport is an institution largely influenced by the agency of the participants in it, which suggests the possibility of sport to act as an institution of social change. Additionally, because of the multi-layers of analysis used in critical theory (Marxism, socialism, feminism, critical race theory, cultural theory), some of the shortcomings of functionalism and conflict theory are overcome.

Filling in the gaps of functionalism

According to Coakley (1990) there are three major problems with a functionalist approach to understanding sport. The first of those is that the functionalist analysis tends to exaggerate the positive impact of sport. Seeing sport as a direct outcome of the needs of the political and economic systems, functionalists often fail to see that sport has the potential to distort values. The fact that functionalists see the social order as based upon a consensus upon common values leads them to perceive sport as an institution which serves to positively reinforce those values. While this may be true to some degree, equally important in an analysis that interrogates the ways in which sports promote ill-conceived values. As Eitzen (1999) puts it:

> [S]port mirrors society...It shares with the larger society the basic elements and expressions of bureaucratization, commercialization, racism, sexism, homophobia, greed, exploitation of the powerless by the powerful, alienation and ethnocentrism (3).

What Eitzen points out here is one of the major gaps in a functionalist critique of sport. Functionalism certainly illuminates our understanding of sport in showing us the ways in which it promotes positive social values (i.e. striving for excellence). The shortcoming, however, is that functionalism does only that, and no more. Ultimately, it fails to help us see that sport can also promote values that should be questioned and challenged (i.e. winning at all costs).

The second major flaw in the functionalist analysis of sport lies in its failure to account for the diversity of individual needs in a society. Functionalism sees society as having homogenous cultural needs, and in a heterogeneous cultural climate such as the United States, this leaves too much unsaid. This often results in the shortsighted assumption that what is good for one group, usually the dominant cultural group, is good for all groups. The outcome of this is frequently a breakdown or silencing of dialogue from non-dominant groups that are working toward social change.

This failure to account for the capacity of non-dominant agency is the root of the third problem with a functionalist analysis of sport. The fact that sport is perceived to be an institution acting in the best interests of the larger society leads to the virtual absence of a discussion about the ways in which non-dominant individuals and subgroups can define and recreate elements of sports participation. Alternate meaning making in sport goes virtually unrecognized, taking from groups the ability to use sport as an institutional tool for promoting cultural and ideological differences.

In each of these gaps, critical theorists posit interrogations of sport that prove more promising. Critical theorists recognize that sport functions as a reflection of society in ways that lead to the reproduction of important and empowering cultural trends, such as teamwork and discipline. They also see sport as mirroring the trends of society that lead to oppression and inequality for some, and profiteering and luxury for others. Critical theorists' recognition of the potential of the individual and subgroups to exact their powers of agency to influence cultural trends, creates an analysis that is the most promising in the search to understand social institutions like sport. Such understandings are critical to our understandings of how cultural institutions can be spaces for both reproduction and conflict; perhaps no two institutions are more reflective of this tension than sports and schools. What critical theory gives us is a more broad and accurate cultural view of what goes on in sport, and this creates the possibility for discussions on how sport can be an institution of change.

Filling in the gaps of conflict theory

Most of the major theoretical shortcomings of using conflict theory to examine sport center around the same issues discussed in the criticism of functionalism. And, like functionalism, most of these problems emerge from the failure to recognize the impact of agency. Conflict theorists do not see the potential of agency to create change via the institution of sport. They see sport, and therefore its participants, as subject to the economic system, unable to influence or change it. In the conflict theorist's analysis, capitalism is the warlord of cultural institutions, ruling with an iron hand over the production of all cultural activities. Sport, therefore, becomes subject to the needs of the capitalist economy, reproducing economic factors and conditions. While Coakley (1990) recognizes that economics is important in explaining the relationship between sport and society, he calls the critical theorists' approach "unreasonable and self-defeating" (29). This may be so because of the limitations that it imposes on our understanding of sport as a potential site of social change. These limitations emerge largely from an overly critical perspective that sees only the shortcomings of sport in society. To be sure, those inadequacies are real. However, to focus exclusively on those is to overlook the potential of sport to act as a conduit for social empowerment and change.

Conflict theory also overemphasizes corporate influence by looking almost exclusively at revenue producing professional sports. In that analysis, they see sport as controlled largely by big business, discounting the millions of youth and recreational participants in sport. This focus on the business of sport leaves out the overwhelming majority of sports participants, and ignores the potential of sport to be a culturally empowering space where individual creativity and expression are encouraged. As Bourdieu (1991) notes, we must not reduce sport to the product of the needs of the mass media:

> It is not sufficient to invoke the relatively autonomous logic of the field of production of sporting goods and services or, more precisely,

the development, within this field, of a sporting entertainments industry (364).

A proper analysis of the institution of sport, its origins and its cultural significance, must extend beyond a purely economic critique, which conflict theorists mostly fail to do. Critical theory, with its attention to broader analysis that includes evaluating the interplay between agency and structure, offers the potential of a more complete discussion of sport as a social institution.

Critiquing critics of critical theory

All of this is not to say that critical theory is beyond reproach. Like any theory, it should address its critics and adapt to changing social conditions. One common critique of critical theory is that it lacks theoretical focus because of its use of multiple lenses of analysis. The potential for this shortcoming can be seen in the fact that critical theorists have differing definitions for which relationships most influence sport. "Some critical theorists focus on the relationships between different social classes in society, while others focus on relationships between men and women" (Coakley, 1990: 36). This variance can lead to confusion about the theoretical stance on certain key issues. However, Coakley points out that the flexibility to investigate sports at various levels is also a strength of this approach. As more research on sport is done, critical theory will provide the flexibility to address the breadth of influences over it.

Detractors of critical theory have also argued that the approach lacks the empirical data of "actual people in everyday life settings" (Messner, as cited in Coakley, 1990), which can lead critical theorists back into somewhat deterministic conclusions like those found in conflict theory. Namely, that sport tends to reinforce the status quo rather than to provide social spaces for the emergence of oppositional agency. Without qualitative study and empirical examples of sport acting as a pathway to individuals seeking social change, critical theory will likely continue to come under fire.

This book hopes to address concerns with critical theory by combining critical and cultural theory into a theory of critical pedagogy in sports (Duncan-Andrade, & Morrell, 2008). This theoretical approach will combine the flexibility of critical theory with qualitative study. By using the multi-leveled approach of critical theory, considering a variety of social, economic, political and institutional factors on the student-athletes discussed in the later chapters, this hybrid approach promises to avoid the overly dogmatic and deterministic flaws of functionalism and conflict theory. In addition, the use of empirical data to support critical theory's claims about the potential of sport to have a positive influence on young people allows this undertaking to overcome criticisms of a lack of investigation into the ways that actual people experience sport in society.

NOTES

1   Originally coined by Durkheim to mean "without norms," but later advanced by Merton (1949) to include social situations, and individual orientations, in which a mismatch exists between culturally defined goals and the availability of institutionalized means of achieving these goals (Jary, 1991).

2   This critique of the benefits of the professional athlete will be explored in greater detail in the later section entitled "Victors or Victims?: Reconceiving Professional Athletes."

3   In his more recent work, Edwards still finds himself critical of the institution of sport, particularly major college and professional sports for much the same reasons as the past. However, his criticisms are no longer so absolute. Much of his more recent work focuses on the fact that sport may be one of the only institutions which can act to positively influence young black men. Much of this new work focuses on the role that sport can play in re-enfranchising poor and working class youth. See Edwards (2000, 1994).

4   Title IX of the Civil Rights Act guaranteed that sports funding in schools would be equally distributed between girls/women and boys/men.

5   Here, Coakley cites Birrell, 1988 (see works cited for complete reference).

6   Used here to mean the ability of individual actors to act independently of their social constraints in ways that might influence and/or subvert the process of social hegemony, social change and social reproduction.

7   See Tuhiwai-Smith (1999) for a more detailed description of the concept of non-dominant group. In essence, this is a term used to describe groups that are marginalized from the dominant culture.

8   Defined in the Dictionary of Sociology as "the power of actors to operate independently of the determining constraints of social structure" (Jary & Jary, 1991).

CHAPTER THREE

THE IMPACT OF SPORT ON SOCIETY AND YOUTH: A CASE FOR SPORT IN SCHOOLS

The Associated Press reported that, in a survey of African-American children, [Michael] Jordan had tied with God as the person they most admired after their parents. A radio station in Chicago asked listeners if Jordan should be named king of the world, and 41 percent of the respondents said "yes." And fans were spotted kneeling and praying at the foot of Jordan's statue in front of the United Center. (Jackson, 1995: 17)

Sports sociologists like John Hoberman (1997), who use a cultural deficit framework to critique black social investment in sport, are misguided. Hoberman's analysis of black participation in sport continually references popular images of menacing urban youth to make unsubstantiated sweeping claims about black culture.

...the black male style has become incarnated in the fusion of black athletes, rappers, and criminals into a single menacing figure who disgusts and offends many blacks as well as Whites. (xix)

He goes on to imply that black social investment in sport is pathological, a fixation "emblematic of an entire complex of black problems, which includes the adolescent violence and academic failure that have come to symbolize the black male for most Americans" (Hoberman, 1997: xxv).

The racist elements of Hoberman's claims are weakly veiled behind his rhetoric of concern for the black community. After citing *The Bell Curve* (Murray and Hernstein, 1994), a book which makes a quasi-Darwinian argument that black people are intellectually inferior to other ethnic groups, Hoberman references the book's suggestion that black Americans form "clan pride" in "superior athleticism" to deal with their place at the bottom of the social ladder. Rather than directly critiquing the racist overtures of Murray's and Hernstein's argument, Hoberman attempts to use their argument to prove that black Americans have effectively fallen in line with *The Bell Curve's* expectations. Hoberman does this by stating, "the celebration of black athleticism as a source of clan pride does not need to be predicted, because it already exists on a scale most people do not comprehend" (Hoberman, 1997: 3).

CRITICALLY INTERPRETING SOCIAL INVESTMENT IN SPORT

Hoberman is certainly correct in saying that some members of the black community are highly invested in sport. However, he does not properly interrogate the reasons for this investment, and this glaring oversight exposes one of the major flaws of the cultural deficit model—the absence of an analysis of the inter-relationships between institutions, society, and culture. Hoberman uses investment in sport as a proxy for blaming black culture as the root cause of poverty in black communities. He patently suggests that people of African descent should move away from their investment in sport and rely on schools to improve their social position. This overlooks two very important reasons for the existence of black cultural investment in sport, and implies that participating in sports is antithetical to intellectual development (a point discussed later in this chapter).

To properly understand any group's cultural investments, the context of the broader society must be considered. First, sport is one of the only places in United States society where the playing field is even close to level for poor and working class people of color (Edwards, 2000). Secondly, other avenues for social mobility are made virtually unavailable to many youth of color due in large part to failing urban school systems (Anyon, 1997, Darling-Hammond, 1998, Kozol, 2005). Under these conditions, sport takes on a significance much more complex than just some cultural pastime that replaces intellectual pursuits.

The majority of the most visible athletes at virtually every level (prep, college and professional) are people of color from poor and working class communities. With the vast majority of professional athletes in major revenue sports being of African or Latin/South American descent over the last four decades, it seems logical that these two groups would have significant control over these professional arenas. But, they do not. In fact, they have little control over the sports that they keep in business. The result is what Coakley (1997) calls "stacking," what Marx (1867) referred to as social classification, and what sociologists often call social stratification. Rather than athletes of color being perceived as the most experienced people in the business, and thereby the most qualified to be groomed for positions as owners, managers, and front office positions, talk turns to their physical prowess. According to Wiggins (1994), this mischaracterization of the black athlete has been noted before:

> One black athlete who publicly expressed his resentment over the divergent characterizations of black and white athletes was Isiah Thomas, the outstanding guard of the Detroit Pistons. ...Thomas told reporters he agreed with the earlier comments of his Piston teammate, Dennis Rodman, that Larry Bird was a very good basketball player, but if he were black, "he'd just be another good guy." In an attempt to explain what he meant by this comment, Thomas later told reporters that he was not referring to Bird so much as he was "the perpetuation of stereotypes about blacks." "When Bird makes a great play it's due to his thinking and his work habits," noted Thomas. "It's all planned out by him. It's not the case for blacks. All we do is run and jump. We never practice or give a thought to how we play. It's like I came dribbling out of my mother's womb" (Wiggins, 1994: 151).

Thomas deserves critique for his recent legal troubles with the New York Knicks, but this does not change the fact that he is right about the perpetuation of racial stereotypes regarding athleticism. Despite being well refuted, the argument about natural black athleticism over intellectualism persists in works like those from Hoberman (1997) and Entine (2000), who argue, respectively, that black dominance of sport is due to cultural over-investment and genetic physical superiority. What this amounts to, according to Edwards (1989, as cited in Entine, 2000), is that "what is really being said in a kind of underhanded way is that blacks are closer to beasts and animals in terms of their genetic and physical and anatomical make up than they are to the rest of humanity. And that's where the indignity comes in" (2).

Edwards's analysis of sport is an important challenge to the overly deterministic arguments of Hoberman. Like Edwards, Coakley (1990) sees a host of institutional factors at play that result in black cultural investment in sport, describing the perpetuation of an athletic gold mine myth for black males as fraud:

> ...if some other business organization tried to encourage all young black males in the United States and Canada to train for a very specific job only available to a mere 3, 000 employees, it would be fraud. Yet this has been done for years in connection with pro sports. And sports have been praised for their supposed "contributions" to mobility among blacks! (244).

Academics like Edwards and Coakley are expected to critically analyze social institutions like sport. However, it is rare to find critics of the dramatic impact of sport on urban adolescent identities among the ranks of those involved with sports. Perhaps that is because they can see the positive elements of sport in the lives of young people. Whatever the reasons, those involved in sport are the people best positioned to lead discussions of how sport can be better used in schools. Joe Paterno, head football coach at Penn State University for over 40 years, is one such critic who expresses concerns over how sport has been misused:

> For fifteen years we have had a race problem. We have raped a generation and a half of young black athletes. We have taken kids and sold them on bouncing a ball and running with a football and that being able to do certain things athletically was going to be an end in itself. We cannot afford to do that to another generation (Coakley, 1990).

The fact that Paterno is the all-time winningest coach in NCAA college football history makes his call for change that much more powerful. Despite his success by the industry's standards, he remains openly critical of a feeder system that develops athletes as commodities, rather than as scholars.

Years after these stinging indictments of sport, very little has changed. It would seem a logical progression that after 40 years of overwhelming representation on the playing field, athletes of color would be sufficiently trained in the business of sport to matriculate into management positions. Instead, while players of color continue to dominate in basketball, football, and baseball, their succession to the reigns of power in the business of sports has not been forthcoming. As Coakley notes:

> The exclusion of blacks from coaching and management jobs in sport has evoked massive media coverage since 1987, when Al Campanis, the longtime director of player personnel for the Los Angeles Dodgers,

said that blacks were excluded from these jobs because they "lacked the necessities" to handle them… [Additionally], blacks hold almost none of the management jobs in amateur and college sports, even in those with high rates of participation among black athletes (247).

Despite these obvious racial barriers at the higher levels of sport, many youth of color continue to find reason to pursue athletics. Various scholars have pointed out reasons for this investment, mostly attributing it to the lack of other viable institutional options (Braddock, Royster, Winfield, & Hawkins, 1991; Edwards, 1994, 2000; Harris and Hunt, 1984; Mahiri, 1994). The fundamental connection between the arguments made by these scholars and the position I take in this book is that this commitment by young people of color is *not* a social problem. Instead, it is an opportunity that is often overlooked by schools and communities, and one that should be better capitalized on to facilitate increased social and academic growth among youth of color.

UNDERSTANDING YOUTH CULTURAL INVESTMENT IN SPORT

Othello Harris and Larry Hunt (1984) characterize the investment in sports by urban youth as an outcome of perceptions of inequalities in access to other arenas of opportunity. Edwards (1992) argues that this investment in sport for the black community began with the 1946 signing of Jackie Robinson to a professional baseball contract.

…a door was thrown open in what had been virtually a solid wall of discrimination obstructing black access and participation across the spectrum of national institutional life (128).

As black Americans continued to experience racial discrimination and exclusion from other institutions, sport came to be perceived as a viable vehicle to financial freedom. Edwards (1992) goes on to point out that "[s]ince the 1950s, with the exception of the military and the penal system—both of which have serious downside risks and/or consequences related to involvement—no institution has provided access proportionate to the representation of blacks in major sports" (128). Although much of my analyses of participation in sports has focused on black males to this point, the argument can easily be extended to other young men of color, and an increasing number of young women of color.

A prime example of the logic that drives young people of color toward sports can be found in the book *Hoop Roots* (Wideman, 2001). Wideman relates the ways in which participation in basketball was something he needed precisely because his family was poor and non-white. He explains that for him, sport was one of the only available avenues for exploring his potential self-worth, a "door cracking between known and unknown" (7). A poor black child growing up in Pittsburgh (PA), Wideman found himself in a world where there was a continual fear that he would not measure up to the standards established by white people. He believed, at some level, that he was fated to some otherized existence because he was who he was, and that would never be good enough. For Wideman, this fear was magnified and complicated in most every place except home, music, and sports. His interpretation of the role that sport played in the development of his self-identity and self-worth are important enough to quote at length here:

> It's probably accurate to say that anybody, everybody wants more. But how strong is the desire. How long does it last. What forms does it take. How many young people are convinced they deserve more or believe they possess the strength required to obtain more or believe they actually have a chance for more. The idea of race and the practice of racism in our country work against African-American kids forming and sustaining belief in themselves. Wanting more doesn't teach you there are ways to get there. Nor does it create the self-image of a deserving recipient, a worthwhile person worth striving for. You need the plausibility, the possibility of imagining a different life for yourself, other than the meager portion doled out by the imperatives of race and racism, the negative prospects impressed continuously upon a black kid's consciousness, stifling, stunting the self-awareness of far too many… Imagining a different portion is the first step, the door cracking between known and unknown. A door on alternative possibilities. If you want more and you're lucky enough, as I was, to choose or be chosen by some sort of game, you may then begin to forge a game plan. If you believe you're in the game, you may be willing to learn the game's ABCs. Learn what it costs to play. Begin making yourself a player (6–7).

The crack in the door provided by sport was enough for Wideman, like many young men and women of color, to begin investing in himself again. For Wideman, it was sport that created the desire to take risks at bettering himself. It provided him with a sense that someone cared, someone rooted for him, and someone expected him to do well (7). It was here that he knew that he could dare to fail, and that he would have the support of those around him whether he succeeded or not. In institutional endeavors such as school, adults in Wideman's family could provide little support, and those that were expected to help (teachers, counselors, and school personnel) seemed to care very little. He argues that for children denied access to equitable opportunities for social empowerment, endeavors such as sport have served as one of the only paths for them to invent themselves, make more of themselves, and to become players in the game of life (7).

Like Wideman, I believe the continued trend of athletic participation by socially marginalized youth holds the possibility for academic and social empowerment. With the level of investment already being made by young people in sport, it seems logical to tap that investment as a way to guide them toward avenues of success that are less limited than the pursuit of a professional sports career. Edwards, a major critic of black investment in sport during the 1980s, now shares a similar outlook on the potential of sports. His more recent work argues that:

> ...for increasing legions of black youths, the issue is neither textbooks nor playbooks, it is survival and finding some source of hope, encouragement, and support. [I]f community and school sports can provide a means of reconnecting with at least some of these black youths whom we have already lost, and of strengthening our ties with those who have managed to stay the course, then these sports programs deserve our strongest support (Edwards, 1994: 87).

The potential of youth cultural activities, such as sports programs, to reconnect America's most dispirited youth to opportunities in the larger society remains largely untapped. If we were truly committed to ameliorating the downward spiral of conditions facing numerous urban youth, it would make sense for us to make better use of areas that already draw their attention. In the case of youth sports, programs should use student participation to provide academic support and to develop the tools of critical thinking so that young people are better prepared to confront and overcome persistent racial and social inequities.

As I encourage educators to make better use of youth popular cultural activities such as sports, it is important that we are critical about how this is done. The point here is not to overvalue the popular cultural endeavor (sports, music, media). Instead, we should see youth investment as a chance to teach other skills that will create a broader set of opportunities.

The duality of sports participation is a great example of why educators must think critically about how they use youth popular culture. The impact of sport on adolescent identities has two sides—"sport is healthy, sport is destructive" (Eitzen, 1999: 59). On the one hand, if properly utilized, sport provides critical development in the areas of discipline, self-esteem, motivation, goal setting, problem solving, teamwork, and connection to the institution of school. On the other hand, if misdirected, sport can create incidents of unnecessary pressure to perform, social elitism, and physical injury. Despite these potentially negative elements of sports participation, research suggests that involvement in youth sports yields positive results, particularly for participants of color (Braddock, J.H., Royster, D.A., Winfield, L.F., Hawkins, R., 1991; Melnick & Sabo, 1994; O'Bryan, S., Braddock, J., and Dawkins, M., 2006).

This potential of sport to provide solid ground for youth in schools is being recognized by scholars, like Edwards, who were once outspokenly critical of youth over-investment in sport. After criticizing a "single-minded pursuit of sports" as a major problem in the black community, Edwards commented in a recent interview that:

> There is still, thank God, a disproportionately high emphasis on sports achievement in black society, relative to other high-prestige occupational career aspirations. Given what is happening to young black people, who have essentially disconnected from virtually every institutional structure in society, sports may be our last hook and handle… The street is their temple; the gang leader is their pastor. They don't seek the respect of anybody but each other. But they still want to "be like Mike" (Edwards, 2000: 23).

This is not to say that sports alone can right the wayward ways of urban schools. Nor is it a statement that all athletes are an example of the potential of sports to propel poor and working class children into positions of academic and social success. Rather, as Edwards suggests, if we can effectively tap into these types of investments on the part of our youth we can begin to curb some of the trends currently destroying educational aspirations.

In that sense, sport is a point of inquiry. It is a cultural tool that demands deeper investigation. Some of the same students that are miserable and failing in our public school system are investing themselves in the sports programs there. If we investigate the nature and underpinnings of this investment, we are on our way to better understanding how to meet their needs.

SPORT, YOUTH POPULAR CULTURE, AND SCHOOLS

Recent investigations into popular culture and its relationship to schools and student academic and social development, have opened up new spaces for educators (Duncan-Andrade, 2005; Giroux, Lankshear, McLaren, & Peters, 1996; Mahiri, 1998; Morrell, 2005). Studies such as these invite educators to consider accessing youth popular culture as a way to increase student investment in school. Hall (1993) argues that educators must gain a better understanding of the complexities and power of culture; that the ability to make and remake culture is one of the few empowering acts available to disenfranchised groups. While the culture created by these groups is often commodified and marketed back to the larger population (see Hip-hop culture as one example), the initial freedom of this process is largely unfettered by capitalist controls. This freedom makes popular culture a space for expression and self-empowerment that is largely unmatched in mainstream social institutions. Hall (1996) describes popular culture as a complex, hybrid form of culture, one that cannot be easily reduced or attached to a specific racial or ethnic group. This argument logically extends to youth popular culture as well, as youth develop their culture both inside mainstream opportunities and at the margins of mainstream cultural expression.

Sport is a good example of youth popular culture. In sport, students are presented with a specific set of rules that they are expected to follow to play the game properly. There are specific guidelines surrounding rules of play, the uniform, and disciplinary expectations. Where sport becomes a cultural form of expression is in the opportunities it provides for cultural expression within, and at the margins, of the rules (Boyd, 1997). Through sport, student-athletes are able to negotiate new and changing identities around issues such as style, language, representation, and play. The "bending" of the rules, which amounts to the testing of the boundaries of the rules governing play and participation, presents opportunities for the cultural production referred to by Hall (1996).

In cultural spaces such as sport, new and changing notions of style emerge that impact the broader society. Take hairstyles in basketball for example. In the 1970s the natural "Afro" became popular in the American Basketball Association (ABA) (Boyd, 1997). In this league, seen largely as the "showboat" version of the more conservative National Basketball Association (NBA), players such as Julius Irving (Dr. J) made basketball a place where culture was produced and re-defined. Using a red, white and blue basketball to highlight the expressive culture of the league, players tested the limits of an otherwise very conservative game. Mastering moves such as the behind the back dribble and the no look pass, basketball became a place of new cultural production. We have seen this trend of cultural expression through sport continue into present times with slam dunks, "killer crossovers," "And-One," end zone and goal scoring celebrations, and home run trots that teeter on the edge, and sometimes breech, the rules of the game (Dyson, 1993).

On the playgrounds, youth imitate, refine and augment these expressions of cultural creativity. All of this happens amidst a fashion show of styles, which further express the cultural character of sport. In basketball, baggy shorts and high socks challenge notions of appropriate attire. The limits are tested and re-tested as young people sag their shorts deeper down their backsides, seeking more and more ownership of the games they love. What is hip today might be two high socks, bringing back trends of the Los Angeles Laker's Michael Cooper. But in the next breath, young people switch to socks cut just above the ankle—so low that it appears they have no socks on at all. In the next moment, we see a young player wearing one black stocking, and in the next a single long white sock. The spaces for defining and redefining one's style and attitude abound in sport, making it an excellent example of youth popular culture (Hall, 1996).

If school sports programs are going to become a successful social and aca-demic intervention strategy for students, we will need to value sport as a space for cultural production. Sports must be understood as hybrids of youth and mainstream institutional cultures. Sports act as a space where students take on multiple roles. Participants engage in levels of self-expression and style, while at the same time conforming to traditional standards of behavior and disci-pline.

As it stands now, sports are perceived as an "extracurricular activity," very much at the margins of the school day. Practices and competitions are held after school hours, or on weekends, and are frequently not considered a part of the learning that goes on in school. As a result, student-athletes often separate their participation in sport from their identities as students because their invest-ment in sport is rarely honored, or capitalized on, in the classroom. It is not uncommon for student-athletes, particularly students of color, to be associated with stereotypes of the "dumb jock," which result in unacceptably low expecta-tions of them in the classroom. These lowered expectations ultimately reinforce misguided correlations between youth cultural activities and low-level intel-lectual endeavors. This same analysis can be applied to youth investment in music, media (television, video games, etc), and fashion.

The double-sided identity for student-athletes (in school I am a student and after school I am an athlete) is so prominent that "student-athlete is the only hyphenated role in academia. We never refer to student-musicians or student-workers, regardless of the time commitment required by such activities" (Goldberg and Chandler, 1995, p. 39).

Student-athletes or not, the significance of sports in the lives of school-aged children is undeniable. Through interscholastic and intramural sports alone roughly 16 million students participated in sports (Svare, 2003). This does not include the millions more that participate recreationally and vicariously through the media. While this is only a portion of the students attending schools (approximately 1 in 3), the study of effective sports programs expands the dialogue about how schools can use youth culture more generally to improve students' experiences.

With that intention, the remainder of this chapter examines sport as an area of school and youth culture where some students of color make large-scale investments of time, energy, and intellect. This discussion begins with the premise that to fully tap the potential of sports in urban schools, we will need to be more critical of how we define success in sports programs.

REDEFINING SUCCESS IN ATHLETIC PROGRAMS

Most athletic programs measure their success based on their win-loss record. While other factors such as team grade point average, commitment to the community, graduation rates, and college admission rates are becoming more popular in assessments of athletic programs, they still remain as the "other" categories to consider. More than any factor influencing school sports programs, these misguided determinants of "successful" programs need to be re-evaluated.

Adler and Adler (1985) problematize the priorities of collegiate revenue athletics in their article, "From Idealism to Pragmatic Detachment: The Academic Performance of College Athletes," citing a sophomore college athlete in their study as saying:

> The day before class you go up to the office and they hand you a card that got your schedule all filled out on it. You don't say nothin' or think nothin' 'bout it, you just go. And it kinda make you feel like you not in it, 'cause you don't have nothin' to do with it. Like it's they's job, not yours (244).

While stories such as this make it seem like the term student-athlete should be athlete-student, the problem starts long before college, and responsibility lies first with athletic programs, not with the athletes. A lack of academic preparation and motivation starts long before athletes ever set foot on a university campus. While I do not excuse the collegiate programs for their hypocritical behavior, stronger elementary, junior high, and senior high school programs must precede the athlete's admission to a university so that issues of academic preparedness are no longer applicable to the plight of the college athlete. This change is best instituted from within the primary and secondary sports programs through re-evaluating and redefining what will constitute excellence, and that begins with the coach.

THEY CALL ME COACH: LESSONS FROM AN AFTERNOON WITH COACH JOHN WOODEN

In their article "What a coach can teach a teacher," Tharp and Gallimore (1976) describe the coaching philosophy of John Wooden, college basketball's most successful coach, in the following way:

> He teaches that "basketball is not the ultimate. It is of small importance in comparison to the total life we live." He says, convincingly, that though he has had players whom he has not admired, he has loved every one (75).

Wooden insisted that his players prioritize their excellence as human beings, a trait that is not typically emphasized, or measured, for teachers or coaches. His vision of life clearly sees beyond the traditional measure of athletic success, such as "simple numbers on a scoreboard" (78). This is evident in the pregame speech he gave to his players before the last game of his career at UCLA, one where he won an unprecedented 10th national championship.

Facing an athletically superior Kentucky team, Wooden concluded his remarks to his players by saying:

> Each player should come out of the game, win or lose, with your head high; only you and your Lord will know, but the only thing that matters is that you really meant it (78).

On the biggest stage, before the biggest game of their basketball lives, Wooden's message to his students was not about executing basketball strategy. He was asking them to make a statement about how they wanted to live their lives. He was asking them to show that they understood the definition of success that he had been teaching them since their first meeting:

> Success is peace of mind which is a direct result of self-satisfaction in knowing you did your best to become the best that you are capable of becoming.

Almost 25 years after this game, I had the distinct honor of spending an afternoon with John Wooden in his apartment. Although I was a high school basketball coach at the time, we hardly discussed basketball at all. We mostly discussed teaching and literature. Nearly 90 years old at this point, Coach would stop our discussions about building character or confidence in young people, and say, "that reminds me of poem." He would proceed to recite lengthy poems that he had committed to memory that seemed to capture with remarkable accuracy the very point we were driving toward in our dialogue. I learned many lessons on that day with Coach Wooden. But, there are two that I have incorporated into the core of my teaching philosophy, having found them useful on almost every day I have been in the classroom.

The first of these lessons from Coach Wooden was his statement to me that he "treated everybody differently under the same set of rules." Wooden, like any successful teacher, understood that every student he had was different and that they would have to find their own way in this world. This does not mean that we must not have standards or rules in our teaching practice, but rather that those standards must operate as a framework for success, rather than a cage that prevents it. By setting standards for behavior and performance with our young people, we are providing them the preparation and disciplined framework that all young people crave. But, what Wooden emphasized to me was that our standards had to be dynamic enough to respond differently to the unique talents and needs of each student, without sacrificing those standards—everybody treated differently under the same set of rules. Wooden admitted to his students that he was going to make mistakes and invited their input, but never waivered on his commitment to understand each student's needs or his understanding that the final decision on the rules rested on his shoulders.

The second piece of advice that has stuck with me from my time with Coach Wooden was the importance of keeping things simple. An hour or so into our conversation, the discussion took a quick turn to basketball strategy. Coach asked me what I wanted our team to be great at, and I started to rattle of various traits of championship teams that I admired.

After a half-dozen or so, Coach politely interrupted my list, and said, "Oh my, you are a better coach than I ever was."

He proceeded to tell me, "you can be good at a lot of things, but only great at a few."

Teams that are good at many different aspects of a game will certainly win their share of contests, but eventually they will lose to teams that have formed a culture of greatness around a few essential aspects of the game. This simple advice changed how I coached, and how I taught my English classes, by forcing me to narrow my teaching down to a very few areas that I believed were indispensible to greatness. Once these had been identified, I could set about planning my lessons and my personal development around those key areas. This raised my own confidence in the things I was teaching, it also raised my students' confidence in me as their teacher, and it buoyed their self-confidence in those areas because they were given clear goals, quality instruction, and the opportunity to continually practice toward mastery.

Before I left Coach Wooden's apartment that day, he handed me a card, folded into four sections, that I keep in my wallet to this day. On the card are some of Wooden's favorite maxims, his definition of success, and his "seven-point creed" that he was given by his father when he was 12 years old:

- Be true to yourself.
- Make each day your masterpiece.
- Help others.
- Drink deeply from good books.
- Make friendship a fine art.
- Build shelter against a rainy day.
- Pray for guidance and give thanks for your blessings every day.

When you are with Coach Wooden, you are clear that you are in the presence of a master educator because it is obvious he has spent the better part of his life crafting a pedagogical philosophy that is a direct extension of his philosophy of life. When you hear his former students speak about the influence he had over their lives, there is no doubting that his life modeled the very philosophy he was teaching them.

In fact, Wooden's teaching philosophy, what he refers to as the "Pyramid of Success" (see Appendix A), probably best explains his legendary success as a basketball coach. Wooden spent fourteen years developing the pyramid, while teaching and coaching in the Indiana public schools. He describes it as "the result of my trying to develop something that would make me a better teacher as well as give those under my supervision something to aspire to other than a higher grade in my English class" (Hill & Wooden, 2001, p. 9).

As a teacher, I was deeply influenced by the pyramid for two reasons. First, the logic of Wooden's framework is profound and contains some of the most important lessons we should be adhering to in our lives as educators, and that we should be sharing with our students; interestingly, none of the blocks on the pyramid are state content standards in California. Secondly, it planted in me the idea that part of the process of becoming the best educator I could be meant accepting the fact that I needed to be able to articulate my own philosophy of life before I could truly help my students shape their own.

Following Wooden's guidance, I have spent the last twelve years of my life, developing my own philosophy, what I refer to as the "Definite Dozen/La Docena Definitiva." I began using the Definite Dozen as a coaching tool in our basketball program, after hearing Pat Summitt speak at a coaching clinic. Summitt designed something she called the "definite dozen" to establish a set of 12 core values in her basketball program at the University of Tennessee. My initial adaptation of the Definite Dozen (see Appendix B) borrowed heavily from Summitt's version. However, the version that I currently use in my classroom (see Appendix C) looks almost nothing like the original. The document has also become a central instructional tool in my teaching, just as Wooden's pyramid was in his practice. In my class, one of the primary rites of passage is the requirement that students memorize and recite the definite dozen, as well as begin a draft of their own philosophy that, it is my sincere hope, they will spend their lives revising. Two years ago, several of my students suggested that we should also memorize the document in Spanish and so with the help of my mother and those students, we produced "La Docena Definitiva" (Appendix D), and we have added this as an additional rite of passage.

Like Coach Wooden, I have found countless similarities between good coaches and good teachers. In my own life, I find that so much of what I do well as a classroom teacher I learned from coaching, and so much of what I did well as a coach I learned from teaching in the classroom. One of the goals of this book is to explore the relationship between those two so that we can give young people better sports programs *and* better classrooms.

A LESSON IN CONTRAST

In contrast to my use of Wooden as a coach that has much to teach teachers, the 1994 documentary *Hoop Dreams* (James, 1994) presents us with Gene

Pingatore. Pingatore is head basketball coach of suburban Chicago's St. Joseph High School and has the most all-time coaching wins in Illinois high school basketball history. On his way to the record books, he has frequently seen his way clear to recruit black athletes from urban Chicago to come star in his program, the most famous of whom was Isiah Thomas. In this documentary, his relationship with the young superstar, William Gates, is counter to many of Wooden's most valuable teaching methods as a coach. In some ways, the portrayal of their relationship reflects a troubling trend in classrooms and sports programs around the country. What is unveiled is the damage done to young people, as a result of our growing obsession with associating the value of our students with the scores they produce (sports or tests, take your pick).

Due to Gates' obvious star potential, Pingatore sees to it that Gates is privately funded through some "friends of the program"—bare in mind, this is a high school program. Was Gates privately funded because Pingatore saw the potential for Gates to go on to become a doctor, a scientist, or a literary genius? Or was Gates funded because he could help the program win games? The answer to that question lies not in Gates, but in Arthur Agee, another black student recruited at the same time as Gates. When it became clear that Agee would struggle academically and would not contribute immediately to the varsity program, the money from the numerous "friends of the program" suspiciously ran dry.

When Gates has a near career ending knee injury and struggles to regain his confidence as an athlete, Pingatore's attitude toward his star player changes. He is no longer impressed with Gates' potential, but becomes critical of his desire and commitment. Rather than accepting the fact that a 16-year old child has a torn ligament in his knee, Pingatore can only see his team's chance to win a state championship diminishing before his eyes.

Pingatore's obsession with winning is so transparent that even Gates, a teenager, picks up on it. Already struggling with his injury, Gates begins to have family problems. However, even after having played four years for Pingatore, Gates says that whenever he had problems he could not turn to anyone in the St. Joseph's program for help. He makes this assessment based on his own perceptions of his relationship with the staff and on the bitter memory of the one time he did ask Pingatore for help in dealing with life outside of basketball. In that instance, Gates met with Pingatore to explain that his girlfriend's (who is the mother of his daughter and later becomes his wife) family was putting a lot of pressure on him to become more involved with his daughter. Coach Pingatore's advice was to "just write them off." Gates' frustration with that statement manifests itself in his unwillingness to open up to the coach, and his own critique of that advice with the rhetorical question: "What kind of advice is that?"

The possibility that this was an isolated incident, or that Pingatore's callousness is misread by Gates, has little foundation based on two statements Pingatore makes during the documentary. The first was a response to a mediocre athletic performance in one of Gates' final games, in which Pingatore implies that Gates' effort was substandard and undeserving of a scholarship.

"It's business. It's big business, and that's what the scholarship is for" (James, 1994).

The irony in this statement is Pingatore's ambiguity as to whether he is referring to Gates' scholarship to St. Joseph's, or his recent decision to take a scholarship from Marquette University. Either way, Pingatore's meaning is the same. He is explicitly clear that Gates is getting a scholarship to play basketball, not to learn, and not to decide what he wants his "dream" to be.

The second statement from Pingatore comes as Gates leaves his final meeting with the "coach," and Pingatore articulates his concept of his own program:

"Well, another one walks out the door, and another one comes in. That's what it's all about" (James, 1994).

Pingatore's cliché definition of "what it is all about" is indicative of the exploitation seen in any factory-like sports program. Rather than turning out strong-minded, intelligent individuals, Pingatore takes two young black men and turns them into nameless products of a callous system.

Wooden saw his relationship with his players quite differently. In his autobiography he writes:

I often tell my players that next to my own flesh and blood, they are the closest to me. They are my children. I get wrapped up in them, their lives and their problems (Tharp, 1976: 77).

Wooden's obvious investment in his players and their lives earned him their respect, something Pingatore did not gain from Gates or Agee.

Mahiri's (1994) analysis of the coach-player relationship shows the importance of a coaching philosophy based on "the value and practice of mentoring." He cites numerous examples of men contributing back to their communities through youth sports programs that recall transformative experiences with coaches in their lives.

Roger was one of these young men that Mahiri worked with, describing one of his coaches as someone that "believed in me to the point where I started believing in myself. And like now, anything I believe I can do, whether it's sports or out here in the work world, I can do it. It's like a positive thing" (368).

Notice that Roger does not ramble into musings of past championships or the coach's ability to help the team win games. Instead, in keeping with Wooden's philosophy, Roger's coach reached his player in a manner that extended far beyond the playing field. He fostered a relationship with Roger that built a connection between the skills necessary for athletic success and those necessary to finding success in life. The act of imparting that invaluable knowledge from coach to player is the defining trait of a successful program, just as it is the defining trait of a successful classroom. The relationships between students and teachers/coaches are what build successful attitudes in young people, whether they win championships or not. As Roger points out, that attitude develops a person that is more effective in all areas of life. For many students, particularly students of color, these types of relationships with adults in schools are often the difference between feeling connected to school and feeling that school is not a place for them.

WHAT TEACHERS CAN LEARN FROM SPORT

The contrast between Wooden and Pingatore highlights the importance of educators having a philosophy guided by a moral integrity, one that transcends game scores or test scores. However, the lessons for classroom teaching from the coaching world do not stop with philosophy. A growing number of educational researchers are encouraging the use of coaching to assist teachers in transferring skills from professional development into their practice (Kise, 2006; Dunne & Villani, 2007). As well, there are practical instructional strategies used in coaching that teachers can make use of in the classroom. One of the leaders in this strategy is the Promoting Academic Achievement through Sport (P.A.S.S.) program. P.A.S.S. uses what they call FAMs (Fundamentals of Athletic Mastery) to build success in classrooms (Kirsch, 2002). Using eight FAMs (concentration, relaxation, rhythm, instinct, balance, power, flexibility, and attitude), the program operates under the premise that the fundamentals of athletic mastery are the same fundamentals necessary for academic success. By allowing students to understand what is allowing them to master a sport, the P.A.S.S. program opens the window of opportunity for those skills to be applied in other areas of the students' lives. According to the American Sports

Institute, the program operates on the principle belief that "the positive aspects of sport culture and the fundamentals that lead to success in sport can be brought into the classroom to create an environment that is as attractive, spirited, and fulfilling as that which takes place on the fields and courts" (American Sports Institute, 2008).

Studies of the P.A.S.S. program reveal that it has had consistent success in raising the academic achievement of the participants (McClendon, 1998; McClendon, Nettles, & Wigfield, 2000; Kirsch, 2005). McClendon (1998) upheld this claim in her study that examined the impact of the program on black students. The data from her study uncovered that black students enrolled in the program had significantly higher post GPAs than students that were not in the program. While such success stories are hopeful, it is important to note that these studies did not control for socioeconomic class or school conditions. If PASS aims to find similar success in schools serving poor and working class children of color, they will need to develop a programmatic focus that gives more explicit attention to matters of social inequity such as poverty and racism.

Still, there are a number of elements used in the PASS program that are transferable to educational environments serving urban youth. In one study that compared PASS and non-PASS classes (McClendon, Nettles, & Wigfield, 2000), six dimensions of effective classrooms were used for evaluation: depth of knowledge, higher order thinking, social support for academic achievement, academic engagement, and connectedness to the real world. The classes using PASS scored higher on all six of the evaluation criteria. PASS achieves their success by creating largely student-centered classrooms, meeting each individual where they are, and building on the skills they already exhibit (see references to Vygotsky's zone of proximal development in upcoming chapters). Studies of the program also revealed important deconstructions of athletic myths, such as the belief that skills necessary for athletic success are distinctive from those required of scholars. PASS takes the position that as students recognize that they already display the skills necessary for academic success, they are more likely to apply the FAMs to athletic, academic, and personal goals (Kirsch, 2005). PASS reveals an important lesson for all educators; every student is good at something when they come into a classroom and teachers that tap into those existing skill sets are more successful. Numerous studies suggest that this teacher skill is particularly important when working with students from outside the dominant culture (Akom, 2001; Duncan-Andrade & Morrell, 2008; Howard, 2001; Ladson-Billings 1994; Valenzuela, 1999).

The PASS program also uses a well-planned curriculum for parents. Their attention to structured and meaningful parental involvement empowers prominent adult figures in the student's education and creates a sense of community attachment to academic elements of the school, something sorely lacking in urban public schools. This parent involvement presents numerous avenues for increased student success such as the development of a community culture, informed parental participation for college preparation and admissions, and strategies for providing students with social and academic support at home.

Although the PASS program is not designed exclusively for student-athletes, it tends to draw primarily from that group because of its explicit focus on the principles of athletic mastery. Recalling the earlier arguments that revealed problems with the separation of athletes from the larger school community, the tendency of the PASS program to serve primarily student-athletes can be seen as a challenge. However, as the American Institute of Sport argues, instead of using PASS to impart these skills to student-athletes, maybe it is time that whole schools investigate the relevance of this program for raising student engagement and achievement.

The mental training required for academic success is remarkably similar to the mental training that takes place with intense athletic practice habits, and other forms of intense cultural engagement (see Gee, 2003 for a similar analysis of video game play among youth). What is mostly missing in classrooms serving poor children is not the potential of youth to accomplish rigorous tasks, but the design of material that youth believe is worth their investment (see Duncan-Andrade and Morrell, 2008 for discussion of classroom content as the vehicle of delivery for successful pedagogy). Successful sports programs have grasped this concept and this has much to do with why they are able to generate such intense investments from urban youth. When urban classroom cultures show a similar capacity, shifting toward more rigorous and "culturally relevant" pedagogy (Ladson-Billings, 1994), non-dominant culture students will be more likely to perceive school as a viable option for social and economic success.

NOTES

1   This book refers to Edwards's scholarship on the sociology of sport, but he also remains a prominent public commentator on sports.

2   The title of this subsection is taken from a book written by John Wooden. Wooden was wildly successful during his tenure at UCLA from 1948–1975, winning 10 national championships over his last 12 years at the school. The NCAA has since named their national

player of the year award after him. He was also the first person to be inducted into the Basketball Hall of Fame as both a player and a coach. Wooden worked as a high school English teacher and basketball coach in the Indiana public schools before he began his college coaching.

3   The portrayal of anyone in a film can be problematic. My critique of Pingatore's approach to working with the two black players featured in this film is based solely on my analysis of his coaching/teaching in the film. I have seen my share of coaches that fit the characterization of Pingatore, but it would not be totally fair to consider this book's critique of his coaching as a thorough review of his coaching pedagogy. Instead, the film is used to create a discussion in contrast to Wooden's approach to coaching.

CHAPTER FOUR

YOUR BEST FRIEND OR YOUR WORST ENEMY: THE SIGNIFICANCE OF YOUTH POPULAR CULTURE IN EDUCATION

As I stated in the introduction of this book, I have argued in my previous work my belief that urban schools are designed to fail (Duncan-Andrade & Morrell, 2008) and this has led me to favor a critical pedagogy that draws from the culture of my students. This idea of a "culturally relevant" approach for students of color is not new (Banks, 1994; Gay, 2000; Ladson-Billings, 1994; Nieto, 1992), but it has not produced notable gains in engagement or achievement. This is due, in large part, to conservative applications which equate cultural relevance with the incorporation of more authors of color in the curriculum while using the same delivery strategies (i.e. textbook learning, teacher-centered classrooms).

The misapplication of the principles of culturally relevant pedagogy is, in part, the result of an incomplete analysis of culture. The expectation of many culturally relevant pedagogues is that in classrooms that are mostly students of color, a curriculum that includes authors of the same ethnic background will somehow be more engaging. While I would certainly include race at the forefront of a discussion of culture, my work has sought to expand educators' analyses of culture to include the actitivities that our young people voluntarily engage in (i.e. sports, music, media). I believe that much of my success as an urban educator is connected to my willingness to pay attention to youth culture, which includes elements of race, class, language, style, and form. This

broader concept of culture has led me to engage in culturally relevant pedagogy that incorporates youth popular culture into my curriculum, as well as my
pedagogical delivery.

POPULAR CULTURE AND PEDAGOGY

It is important to begin this chapter with a discussion of the term youth popular culture and its relevance to pedagogy. Broadly defined, youth popular
includes the various cultural activities that young people invest their time in,
including but not limited to: music, television, movies, video games, sport,
internet, text messaging, style, and language practices. Central to a discussion
of youth popular culture is the point that culture is not just a process of consumption (critical or passive); it is also a process of production, of individual and
collective interpretation (meaning making) through representations of styles,
discursive practices, semiotics and texts. The complexity of this relationship
between cultural consumption and production warrants some attention here in
order to more fully understand youth popular culture as a pedagogical tool.

Recent theoretical notions of the purpose and role of popular culture in
society suggest that it is a "rapidly shifting…argument and debate about a society and its own culture" (Hall, 1992). Williams (1980) argues that any discussion of culture must pay attention to the dynamic nature of culture as a set of
"activities of men [and women] in real social and economic relationships, con-
taining fundamental contradictions and variations and therefore always in a
state of dynamic process" (410). West's (1990) "new cultural politics of difference" and Hall's (1992) discussion of popular culture echo Williams's insistence
that modern discussions of culture recognize popular culture as a simultaneous
site of resistance and commodification. For West (1999) there is "a new kind of
cultural worker in the making, associated with a new politics of difference"
(119). This cultural worker grapples with what West calls "an inescapable dou-
ble-bind" as their cultural participation and production "is a gesture that is
simultaneously progressive and co-opted" (120). This description of a new century popular cultural participant fits with Hall's insistence that the struggle over
cultural hegemony is "waged as much in popular culture as anywhere else" (468)
and that that space is inherently a contradictory space.

Nowhere is the contradictory nature of popular culture more clear than in
youth popular culture—a socio-politically charged space because of its increasing influence on the cultural sensibilities of this country's next generation. The
growing sophistication of the culture industry and its increasing focus on

youth, has spurred debate over the implications of popular culture for the field of education, particularly around issues of pedagogy. To better understand the competing pedagogical ideologies, it is worth drawing from Grossberg (1994) at length. He suggests that there are four types of pedagogical practices, all of which differently engage the value of popular culture in education.

Grossberg's first model, "hierarchical practice," is one where the teacher is judge and jury of truth. He is careful to recognize that there are times when it is appropriate for teachers to take this sort of authoritative stance, but that the problem emerges when:

> ...the teacher assumes that the or she understands the real meanings of particular texts and practices, the real relations of power embodied within them, and the real interests of the different social groups brought together in the classroom or in the broader society (16).

This culturally imperialistic approach to teaching, what Freire (1970) referred to as the "banking concept of education" is symbolic of a set of material relations to power where teachers control the creation, interpretation, legitimation, and dissemination of knowledge and students are expected to "patiently receive, memorize, and repeat" (53) that information.

Grossberg's second model, "dialogic practice," attempts to avoid a teacher-centered system of knowledge control by creating opportunities for the silenced to speak for themselves. To be sure, it is important that educators actively engage their students in Hall's argument and debate of cultural sensibilities. However, as Grossberg points out, educators seeking to give voice to the voiceless, often wrongly presume that these groups have not already created these spaces for themselves (16). They fail to recognize that historically marginalized student groups often develop sophisticated ways of cultural participation that schools do not acknowledge or legitimate (MacLeod, 1987; Willis, 1981), and that these cultural activities are often responses to structural and material conditions of inequality.

Similar to dialogic practice, Grossberg's "praxical pedagogy" can underestimate the cultural activity that is already taking place in the lives of students. The praxical pedagogy model draws heavily from critical pedagogy's aim to develop agency among marginalized groups to change their material conditions. It moves from critical dialogue for understanding toward a pedagogy of action where students are given tools to "intervene into their own history" (16). Grossberg points out that this approach can be doubly problematic. First, it can lead teachers to operate from the deficit perspective that students are coming to the classroom as "empty vessels" (Freire, 1970), lacking the skills and experiences that would allow them to be active agents for change. Secondly, teachers run the risk of replicating the shortcomings of hierarchical pedagogy if they presume that there are a fixed set of skills that will empower students to engage in critical action. Teachers must be aware that a scripted approach to developing agency in young people discounts critical cultural activities that are already there and over-looks the fact that oppressive conditions require context-specific solutions.

To manage the complexity of fulfilling the role of instructional leader, while avoiding a replication of oppressive relations of power, Grossberg suggests that teachers "locate places from which [they] can construct and disseminate knowledge in relation to the materiality of power, conflict, and oppression" (17). He describes a fourth pedagogical model, a "pedagogy of articulation and risk" that avoids the pitfalls of the first three models while maintaining some claims to authority and a commitment to developing the capacity of students as critical civic participants. It is a pedagogy that:

> ...neither starts with nor works within a set of texts but, rather, deals with the formations of the popular, the cartographies of taste, stability, and mobility within which students are located (18).

This fourth space admits to an understanding of the complexity of culture and the role of the pedagogue in navigating that complexity. A pedagogy of articulation and risk recognizes that popular culture is a pre-imminent site for contesting cultural hegemonic practices (Hall, 1996). It denies false binaries which suggest that students are at once either passive or critical recipients and producers of culture. Finally, it bares false witness to the paralyzing notion that cultural hegemony is a zero-sum game by insisting that cultural activity is "always about shifting the balance of power in the relations of culture" (468).

RETHINKING THE VALUE OF YOUTH POPULAR CULTURE IN SCHOOLS

Teachers are often the group of outsiders most familiar with youth popular culture, from style to media to language practices. This rich database of information is, at best, untapped by schools. At their worst, schools reject and debase youth culture as academically irrelevant and socially reprehensible. This adversarial position, often taken by teachers, contributes to many students' perceptions that school is at odds with their personal and cultural interests.

Regardless of teachers' and school officials' good intentions, the choice to make youth culture one of the central battlegrounds over cultural sensibilities creates needless and destructive cultural distances instead of opening access to knowledge and supporting, trusting relationships.

To understand the potential of youth culture as a pedagogical scaffold, it is important to explore two dimensions of it: 1) youth culture as an avenue that can provide teachers with access to knowledge of and relationships with their students; and 2) youth culture as an avenue that can provide youth with access to the broader society's valued knowledge. A final caveat that is important to include in all discussions of teachers' accessing youth culture for pedagogical and democratic ends: Nothing said here suggests that the teacher abrogate her or his own cultural predilections or "standards" in favor of what may be, almost by definition, transient styles, language, and so forth. Not all cultural discontinuities can be or should be resolved. Perhaps the most important lesson here is that the cultures present in classrooms and under examination here should be seen as additive, rather than as zero sum.

With the growing pervasiveness and persuasiveness of 21st century youth culture, most particularly the media (television, music, video games, movies, magazines), traditional school curriculum, coupled with traditional pedagogies, stand little chance of capturing the hearts and minds of young people. Traditional teacher education has approached this attention to "hearts and minds" from psychological (largely behavioral) perspectives. Some educational theorists have become increasingly more critical of this treatment of learning as a largely individual matter, "culture" as an impediment to learning (Hull, Rose, Fraser, & Castellano, 1991; McDermott & Varenne, 1995; Valdes, 1996). Building on criticisms of cultural deficit models, an increasing number of studies have focused on culture as additive, encouraging schools to make better use of students' cultures (Gay, 2000; Howard, 2001; Moll, Amanti, Neff, & Gonzalez, 1992; Valenzuela, 1999). This "culture as additive" scholarship emphasizes that the ready access that schools have to students' cultures can be an important tool for teachers attempting to create more engaging educational environments.

Basic teacherly sensibilities, honed through attention to the lives of students (sometimes referred to as 'caring' (Noddings, 1992; Valenzuela, 1999), give teachers tremendous access to youth cultural interests. Through an ongoing analysis of these popular cultural interests, teachers will be better able to design curriculum that keeps pace with modern media's cultural production machine. This knowledge of youth culture will also permit teachers to provide their students with productive critiques of the more negative elements. Without this grounding, teachers are left to moralizing sermons and culturally isolating out of hand dismissals that have been problematized by the aforementioned literature that critiques cultural deficit models.

Why is this is a useful goal for classroom teachers? Many educators agree that schools should give young people access to critical thinking skills. The place where the ideological road splits is over the question of how to best accomplish this goal. For most, critical thinking means that students can engage in analysis and critique of a set of texts similar to those examined in the teacher's schooling experience. In this model, academic literacy is imparted using time honored curricula (often referred to as the canon) and pedagogical strategies. This method of schooling positions students as empty vessels and teachers as the depositers of knowledge into these vessels (described by Freire (1970) as the "banking concept of education").

Valenzuela (1999) refers to this pedagogical approach as "aesthetic caring," and differentiates between this sort of schooling and "educación," an approach that foregrounds an ethic of "authentic caring." According to Valenzuela (1999), "schooling" emphasizes an aesthetic caring for students, one that brokers caring as a trade-off; that is, students are cared in proportion to their willingness to exchange their own cultural sensibilities for the dominant cultural preferences of the school. Teachers that promote "education" (or educación) over schooling employ an ethic of authentic caring; that is they create a classroom culture that draws from the cultural sensibilities of young people as a point of strength for increasing intellectual development (Valenzuela, 1999 (see also Moll et al., 1992)).

Critical theorists such as Apple (1990) argue that these competing pedagogical ideologies are the result of the fact that education is inherently a political act. For that reason, Apple suggests that a liberatory education should focus on the development of critical literacies and sensibilities that challenge traditional ways of schooling. Likewise, Delpit (1995) and Darling-Hammond (1997, 1998) both remind us that power and politics are being brokered every day in schools. From this more critical perspective on schooling, teachers recognize school as an institution that mitigates the distribution of power and the development of identity; they also stake a claim to their capacity as agents of change, disrupting the business as usual approach to pedagogy and curriculum. The tool for this raised consciousness is self-critical reflexivity. This process challenges one's own political and cultural subjectivities as they are manifested in the choices made about what is taught and how it is taught. Ultimately, the goal of such a process is to better understand what works for kids, why it is working, and how schools can become more adept at incorporating those things into the classroom and the larger school culture.

THE RELEVANCE OF YOUTH POPULAR CULTURE
FOR CURRICULUM DESIGN

According to Nielsen's "Report on Television" (1998) the average child watches three hours of television a day. The Kaiser Foundation (1999) reports that this engagement with electronic media more than doubles to six and one half hours per day when various forms of electronic media are included (i.e. television, movies, video games). This increasingly intense investment of U. S. youth in the media has led the American Academy of Pediatricians (2001) to issue a policy statement regarding the impact of this issue on children's health. The policy statement lists several recommendations for parents and educators, including the following:

- View television programs along with children, and discuss the content.
- Use controversial programming as a stepping-off point to initiate discussions about family values, violence, sex and sexuality, and drugs.
- Support efforts to establish comprehensive media-education programs in schools (Committee on Public Education, 2001).

More recent studies of youth and the media indicate that the hours spent with electronic media are even higher among poor students of color (Goodman, 2003; Nielson Media Research, 2000). Given this data and the Academy of Pediatrician's recommendations for addressing the growing relevance of the media in the lives of young people, three questions seem particularly relevant for teachers to investigate when pursuing a pedagogy and curriculum that addresses the cultural needs of urban children: 1) What are students investing themselves in? 2) How are they investing themselves in these areas? 3) Why are they investing in these areas? Answers to these questions, although requiring on-going inquiry, are readily available to educators if they talk with and observe their students.

A TEACHER'S PERSPECTIVE ON YOUTH CULTURE

I spend significant amounts of my time studying the popular culture of my students. I seek to make their engagement with popular cultural texts (particularly films, music and television) a centerpiece of intellectual inquiry in the classroom. One tool I use to inform myself about youth popular cultural texts is interviews with students. I typically interview students from across the academic performance spectrum to allow for multiple perspectives. The interviews used in this piece, are from three of my African American male 12th grade students. Isaiah was a consistent honor roll student that attended Howard University after graduation. Shaun was a student whose grade point average hovered around 2.5 for most of his high school career; he briefly attended Hayward State University before dropping out to work full time. Yancey was a student that struggled to be consistent in school, but did just enough to pass most of his courses; he managed to gather enough credits to graduate and was considering a local junior college before dropping out to work full time.

STUDENTS' PERSPECTIVES ON POPULAR CULTURE IN THE CLASSROOM

Yancey: If you show someone how to handle popular culture, if they can understand that, then I think they can understand [the] canonical. Yeah. They can definitely relate…and take it together [putting his hands together to make a ball].

Shaun [pointing at Yancey]: Yup. I agree with him.

Yancey: Yeah, I agree…if you can understand popular culture, if you're taught how to understand it as popular culture, if you're taught to look at it in a certain way and analyze it in a certain way…

Shaun [interjecting]: Critique it, yup.

Yancey: …then I think, definitely, you can take that knowledge and analyze anything.

My students' sensibilities about the pedagogical power of popular culture in classrooms is not a particularly novel idea—theoretical positions on the value of this instructional approach date back to the early 20th century (Dewey, 1938).

In his insightful text on the importance of incorporating learned experiences into the curriculum, Dewey (1938) argues:

…[it is important to] emphasize the fact, first, that young people in traditional schools do have experiences (26). …A primary responsibility of educators is that they not only be aware of the general principle of the shaping of actual experience by environing conditions, but that they also recognize in the concrete what surroundings are conducive to having experiences that lead to growth. Above all, they should know how to utilize the surroundings, physical and social, that exist so as to extract from them all that they have to contribute to building up experiences that are worthwhile (40).

Modern educational theorists have continued to make the case for valuing critical examinations of youth cultural experiences (Duncan-Andrade & Morrell, 2008; Gee, 2004; Giroux, 1997; Morrell, 2007). Critical educational theorists have also maintained that school curricula and pedagogy should more profoundly reflect the popular cultural interests and social needs of students (Akom, 2003; Giroux, Lankshear, McLaren, & Peters, 1996; Ladson-Billings, 1994; Lee, 2004; Morrell & Duncan-Andrade, 2002, 2003; Noguera, 2008).

For Giroux and Simon (1989), this challenge of using popular culture in classrooms can place teachers at an intellectual and pedagogical crossroads:

Popular culture and social difference can be taken up by educators either as a pleasurable form of knowledge/power…or such practices can be understood as the terrain on which we meet our students in a pedagogical encounter informed by a project of possibility that enables rather than disables human imagination and capacities in the service of individual joy, collective prosperity, and social justice (25).

Some of my other classroom-based studies support the merit of the latter of these two roads; that is, educational practices that engage urban students of color in critical intellectual interactions with youth popular cultural forms:

When challenged by a critical educator, students begin to understand that the more profound dimension of their freedom lies exactly in the recognition of constraints that can be overcome. They can discover for themselves, in the process of becoming more and more critical, that it is impossible to deny the constitutive power of their consciousness in the social practice in which they participate. The radical pedagogy is dialectical and has as its goal to enable students to become critical of the hegemonic practices that have shaped their experiences and perceptions in hopes of freeing themselves from the bonds of these dominating ideologies. In order for this to happen, learners must be involved in tranformative discourse, which legitimizes the wishes, decisions, and dreams of the people involved (Morrell & Duncan-Andrade, 2003; see also Duncan-Andrade, 2008).

This sort of empowering pedagogy, focused on developing students' capacities as agents of critical awareness and social change, must interrogate the formation of cultural sensibilities resulting from "the power of postmodern literacies such as film and television" (McLaren & Hammer, 1996).

Sadly, my experience is that teachers that do use popular culture often do so in ways that unwittingly reinforce the already present cultural hierarchy. They do this by using the popular cultural texts (usually movies, music or sport) as a reward, given out to students after the "important work" in the class has been done. In the English classroom, this most commonly manifests itself in the form of a movie at the end of a curriculum unit. This usually translates into one or two days of "fun time" where students don't have to learn and teachers don't have to teach. The film is never treated as a text to be studied, and what's worse is that this leads to a tacit agreement between student and teacher that youth popular culture is simply a school's tool of pacification unworthy of intellectual interrogation. In this scenario, young people are never taught to see their engagement with media as a form of intellectual development, nor are they taught how to enhance and refine that development.

This misuse of youth culture operates from the presumption that the vast majority of students spend their free time (upward of 60 hours per week) intellectually unengaged. While this may be true in some senses, I would argue that schools have some culpability in this disengagement with media. Rather than providing young people with the tools for critical media awareness, we have villainized their media culture and unwittingly set off a war between the legitimate knowledge of schools and the nefarious knowledge of youth culture. This is a silly war for educators to fight for a number of reasons: 1) It wrongly presumes the higher cultural and intellectual order of printed texts, an argument for which we have no evidence other than our own imperialistic cultural sensibilities; 2) It wrongly presumes that we could not teach the same higher order thinking skills, across academic content areas, using a rich combination of media texts and printed texts; 3) It wrongly presumes that to turn to a pedagogy and curriculum that emphasizes the use of youth popular cultural texts will insure that children will never learn to love reading printed text and therefore be denied important literacy skills and the richness of the literary canon; 4) It wrongly presumes that education is not supposed to be fun for young people, but is, instead, a right of passage into adulthood where their childlike sensibilities are removed and replaced with the more upstanding sensibilities of adults; and 5) It wrongly presumes that popular cultural texts are more engaging for young people because they are simplistic and nurture a more visceral interaction.

The Nielsen studies (1998, 2000) make it clear that children are reading texts and that they are doing it with the voracity we might well attribute to budding literary scholars. These studies only further confirm Luke's (1997) preceding argument that there is an "urgent need for educators to engage constructively with media, popular and youth culture to better understand how these discourses structure childhood, adolescence and students' knowledge" (xx). The problem with moving this project forward is that many educators do not see youth cultural texts as texts at all. But, young people do:

Shaun: ...there is this magazine called *The Source*. *The Source* will give you some information to make you think about the world. That's how I look at it. *The Source* do have some powerful stuff in it, you just gotta go through and look for it, and look, and look. ...A lot of music is deep [too]. Damn near every single tape Tupac has made you could sit there and write any kind of critique, analy[sis]...Goodie MOB, who else? Fatal.

Isaiah: KRS One.

Shaun: KRS One. Yeah, that's, ooh!

Yancey: That's a deep boy right there.

Shaun: They sit there and tell you what's going on in their lives. And every time they talk about something that's going on in their life, you can always relate it back to your life [Isaiah and Yancey shake their heads in affirmation]. That's how I look at it...I remember we had that assignment where you pick your own song. I had so many rap songs up in my head that it was ridiculous [Yancey and Isaiah laugh and nod their heads as to affirm the feeling]. I had like Tupac, and I had Dogg Pound, I had...man, I must have printed out like three different lyrics. I must have printed out at least three different ones and just sat there and had to look at them to see which one I thought was the deepest, which one I could write the most on.

Yancey: Well, I would relate music as, basically poetry. Sometimes I'll just listen to the beats and the music, not pertaining to the words. But, when I decide, ok, let me pay attention to this artist and see where he's coming from and see what he's saying, they're *real* deep. I mean, they dig in there! It's like, "wow!" It's like, this is just not, you know, "hey baby let's go groove"...

Shaun [interjecting]: [smirking at the stereotypes of music] "kick it"

Yancey: …or whatever. It's politics in there. It talks about, you know, [pounding his fist into his hand for emphasis] society and, and the drugs and…

Shaun [interjecting]: Struggle! The struggle!

Yancey: …yeah, the struggle that people don't see [Shaun nods his head in agreement]. The media, you know, what the media decides to not so much talk about and cover up, it's all out in the music. It's just like books you know, people that read books probably have a better understanding than people that just watch the news or watch t.v. of how hard it is to live in the United States. I think the people that have been through those struggles, when I listen to their lyrics, it's like they've been there and they've done that and the way they tell it's like they bring you right in their face and it's like you begin to understand a lot more. And you're like "wow!" It's *real* deep.

Shaun: The reason I say he [KRS One] is deep is because he talks onto subjects that people usually don't want to talk about. Let me think of one song [pause] (to himself): "I've got so many songs in my head."

Rather than seeing artists such as KRS One or Tupac Shakur as the creators of intellectually meritous texts, we categorize them and other youth cultural texts, such as electronic media and music, as central contributors to national health concerns over youth violence and adolescent obesity (Malkin, 2003; Steele, 1990). I wonder if we would be attributing these same national health crises to books if children were spending the same amount of time on the couch reading as they are currently spending engaging with electronic media? Would we argue that children are dropping out of school and using profanity because they read J. D. Salinger's *Catcher in the Rye* a dozen times over? Would we argue that children were committing patricide because they played Hamlet in the school play? It is difficult to picture a scenario where we reproach a child for reading too much, but we are quick to chastise children for spending too much time in front of electronic media. This speaks to a conservative national mentality so entrenched in historical notions of literacy that it is dismissive of the potential of youth popular culture to be one of the richest sources for critical literacy development to emerge in our lifetimes (Gee, 2004; Kress, 2003; Luke, 1999).

What is worse is that while we do not deny the impact of the media on young people—Shaun has "so many songs" in his head—we shirk our responsibility as educators to prepare young people to critically engage with the media, an endeavor that will better equip them to process what they see and hear.

Young people are well aware of the power present in popular culture. As my students' comments suggest, they are also confident that teachers could use popular culture to teach them the academic skills that schools purport to want to develop in their students.

> **Yancey:** I would pertain KRS One, basically a hundred percent, to *Savage Inequalities.* I would relate those two real closely to one another. For Kozol in *Savage Inequalities*, he's basically just talking about our school system and the way it's corrupted by the government and how our society is built and how there is such a false in the word "United" States; how it's such a free and liberal country. If I didn't read *Savage Inequalities*, I think listening to KRS One basically would tell me everything that was in *Savage Inequalities*. I think he (KRS One) breaks it down the same way, it's just you're hearing it, instead of reading it. And it's got a beat to it, so you're more interested perhaps. I relate those two hand in hand. [Smirking] Students probably could teach the teachers.
>
> **Duncan-Andrade (D-A):** What type of impact do you think that would have on students...
>
> **Shaun: (exhaling loudly, smiling and laughing)** gshhhhh
>
> **D-A:** ...if there was a KRS One class or a rap in literature class, or something like that?
>
> **Shaun:** Well, I know what you're saying. At Cal Berkeley don't they have like a Tupac class?
>
> **D-A:** Yeah.
>
> **Shaun:** I bet you that attendance is like a hundred percent isn't it? It's like I know if they was to have one of those classes here, I don't think there'd be that many people cuttin'. I bet you the class would be overfull to the point that people are still in line in the office trying to get in. And the reason I say that is because if they had a Gooddie M.O.B., 2Pac, or KRS One class, that's automatic. People already know

about them, and they already listen to them, so they already have influence over people. So that's just going to make them want to come to the class even more to learn what they are talking about. And I think they're gonna give them a little more respect than they're gonna give to a regular teacher...Because, the way they'll do it I think it'll get the kids' attention more than what the teachers are doing now. It's like the book I got at the house [that I'm] reading now is about Death Row. It's about how corrupt Suge Knight was and how he did all this, and I know hecka stuff that I didn't ever know about Suge Knight. And I'm still going to certain chapters and reading it all over just cause I'm interested in that kinda stuff.

Worth noting is that both Shaun and Yancey reference printed texts in their discussion about the value of popular cultural texts. They are not arguing for the banishment of printed texts. They are arguing for a more culturally relevant curriculum, one that encourages them to bring to bear the youth cultural knowledge that they possess.

Perhaps the recent test score scare tactics that encourage educators to believe we are dealing with a growing population of illiterate children are wide of the mark. Perhaps student resistance to printed texts that we see in schools is a conscious response by students to what Valenzuela has called "aesthetic caring" (Valenzuela, 1999); Kohl has characterized this as willed not learning (Kohl, 1994). This way of looking at student performance in schools drastically changes our notions of what is actually causing trends of failure. It encourages educators to do away with deficit notions of diminished intellectual capacity on the part of the student by considering acts of resistance to the curriculum as a form of student agency; that not learning is a statement on the part of students to say that they will not be subjected to a curriculum and pedagogy that is dismissive of them and their cultural knowledge.

Both Yancey and Shaun suggest that educators need to rethink their position on "official knowledge" (Apple, 1993):

Yancey: I think those types of artists such as KRS One, Goodie MOB, so on and so forth, should definitely be accepted into our school system. For the simple reason that they basically have the same qualifications as any other writer. I mean basically when they're writing, they're putting it down on paper and they're just saying it with a beat and rhyming it out to you. But, that shouldn't mean...

Shaun [interjecting]: That's even more complex.

Yancey: ...yeah, basically. It shouldn't even be looked upon differently. I think that maybe the way the school system is set up they're maybe intimidated by bringing such a thing out. That the students might actually want to learn this and be able to get something out of it to use in each day of our lives, to be able to push, strive to excellence through that literature. I think they see it as kids will probably understand that better so why don't we make it difficult for them. And if they can make it through this difficult process then they can make it through another difficult process. And, I disagree with that. ...You can take music to a whole different level. It's on you, how you teach it, how far down you dig into the music. If you just let it go through your ears and you're just dancing to it, that's another story. But, if you're sitting there and you're actually writing what he says down and, or she says down, and you look at it and you study it, you can get a lot out of that.

These student perspectives resonate with an increasing body of research (Duncan-Andrade & Morrell, 2008; Finn, 1999; Moll et al., 1992; Morrell & Duncan-Andrade, 2003; Valenzuela, 1999) that has found that urban students, particularly urban students of color, are misportrayed as being intellectually disengaged. In fact, what we find in discussions with urban youngsters is not necessarily that they want less time in classrooms; rather they want classrooms that are more worth spending time in.

D-A: What would you change about this class, or the unit, or the way that the class incorporates popular culture and the canon?

Shaun: I remember before when someone said that the class should be longer. And I agree with him that the class should be longer because when we watch a film like *The Godfather* or something, we'd watch it for like the first 15 or 20 minutes of class and then we've only got like 30 minutes left to discuss it. But, if we're going to discuss *The Godfather* it's going to take longer than 30 minutes to discuss a little, like, one and a half scenes. So, I mean, that's why I think class needs to be at least two hours long.

Yancey: I would agree to class being longer, as to this class. But, pertaining that to my other classes...

Shaun [interjecting]: Yeah, that's true.

Yancey: ...I think I would definitely suffer to sit in one of those other classes for two hours, for the simple fact that the teacher doesn't have enough curriculum set up for us to participate in. So, basically, all you're doing is, I mean going in there to be sitting there, and you know...

Shaun [interjecting]: Waste of time.

Yancey: ...there's nuthin' to do, basically. I've literally dropped a class, completely, because of that situation. Where I would walk into the class and the teacher had nothing set up and it's basically talk time, you know, social time, social hour. And, to make it two hours, for all classes, it would be good, but they would have to evaluate each class a lot more and justify as to why that class should be longer.

Isaiah: Yeah, I mean I've had the fortunate experience of being in your class all but one year since the 8th grade. Prior to that it was more or less you read short stories, novels, etcetera and it's just a story. You basically just summarize the plot and the characters, and "why did Peter do such and such." I think it's very important that the way we take it in here is a much more in depth analysis of the text and that it's texts that mean something to us. And it is, as far as just understanding it not just from the words, but also for the implications of it in a person or the individual's circumstance...it's not about just knowing what a character did or just the basic plot, but the implications of their actions and a character's motives. That's very important in understanding any text, and most teachers don't do that.

In my experience, these three students' comments reflect the sentiments of many urban students in their desire for a more intellectually rigorous curriculum that employs youth popular culture as a bridge to traditional academic skills. To be sure, young people want the opportunity to represent their own cultural knowledge, but they are also clamoring for pedagogies that employ this knowledge as a scaffold into skills that allow for more complex intellectual analyses. To some degree, this request is quite the opposite of current curriculum and pedagogy trends in urban public schools, which are often focused on the use of corporate textbooks and curriculum packages geared toward raising test scores.

BACK(WARDS) TO BASICS

Steven Goodman, a renowned educator of urban youth in New York City, critiques conservative cultural and literacy theorists for their unwillingness to recognize the cultural and linguistic assets urban youth develop in their homes and communities. He highlights the work of E. D. Hirsh Jr. (2001) as a prime example of the increasingly powerful conservative voice in urban school literacy programs; a voice that is calling for a return to drill-and-practice exercises that frequently cause "low income urban students to become even more detached and disengaged from school because it widens the disconnect between what students are exposed to out of school and what they are force-fed in school" (Goodman, 2003: p. 32).

Rather than approaching the problem from Hirsh's deficit model which calls for educators to see poor students, particularly students of color, as culturally deficient, more progressive educational theorists see the challenge of improving achievement as resting largely on the shoulders of the school (Akom, 2003; Finn, 1999; Gee, 2004; Lee, 1993; Mahiri, 1998; Morrell & Duncan-Andrade, 2003). These perspectives recognize that there are a variety of ways to display academic skills, but that schools continue to harbor a narrow and increasingly outdated view on how this should be done. In short, the debate should not be over whether traditional academic skills are important, but over how schools can better use the skills young people already have to develop those traditional skills.

RETHINKING CULTURAL RELEVANCE IN CLASSROOMS

The 1980s gave rise to a multicultural education movement that called cultural awareness to the front of educational debate. The positive impact that emerged out of this discourse cannot be overstated. It has made teachers around the nation more sensitive to the needs of students of color, particularly in the selection of curriculum. James Banks, one of the leading thinkers in this dialogue, insists on the need for a multicultural pedagogy and curriculum:

> Teachers should also select content from diverse ethnic groups so that students from various cultures will see their images in the curriculum. Educational equity will exist for all students when teachers become sensitive to the cultural diversity in their classrooms, vary their teaching styles so as to appeal to a diverse student population, and modify their curricula to include ethnic content (Banks, 1994)

Banks, like other multicultural educators, is correct to demand more ethnically diverse content in the curriculum. However, the practice of multicultural education has employed an all too narrow definition of culture. The term "culture" in school curriculum has largely been a proxy for "race/ethnicity," and while this has resulted in some attention to a more ethnically and gender diverse set of readings and perspectives, it has not considered other central aspects of culture.

Educators must expand multicultural education to include a broader definition of culture. This will mean developing curriculum, as well as pedagogy, that empowers students to critically engage the electronic media and other forms of youth popular culture (i.e. music, style, sport). Inside of these cultural spaces, students often display the same academic skills (critique, analysis, memorization, recitation, oral presentation) that we are asking them to produce in the classroom. A multicultural curriculum and pedagogy should be using youth culture to scaffold these skills into academic success.

Our students come to the classroom with many of the skills that teachers expect to teach them. They think critically and analytically. They develop and present arguments. They are creative. They have the discipline required for memorization and recitation. They display these skill sets almost every day when they talk about things that are relevant to them as teenagers—these are the things that I refer to as youth culture. To bridge this gap between youth culture and the culture of the classroom, educators must learn about the interests of their students and find ways to value them in their classroom pedagogy. A classroom would not have to become a live version of MTV (Music Television) to incorporate youth culture in the pedagogy. The goal is to help students to understand that the skills they use to interact with cultural forms of their choosing are actually quite similar to school-based skills that they often reject as irrelevant. At its core, this approach to pedagogy believes that a rigorous multicultural curriculum should utilize elements of student culture along with components of the canon.

Not surprisingly, students intuitively understand the potential of this sort of pedagogical scaffold:

> **Shaun:** If you learn one way to cook on a stove, you can always go to another stove and learn to cook. That's just like if you learn popular culture, you can come back and learn how to use canonical culture. Because learning, basically all you have to do is use your mind and be interested in what you are learning. Because if you are bored in class you are just going to doze off in class and sleep (aside: cause some teachers will let you sleep. I ain't even gonna lie.) If it's interesting though, you'll stay up and you'll participate and you'll try to get some points of information in. But no matter what you'll always try to learn. But I think if you are allowed to learn from pop culture and then that teacher tried to bring you into the canonical, or the regular text, then the person will learn both ways. I can say for myself that I did that in this class.

Shaun makes use of a vivid metaphor to articulate a common sense principle of learning theory: if the curriculum and pedagogy are interesting to young people, they'll be excited about learning. For both Shaun and Yancey, the use of popular film and music as legitimate academic texts provided a variety of opportunities to develop skills of analysis and discussion. More importantly though, it has added to their media literacy tool kit, challenging them to change the way they interact with the media in their lives.

> **Yancey:** I think also from this class, instead of just watching a film or reading a book for entertainment, I have the want, it's like a challenge to me, to figure out what the writer of that book or the producer of that film is thinking. Or, what his motive is, as to why he's doing this, like why, why. That question "why," always revolving through my head.

Notions of academic skill development should not be tied exclusively to typical school-based practices. A smarter approach would recognize and find ways to incorporate the intellectual activity that engages students beyond the classroom walls. This pedagogy of articulation and risk (Grossberg 1994) values and learns from the cultural skills students bring to the classroom and assists them as they expand those skills and develop new ones. For Freire, this is the ultimate form of critical pedagogy; that is, engaging young people in critical dialogues over various cultural skills, providing space for production of those skills, and then valuing those products enough to engage in critical dialogue over them. If, indeed, urban schools hope to advance the spirit of critical pedagogy and the multicultural education movement, then they would do well to listen to young people and make better use of youth culture in their pedagogy and curriculum.

This chapter focused primarily on the use of this pedagogical approach in my high school English classroom. For many educators, the discussion was probably more affirming than it was earth shattering. The remainder of this book turns to a discussion of my efforts to apply some these pedagogical principles in the pedagogy I used with the girls' basketball program at this same high school.

NOTES

1   Chapter 4 draws heavily from an article I wrote in 2005 (see Duncan-Andrade, J. (2005). "Your Best Friend or Your Worst Enemy: Youth Popular Culture, Pedagogy and Curriculum at the Dawn of the 21st Century." *Review of Education, Pedagogy and Cultural Studies*, 26:4, pp. 313–337).

2   The issue of student disengagement is well documented (Finn, 1999; Kohl, 1994; MacLeod, 1987). This paper is not an attempt to duplicate that work, but, instead, aims to discuss promising solutions to the problem.

3   Valenzuela highlights the difference in the U. S. use of the term education, which often means "schooling" for Mexican children, and the Mexican term educación which elicits the expectation of a more holistic, authentically caring relationship.

4   Pseudonyms are used for all three students.

5   Important to consider here are the types of media texts that are employed in the classroom. Students can be just as disengaged with dated and culturally irrelevant films and documentaries as they are with traditional texts.

6   We read Kozol's *Savage Inequalities* in our class at the beginning of the school year as part of a project to examine the educational inequalities at Townville High School.

7   *The Godfather Trilogy*, although stretching back into the 1970s, remains popular with students, particularly because of on-going popular cultural references to the mafia and the godfather (see HBO's hit series "The Sopranos" and Snoop Dogg's album "The Doggfather").

Section Two:
Moving from theory to practice

INTRODUCTION

This section introduces the city and school that housed the Lady Wildcat Basketball Program and then discusses its impact on four students, Ada, Mika, Nancy and Erika, over their final year in the four-year program. This discussion begins with Chapter 5, which gives some background on the school and the city. Chapter 6 uses core tenets of critical pedagogy to provide a general overview of the pedagogy used in the program. Chapter 7 discusses the summer season, covering the months of June, July and August. Chapter 8 covers the brief, but very important, first six weeks of school. Chapter 9 covers the most intense period of the program, the California high school basketball season, running from mid-October to early March. Chapter 10 highlights the Spring, the period immediately following the end of the basketball season until the summer season began again in June.

CHAPTER FIVE

WELCOME TO 'DA TOWN

This study took place during the 2000–2001 school year in the Lady Wildcat Basketball Program (LWBP), a girls' basketball program at Townville High School, located in a major urban center in Northern California. At the time of the study, the school housed approximately 2,400 students and was the first of six major high schools in the Townville District. The school received a score of 3, out of a possible 10, on the 2001 Academic Performance Index, making it the second highest scoring school in the district. The school's ethnic breakdown was approximately 53 percent Asian, 28 percent African American, 14 percent Chican@/Latin@, 4 percent white, and 2 percent Pilipino/Pacific Islander. Of those students, 46 percent were categorized as English Language Learners and over 53 percent were eligible for the free lunch program.

Although the school's ethnic makeup reflects 28 percent African American and 14 percent Chican@/Latin@enrollment, graduation statistics show that only 20 percent of the graduating class is African American and only 7 percent is Chicano/Latino. In a graduating class that had dwindled to approximately 250 students in 1999, only 14 African American students and 6 Latino students were eligible for admission to a California State University. In the year 2000, only 38 percent of African American seniors and only 42 percent of Latino seniors even took the SAT. Their scores were not much better than their turnout at averages of 793 and 815 respectively.

Location

The neighborhoods immediately surrounding the school, stretching approximately 10 blocks to the North and toward the hills, are primarily single-family dwellings. Many of these homes are owned by working professionals who do not send their children to Townville schools. The few multiple family dwellings in close proximity to this side of the school are upscale commuter dwellings, often occupied by 20-something professionals that commute to work in a neighboring metropolitan city. This area is known as the Lakeland District for its close proximity to the city's man-made lake. It is a thriving local business district with all the amenities one would expect to see in an upscale commuter neighborhood. Most of these businesses are within walking distance, or a quick bus ride, from the school. The lake's close proximity to the school makes it one of the more popular places for students to go during their lunch period and for after-school snacks. However, very few of the students actually reside in the homes immediately surrounding the Lakeland area. On weekends, the Lakeland area is often closed down for walking festivals and the lake is a common space for picnicking and other recreational activities. Students often complain that they are unwanted in this area, and that storeowners do not want their business.

Around the time of this study, the lake became a popular cruising area for local teenagers, particularly students and young adults from neighboring East Townville neighborhoods known as the Murda Dubbs/Twomps and Funktown. Within the span of a few months, residents of the upscale apartments lining the city's Lakeland Drive and Central Avenue had petitioned the city council to enforce a permanent "no cruising zone," which has since banned much of the teenage activity in the area. The complaints cited excessive noise and the "potential for gang activity" as reasons for their concerns.

Most of the students attending Townville live in these neighborhoods to the East of the school. A majority of the students come from a neighborhood immediately bordering the East side of the school, comprised mostly of low-income apartments, and A-frame homes that are the remnants of 1940s San Francisco vacationers. The streets there are mostly numbered in the 20s, giving the neighborhood two prominent nicknames: Twomps and Dubbs. During the late 1980s and on into the 1990s the neighborhood became best known as the "Murda Dubbs" when it had the highest homicide rate in the city, in part because of its thriving drug trade. The area became infamous for its "20 dollar baggies," its streets numbered in the 20s, and its intense violence—thus the names "Twomps" or "Dubbs," which are slang for "20s." No small number of the remaining students at the school commute from around Townville, some traveling as far as 70 city blocks.

The school itself sits on the corner of two major city streets, resulting in frequent accidents for students as drivers and as pedestrians. The constant foot and auto traffic is intensified before and after the school day because there is no parking lot for parents or students. This means that students receiving rides from parents, students riding the city buses, and daily commuters all share a major thoroughfare during peek commute hours. This often results in students arriving late to classes due to accidents and traffic jams that slow bus routes and commute times.

Physical plant

At the time of this project, Townville High was comprised of one main building with three levels. This main facility housed the majority of classes, student lockers, all counseling and administration, a small auditorium, 3 student bathrooms, and a gymnasium. As this single building facility became insufficient to house all the school's classes, alternative solutions were sought. In an effort to maximize space in the early 1990s, vocational education classrooms (e.g. the woodshop and the auto shop) were converted into classrooms. By the mid-1990s, these measures had already proven inadequate to accommodate the burgeoning student population. Making use of the little remaining physical space, the school's tennis courts and part of the parking lot gave way to portable classrooms.

The physical plant at Townville High was replete with metaphors for the larger struggles of the school and the district, and was often a site of major friction between teachers and school/district leadership. In the second year of this study, a veteran of 25 years in the Townville District told me a story about the rebuilding of Townville High School that was indicative of the level of mistrust that permeates the school and the district. I heard this story repeated in several circles, including among custodial staff and other veteran teachers.

The story was that in the early 1980s, Townville was slated to be completely remodeled. The principal at the time took bids from two general contractors provided by the district. A school site team, which some of the story telling veteran teachers served on, worked with the contractors to design the physical plant of the school. As the school year wound down, the school advisory team voted to endorse the design plan of one of the bidding contractors. The team left for the summer, presuming that that plan would be implemented and that the school would undergo appropriate remodeling during the summer and on into the Fall. What happened instead was that the principal vetoed the vote and selected another contractor. Her selected contractor informed her that the school would never have to service over 1,200 students and that the other design was excessive and overly expansive. This contractor proceeded to carry out his plan, and remodeled Townville High to serve approximately 1,200 students. This affected everything from the number of classrooms, to the size of the hallways, to the number of student lockers, to the number of restrooms, to the size of the auditorium, to the size and scope of the athletic facilities. As the story goes, information leaked out later that the contracting company selected by the principal was owned by her family member. During this study, the school served over 2,000 students each year.

Whether or not this story is completely factual may not be as important as the impact of its existence. From teachers to support staff, there was a sentiment among many members of the school's staff that leadership in the district was corrupt. The lore of this story leaves a residue of that feeling, promoting mistrust and a sense of helplessness to change things.

The intensity of the staff's attitudes toward school and district leadership only became more entrenched during the summer of 2000 when Townville High School, along with several other schools in the district, once again underwent "modernization." This meant the constant presence of construction workers during the last weeks of school, which included final exam week. Workers boxed up classroom items (books, supplies, computers, desks, etc.) and moved them onto trucks so that they could be shipped to storage, creating constant disruptions in classrooms and in the hallways during class time. There were also numerous reports of crucial instructional materials being moved before the end of the semester. As the school year ended, the discontent amongst the staff was extremely high.

I was on campus quite regularly during the summer of 2000, using the outside basketball courts to work out with the team. During this time, it was not uncommon for the construction workers and painters to take 3-hour breaks. The side of the school that bordered the basketball courts kept the same coat of paint for almost a month, even though there was a painting team of 5 painters "working" on that side every day. When the summer ended, the school was nowhere near being finished. But, school had to open.

When teachers returned to campus for the teacher preparation days that precede the start of the official school year for students, they were welcomed by a litany of problems. Some classrooms had 15 desks with the expectation that they would serve 32 students. Several teachers complained that the wrong teacher's desk had been moved back into their room. Many of the hallway floors were covered with dust and residue from the construction and could not be cleaned because construction in that area was not finished. It was not uncommon for teachers to be told that their supplies were lost and that they would have to put in a "lost item report." Equally as frequent were reports from teachers that they discovered someone else's supplies in their classroom and had to carry them over to their colleague's room. As one teacher put it to me:

> In the military, they would call this situation FUBAR (fucked up beyond all recognition). This is one of the lowest points of my professional career. I have never been as demoralized as I am right now, coming to work in a construction zone and realizing that our kids are expected to learn while sitting on the floor, and I am expected to teach them.

The situation hit its apex when word was passed to the district's superintendent that teachers at Townville were considering walking out. They were citing unfit working conditions and the on-site union representatives had started a petition to walk out. The petition was receiving overwhelming support from staff members, as one account had over 80% of the faculty and staff having signed it. A few days before school was to start, it looked as though Townville was facing a nearly complete staff boycott.

The superintendent called an emergency faculty meeting and came to see the conditions at Townville High himself. On his way to meet the faculty in the school's auditorium, he ran into an angry group of teachers, led by the school's union representative. The union rep waived the stop work petition in the superintendent's face, informing him that a walk out was inevitable. The superintendent snatched the petition, ripped it up, and stated that school would start as scheduled and that he was about to explain why in a staff assembly. He proceeded to meet with the disgruntled staff, taking off his suit coat and rolling up his sleeves, calling for a workman like effort from the teachers to do what was best for the kids. He ordered lunch for the staff and insisted that he was not asking them to do anything that he would not do himself. He spent the rest of the day with his sleeves rolled up, moving boxes and desks around the school.

This leap of faith on the part of the superintendent was enough to get the school opened—ready or not. The remodeling of the school was not finished until well into December. The school remained ridiculously undersized for the number of students that it was expected to serve. Portable classrooms littered the campus as a way to address a burgeoning student population that was nearing twice the size of the school's designed capacity. Hallways were so crowded during passing periods that it was common for students getting materials from their lockers to be bumped into them, slamming them shut. This overcrowding contributed to the school's chronic tardy problem and was a consistent source of conflict and tension among students. The cafeteria, also built to serve 1,200, could barely complete its free lunch service by the time the bell would signal the end of lunch. There was only one athletic field. In the fall, the boy's soccer team shared a practice field with the football team. In the spring, the girl's soccer team had to dodge baseballs because the soccer/football field was also the outfield for the baseball team. I could go on, ad nauseum.

Despite the superintendent's ability to motivate the staff to start the 2000–01 school year, the physical plant remained unchanged and overburdened. The school secretary summed up the school's dilemma:

> Why does everyone want to come to Townville High? Don't they know we don't have any more room? But they just keep coming and coming. They must not know what it's really like here. Well, they'll find out soon enough.

Courses and student performance

At Townville High, the number of Advanced Placement classes fluctuated almost annually (see Table 5.1). All other courses, with the exception of English as a Second Language (ELL) programs, Special Education programs, and very few Honors Placement (HP) classes, were considered "normal" classes, or "P" (Preparatory) classes.

The fact that the school used a tracking system (Oakes, 1986) makes the LWBP a particularly interesting study because the team was naturally de-tracked. Students chose to participate based on criteria outside of academic placement. Each year our program had a range of students sign-up, some with excellent preparation in some subjects but not in others, some with poor preparation in all academic subjects. Outside of sports programs, this heterogeneous array of academic preparation was uncommon at Townville High.

In one of the more telling indicators of school performance, Townville High faired worse than district averages with its African American and Latino students, posting a woeful median grade point average of 1.61 for African Americans and 1.72 for Latinos in A-F courses (see Table 5.2 for median GPA averages by grade, race, and gender). Most significant for this study may be the grade point average of African American females resting at 1.75 because all of the focal students are African American females, and the majority of the program's participants were African American females.

Table 5.1   AP Subject Classes Available

School Year	Number of AP Classes
2001-02	5
2000-01	4
1999-00	2[1]
1998-99	5

[1]District wide, enrollment and availability of AP classes dropped remarkably during the 2000-01 school year. See district notes for more information regarding district underperformance in college preparation and access to AP classes.

Table 5.2   2000-2001 Townville High Average GPA for A-F Courses by Ethnicity, Grade and Gender[1]

Ethnicity	9th grade	10th grade	11th grade	12th grade	Male	Female	Total
African Amer.	1.26	1.48	1.91	2.06	1.45	1.75	1.61
Asian	2.31	2.46	2.71	2.79	2.30	2.81	2.56
Filipino	2.31	2.99	2.03	1.97	2.32	2.57	2.43
Hispanic	1.41	1.63	2.07	2.41	1.4	2.02	1.72
Pac. Islander	1.85	N/A	2.67	1.33	2.02	2.00	2.01
White	2.31	2.21	2.22	2.41	2.03	2.57	2.28
Unknown	2.04	N/A	2.25	N/A	1.69	3.50	2.15
Total	1.85	2.08	2.42	2.55	1.95	2.40	2.18

[1]Data gathered from WASC Self-study Report, 2001.

Like grade point average, the number of AP courses made available to students is a major benchmark of a school's ability to provide college preparation. At Townville High, it is worth noting that in 2001 there were only 8 African Americans out of a total of 59 students enrolled in the school's two sections of AP English. There were only 2 African Americans out of 50 students enrolled in the school's two sections of AP Calculus. There were 7 African Americans enrolled in AP Physics. Of these 17 seats held by African American students in the school's AP classes, 14 were held by females and 9 of those were held by LWBP participants. These trends were constant throughout my time at the school.

The student enrollment trends in the AP classes are unsurprisingly similar in all of the advanced math and science classes at Townville. Consistent trends of exclusion for African American and Latino students showed themselves in virtually every one of these classes. Particularly alarming are the differences in the percentages of African American and Latino students that make it out of Intermediate Algebra into Advanced Math (see Table 5.3). The move into advanced math tends to be a major gatekeeper for access to the University of California (UC) system and other prestigious colleges and universities. Equally as problematic was the under-representation of these two groups in 1st year Physics and Chemistry classes at Townville (see Table 5.3). In stark contrast to these school-wide numbers, all 8 of the 11th and 12th grade LWBP participants were enrolled in Advanced Math or Science courses, and 6 of the 8 were enrolled in both.

Administration and staff

In the six years that I ran the program at Townville High (1996–2002), the school went through four principals, and the turnover rate of its other administrative staff and counselors was similar. This instability in leadership resulted in a faculty deeply entrenched with factions and privately operating political agendas, each jockeying for position when new administrative teams would come on board.

Townville High seemed to defy Ronald Ferguson's (1991) conclusions that teacher qualifications account for some 43% of student achievement. The staff at Townville boasted a relatively high percentage of credentialed teachers, 80%, leaving its failures in the classroom that much more disturbing. One veteran math teacher of over 20 years wrote a letter to the editor of the local paper attempting to explain these trends of academic failure:

> I was recently told about the budget we teachers have to spend on supplies in our classroom. For the year we are allotted $39 of the districts money per class. For my first period class, this means I have about $1.11 to spend per student for the entire year. …Now let me put this in perspective. The district receives somewhere around $6,025 per student from tax money and the state. This does not include special funds for special programs, just money from ADA. This means, for my class of 35 students, the district takes in $140,000. Now lets do the math. Out of that money, which, by the way, is only for this one class, take out my salary and benefits, about $66,000. This leaves $74,000. Now, my room is almost never cleaned, but take out $1,000 per year for maintenance anyway. Also, take out another $1,000 for the electricity and air I use (I think this is pretty generous), and $1,600 if I purchased new books every year for the students (I can't, but it's nice to dream). This leaves

Table 5.3 2000-01 Enrollment in Upper Level Math and Science Courses[1]

School		Female					Male					
Ethnic Group		Intermediate Algebra	Advanced Math	1st Year Chemistry	1st Year Physics	11-12 Enrollment	Intermediate Algebra	Advanced Math	1st Year Chemistry	1st Year Physics	11-12 Enrollment	Total 11-12 Enrollment
AM IND		0 (0.0 %)	0 (0.0 %)	0 (0.0 %)	0 (0.0 %)	0	0 (0.0 %)	0 (0.0 %)	0 (0.0 %)	0 (0.0 %)	0	0
ASIAN		151 (55.7 %)	120 (44.3 %)	91 (33.6 %)	48 (17.7 %)	271	141 (56.9 %)	98 (39.5 %)	95 (38.3 %)	46 (18.5 %)	248	519
PAC ISLD		1 (50.0 %)	0 (0.0 %)	0 (0.0 %)	0 (0.0 %)	2	0 (0.0 %)	0 (0.0 %)	0 (0.0 %)	0 (0.0 %)	1	3
FILIPINO		1 (33.3 %)	0 (0.0 %)	0 (0.0 %)	0 (0.0 %)	3	4 (133.3 %)	0 (0.0 %)	1 (33.3 %)	0 (0.0 %)	3	6
HISPANIC		28 (52.8 %)	11 (20.8 %)	15 (28.3 %)	3 (5.7 %)	53	24 (60.0 %)	3 (7.5 %)	6 (15.0 %)	4 (10.0 %)	40	93
BLACK		67 (50.8 %)	11 (8.3 %)	24 (18.2 %)	16 (12.1 %)	132	48 (41.7 %)	5 (4.3 %)	19 (16.5 %)	10 (8.7 %)	115	247
WHITE		12 (75.0 %)	2 (12.5 %)	3 (18.8 %)	2 (12.5 %)	16	17 (81.0 %)	2 (9.5 %)	7 (33.3 %)	1 (4.8 %)	21	37
MULT./ NO RESP		0 (0.0 %)	0 (0.0 %)	0 (0.0 %)	0 (0.0 %)	0	1 (100.0 %)	1 (100.0 %)	0 (0.0 %)	0 (0.0 %)	1	1
School Total		260 (54.5 %)	144 (30.2 %)	133 (27.9 %)	69 (14.5 %)	477	235 (54.8 %)	109 (25.4 %)	128 (29.8 %)	61 (14.2 %)	429	906
District Total		949 (39.6 %)	377 (15.7 %)	752 (31.4 %)	165 (6.9 %)	2,397	856 (40.8 %)	298 (14.2 %)	648 (30.9 %)	155 (7.4 %)	2,097	4,494
County Total		4,945 (36.6 %)	3,565 (26.4 %)	3,951 (29.2 %)	1,384 (10.2 %)	13,512	4,640 (34.8 %)	3,726 (28.0 %)	3,449 (25.9 %)	1,633 (12.3 %)	13,330	26,842
State Total		120,161 (31.8 %)	97,779 (25.9 %)	107,118 (28.3 %)	35,242 (9.3 %)	378,151	109,292 (28.1 %)	92,443 (23.8 %)	96,764 (24.9 %)	40,393 (10.4 %)	388,757	766,908

[1] Data gathered from http://data1.cde.ca.gov/dataquest/mathcrse4.asp?RptYear=2000-01&RptName=SchMath&cSchool=OAKMOORE'SENIOR'HIGH -- OAKMOORE'UNIFIED -- 0161259-0135905.

$70,400!!! Where is this money?…If I lived in Townville, and was a parent of a school aged child, I would be furious as well!

This letter reflects a larger trend of frustration among a largely white staff (60%), most of whom did not live in the city or have children attending the city's schools, that found themselves struggling to curb trends of failure for its students. Increasing discontent with district mismanagement and lack of direction was often the focus of reform cries. Unfortunately, among the school's teachers, the dominant rationale for consistent trends of academic inadequacy continued to be directed at the students and the district leadership. This focus produced no change in achievement patterns while I was at the school.

Like the administration, the campus support staff—particularly custodial staff and campus security—faced extremely high rates of turnover. In my six years there, there were seven different head custodians (none of whom were hired internally) and approximately 20 changeovers in custodial staff. Campus security officers did not fair much better as there were three different heads of security and approximately 15 changes in security staff during this same period. The lack of stability in these positions resulted in extremely low-levels of performance and little connection among support staff, teachers and the students.

Townville Unified School District

Sadly, Townville High School was considered one of the better schools in the Townville District. With an average district grade point average of 1.8 for African American students—a group that makes up 50% of district enrollment—the district was one of the lowest performing school systems in the country. As a whole, the district was not fairing much better with other ethnic groups, sporting a district wide grade point average of 1.97 for all students enrolled in college prep courses from grades 7–12 (Townville Unified School District, 1997).

As a response to its dismal performance, the district administration and school board produced a focus plan for 1999–2000, and delivered it to school site leadership. At the bottom of the first page of that plan, next to a letter from the superintendent was a statement in bold reading:

As principals and managers, we must ensure that the District meets those expectations, because too much is at stake for us to throw away a real chance of regaining public support (Townville Unified School District, 1997).

In the pages following that statement, a series of mantras are tossed about, along with 11 points of improvement targeted for the district in the upcoming school year. Those targeted areas included issues around test scores, suspension rates, graduation rates, and most other areas we might associate with school performance. One of the district's promised changes was that there would be an increase of 50% in the number of students enrolled in AP classes by 2000–01. This would push the number of students from 992 to 1,488 district wide. However, despite the district's slogan ("It's not about me... It's not about you... It's about the kids!") AP enrollment dropped by 60%, finishing the 2000–01 year with a total of 357 students enrolled in AP courses. In point of fact, 9 of the 11 district goals were measurable by the California Department of Education demographics unit and none of these goals were met in the school year following the plan.

In virtually every category by which we can measure educational quality, the Townville District was failing. According to a January 2002 newspaper article on the state of the district, "nine of the district's middle schools and three of its high schools ranked in the lowest 10 percent for the third year in a row" (Katz & Bender, 2002). Only 1 in 8 of its African American graduates and 1 in 7 of its Latin@ graduates were eligible for admissions to a California State University. Every ethnic group, with the exception of Asians, had over a 20% dropout rate, including whites at 33%. The average SAT score in 2000–01 was 848 for the district, almost 200 points behind the county average and 160 points behind the state average. Similarly, on AP exams district scores lagged way behind county and state averages. Only 17% of the district's senior AP test takers made a passing score of 3 or better, compared to 42% for the county and 37% for the state. According to the California Department of Education Demographics Unit, the entire district only offered a combined total of 10 AP classes in the 2000–01 school year. This, was a number that had actually declined from 19 classes in 1998–99, despite an on-going Civil Rights lawsuit in Southern California over a lack of access to AP courses in urban schools (see *Daniels v. California*).

Unsheltered from the blistering critiques of local newspapers and educational critics, Townville Unified frequently found itself in the crosshairs of unfriendly headlines. One study of access to AP classes in local districts showed Townville Unified to be far and away the most lacking school system for providing these college preparatory services to its students (Minton, 1999). One local district, with only two high schools returned data showing that it offered 38 AP courses to student bodies considerably smaller than most of the Townville high schools.

In a 1998 edition of the city's major newspaper, the top story's headline read "Custodians clean up in OT," and shared the front page with another article with the headline "Schools blasted at mayoral debate" (Schorr, 1998). The first article documented an audit of the district, the content of which revealed that "between January 1987 and February of 1998, the district had paid out $2.6 million in overtime just to custodians. According to the report, that amount would pay the salaries (without benefits) of about 80 new custodians" (Schorr, 1998).

Many of these district shortcomings emerged from unstable and inconsistent leadership. In the ten years between 1992 and 2002, the district went through five superintendents. The latest of these leaders summed up the district's bevy of problems by citing four major areas of past failures that he promised to address:

No system wide expectations for communication;
No expectations for accountability;
No ownership of the system, so no one felt responsibility;
No consistent talk of achievement.

Despite his recognition of past mismanagement and disorganization, the newest superintendent still struggled to right the ship. He too came under fire as a response to his administration's failed efforts to produce the change and growth they had promised. Despite the image of bold task tackling and gutsy management maneuvers, the district faced headlines about its lack of progress. In January 2002, the headlines read "Townville schools rank worst for third year." Comparing the district to schools across the state, the article noted that the Department of Education showed Townville to be "among the worst in the state...[as] almost half of the city's 89 schools included in the report, released Wednesday, scored in the bottom 10 percent of schools statewide." The article went on to note that these comparisons were often skewed because schools with differing resources were unfairly compared. Yet and still, when "Townville schools were compared to schools with similar problems—low socioeconomic status, a high number of non-English speakers and a lack of credentialed teachers—30 city schools still ranked in the lowest 10 percent on the test" (Katz & Bender, 2002).

Beaten at virtually every turn, the district remained open and was expected to serve its almost 60,000 students. No matter what the headlines and statistics were saying, students and teachers were still filling the schools on a regular basis and there was no evidence to suggest that that was going to change. This fact alone was motivation enough for me to urgently seek out profoundly different and more effective ways to educate the youth of Townville.

OUR STUDENTS

Since this book looks at the implications of the program primarily through its impact on four students, it is important that the reader have some brief introduction to them. These four students were chosen because they came to the program with distinct social and academic challenges and skills, and yet each of them experienced success in the program. The remainder of this chapter provides brief descriptions of each student's entry into the program, their racial and family background, and some of their social and academic strengths and struggles (see Table 5.4 for demographic and grade point average data). Additionally, the final chapter of section two provides an update on all the students mentioned in the book and what they are up to now.

Table 5.4   Data on focal students

Name[1]	Ethnicity[2]	GPA (JrHigh)[3]	GPA (9th)[4]	GPA (10th)[5]	GPA (11th)[6]	GPA (12th)[7]	GPA (Cum.)[8]	Socioeconomic Background
Ada	Af.Am./Nat. Am.	2.0	2.2	2.6	3.3	3.0	2.8	Low income
Erika	AfAm/Chicana	2.3	3.4	3.4	2.9	Unk[9]	Unk[10]	Low income
Mika	Af. Am.	2.8	3.7	3.9	4.3	3.9	3.9	Low income
Nancy	Af. Am.	2.1	2.6	2.8	2.4	3.1	2.7	Low income

[1] All names used are pseudonyms.
[2] Ethnicities are as defined by students.
[3] Connotes grade point average from 8th grade as defined by students.
[4] Connotes grade point average from 9th grade year, including summer courses (counts only college courses meeting the University of California A-G requirements.
[5] Connotes grade point average from 10th grade year, including summer courses (counts only college courses meeting the University of California A-G requirements.
[6] Connotes grade point average from 11th grade year, including summer courses (counts only college courses meeting the University of California A-G requirements.
[7] Connotes grade point average from 12th grade year, including summer courses (counts only college courses meeting the University of California A-G requirements.
[8] Connotes cumulative grade point average upon graduation from Townville High School, including summer courses (counts only college courses meeting the University of California A-G requirements.
[9] Erika is a senior this year, leaving this portion of the data incomplete at the time of the printing of this document.
[10] Erika is a senior this year, leaving this portion of the data incomplete at the time of the printing of this document.

Ada

Ada came to the program as one of the most promising young basketball players in the city. A descendant of Native American and African American parents, Ada was tall and remarkably agile for her size. It did not take long for most people to recognize her potential as an outstanding athlete, but she was not as well received as a student. Ada came to the LWBP with extremely low academic self-esteem as the result of past struggles in school. This was not helped by the fact that she was athletically talented and often perceived by her peers as physically attractive. This combination frequently led Ada to heavily invest in the parts of her life that gave her immediate positive reinforcement. This investment meant disinvestment in the classroom because schooling frequently brought her frustration and criticism. Ada admits that, "I have become a better student because of the program. Now, I have a better sense of what to do in the classroom. I believe that it (the LWBP) has helped me become a better person because I know to expect more from myself."

Ada was surrounded with exceptional support at home, even though she did not live with her birth parents. She stayed with a surrogate mother, grandmother and older sister in an apartment a few blocks from the school. None of her immediate family members attended college. Few people in the program were aware of the fact that the family Ada lived with was not her birth family. This was largely due to the fact that she referred to the woman in charge of her care, Monica, as her mother. Monica's mother and daughter also lived in the house and Ada referred to them as her grandmother and sister, respectively. Out of respect for Ada's privacy, the family did not make this information public knowledge. Ada had no contact with her birth mother, and infrequent contact with her biological father who was living in Oklahoma, which sometimes led to bouts with depression and anxiety around her identity.

Mika

Mika entered the program at the same time as Ada, having attended the same junior high school and played on the same basketball team with Ada for the previous two years. Like Ada, Mika too was bi-racial, being half African American and half European American. Unlike the other three focal students discussed in the book, Mika was not an exceptional athlete and found herself struggling to keep up with the pace of high school varsity athletics. She made the varsity team as a freshman largely because the program was in its rebuilding stages, but she was not touted as a potentially good player. She did, however, find considerable success in the classroom, and was considered one of the more promising students in her class. Mika excelled in the math and sciences, rare for an African American in Townville schools, but was less apt to find ease in her social science classes, particularly her A.C.P. (Advanced College Placement) English class.

Mika lived in a rented house in East Townville with her white mother and twin younger sister and brother. Mika's father lived in San Francisco and had infrequent contact with her during her high school years. Mika's older sister had attended school in Townville, but dropped out before graduating. During her time in the program, Mika's younger siblings joined her at Townville High. Her sister, Tanya, a more promising athlete than Mika elected not to join the program, but dropped out of school and was coerced into a teen prostitution ring. This lasted for several months until her pimp was arrested in one of the largest teen prostitution scandals in East Townville. Mika's brother made it to his senior year at Townville as a member of the boy's basketball program but decided to drop out before graduating with his class. Mika's mother is a graduate of the 1960s UC Berkeley, but bounced from job to job and was frequently out on disability from work. The single income and job instability created consistent financial hardship for Mika during her time at Townville High.

Nancy

Nancy came into the program at the same time as Ada and Mika, but from a different junior high. In her first year, Nancy found herself the only member of a very talented group of 9th graders to be demoted to the junior varsity team. Despite being very talented athletically, she had trouble with the demands of the varsity team and showed signs of immaturity that prevented her from keeping up with her newcomer peers. Nancy took her demotion to junior varsity quite hard initially, but later came to call it an "opportunity to show you that I belong on varsity." She dominated most junior varsity games, but did not adjust quite so well academically. Her teachers at Townville High characterized her as an average student, and she had similar expectations of herself, managing just above passing grades her first year at Townville while taking all lower track classes. At one point during and her partner made the decision to move the family 70 miles north to Sacramento when a better work opportunity presented itself. Not wanting to take her out of the LWBP, Nancy's mother commuted back and forth to work in Townville so that Nancy could continue to attend Townville High. This often meant leaving home at 5 a.m. to make it to school on time because of heavy commuter traffic. All this while Nancy took a course load that included her 10th grade year, Nancy's math teacher saw me in the office and commented that, "she is the sweetest thing, but she's just not all that bright."

Nancy's single-parent home was run by her mother who completed high school, but did not attend college. Nancy's older sister and brother also attended Townville High. Her sister dropped out during Nancy's sophomore year, pregnant with Nancy's first nephew. After the baby was born, she did not return to high school, but continued to live with the family while searching for stable work. The inconsistency of her sister's work schedule, frequently resulted in Nancy having to change her plans to provide child care for her nephew.

Nancy's older brother was held back in his earlier schooling years, so he enrolled at Townville High in the same grade and at the same time as Nancy. A prominent baseball player that struggled in school, he flirted with academic ineligibility and was eventually pushed out despite a signing bonus of $75,000 promised from a major league baseball team on delivery of his high school diploma.

In Nancy's senior year, her mother made the decision to move the family 70 miles north to another city when a better work opportunity presented itself. Not wanting to take her out of the LWBP, Nancy's mother commuted back and forth to work in Townville so that Nancy could continue to attend Townville High. This often meant leaving home at 5 a.m. to make it to school on time because of heavy commuter traffic. All this while Nancy took a course load that included AP Calculus and AP Physics.

Erika

Erika entered the program a year after Nancy, Ada, and Mika. She was considered the best 8th grade basketball player in the city and was being heavily recruited by some of the surrounding high schools with strong basketball programs. When Erika did finally enroll at Townville High School, she came touted as the best player to enter the school in recent history. Also of mixed ethnic decent, African American and Chicana, Erika entered Townville an outgoing and gregarious fourteen year-old. She seemed to understand well how to work the urban school system for grades that would have teachers calling her "funny" and "energetic," polite ways for saying that they did not see her as intellectually gifted. Erika's personality won her enough favor in middle school to garner a 'B' average, and upon her entering the LWBP, those marks seemed to fit her perception of herself as a student—better than some, but not one of the best.

Erika lived in an apartment with her mother, two cousins, older brother and younger sister for her first two and a half years in the program. Her mother did not graduate from high school, and worked incredibly long and hard jobs as a housekeeper to provide for the family. Erika's father was murdered outside a nightclub in Texas during her sophomore year. Her older brother dropped out of high school and struggled to find consistent work. Her sister and two cousins were enrolled in a local elementary school.

During Erika's junior year, the family was evicted from their apartment and the exorbitantly high rental market made it difficult to secure housing for the family. For the majority of the second semester of her junior year, Erika bounced from house to house with friends and family members whenever they had room. Toward the end of the school year, she rented an apartment for herself with a close friend who had recently graduated from high school. Her mother, sister and one year old niece sometimes slept on the couch at Erika's apartment. The apartment was located in a neighboring city where the housing market was more accommodating, but this resulted in a 45-minute commute to Townville.

WHAT NONE OF THESE INTRODUCTIONS CAPTURE

For much of my 18 years in teaching, I have had the opportunity to loop with students. In the case of most of the students mentioned in this book, I worked with them year-round for 4 years. The deep and committed relationships that developed as a result of this looping make it difficult for me to write about them. When you know someone as well as I came to know these students, anything you write about them feels incomplete. As I read and re-read the brief introductions above, I became increasingly concerned over the possibility that they would be read as portraits of dysfunctional lives wrapped inside a dysfunctional community—just another ghetto narrative.

In the end, I left them as they are because the remaining chapters focus on their incredible resilience, brilliance, and success. I left them as they are because I want the readers of this book to know that so many of our young people are experiencing forms of social trauma that we conveniently ignore in schools because they are inconvenient for us. Adding insult to that injury, we often use these social traumas as an excuse for why we cannot be more successful with students.

So, I chose to highlight some of the challenges our students faced in their homes and in the community because that is the reality for most of the youth in our community. Times are hard. Lives are hard. People are suffering and struggling, and that includes our young people. Overwhelmingly, these hardships are heaped on the families in our community in ways that people outside of the working poor cannot understand. The families that raised these young people were some of the most committed, resilient, and hard-working people I have known, and I come from a long line of them. In spite of all their efforts, they could not completely protect their children from the harsh realities of urban life.

As educators, we must be honest about the high likelihood of these possibilities in the lives of the families we serve, and our course should be set accordingly. In my mind, this means caring enough to know what is going on in the lives of our students and their families, and developing a pedagogy that is responsive to those realities. This *can* be done without lowering our expectations, but we cannot maintain high expectations without this level of responsiveness.

I would add that this does not mean that we have to have some immediate solution for the failing schools, poverty, homelessness, and violence in our communities. I wanted to offer Erika a place for her and her family to live when they were evicted, but I had no rooms to offer. What I *could* do was to be more flexible with her, make sure she had half my sandwich during study table, and let her know that I could listen if she needed to talk. This responsibility can be summarized as two halves of a whole—we must be aware of the strife in our students' lives and we must respond in every way we humanly can. More often than not, our young people honor that commitment from the adults in their lives by taking advantage of the support and succeeding. In so doing, they are loving us back.

NOTES

1   Data on the school has been collected from Townville's 2001 WASC (Western Association of Schools and Colleges) Report, the California Department of Education website, and the DataQuest website.

2   One high school received a 4 on the API, one received a 2, and the other three high schools received scores of 1.

3   Pseudonym

4   According to California Department of Education, Educational Demographics Unit, "Course Enrollments by District for the year 2000–01."

5   From a guest lecture in Education 40, School of Education, UC Berkeley, September 19, 2000.

6   Looping occurs when you work with the same group of students for multiple years. This practice is more common in elementary schools, and is an obvious occurrence in high school sports programs. But, I have worked to set up looping situations with my students (sometimes formal) since I began teaching because I believe it is an effective way to create sustainable academic growth.

CHAPTER SIX

INTRODUCING THE LADY WILDCAT BASKETBALL PROGRAM[1]

In 1996, I was teaching English at Townville High School. Kendra, the star girl's basketball player was a student in my 11th grade English class. In late September, she asked me to become the varsity head coach because their coach had just resigned. As a former high school basketball player, I knew taking over a program a month before the season began was equivalent to coaching suicide, especially in a highly competitive basketball league like the Townville Athletic League. Having coached boy's basketball in my first four years of teaching, I also knew that coaching was a powerful way to educate young people. I told Kendra that if she could convince Mr. Morrell, also a former high school basketball player, to coach the team with me, I would commit to an interim position with the program while the athletic director conducted a search for a full-time replacement. That search was eventually halted because we enjoyed the coaching so much that we decided to stay with the program.

Morrell coached in the program from 1996–2000 and I stayed with the program from 1996–2002. During those years, the program had tremendous social, academic and athletic success, due in large part to the infusing of the principles of critical pedagogy into the program's ideology and structure.

SPORTS AS A VEHICLE FOR CRITICAL PEDAGOGY

The basketball gym is probably not the first place most people would go to see critical pedagogy in an urban high school. As discussed in Chapters 3 and 4, sports, particularly revenue sports like basketball and football, are often criticized by liberal thinkers as tools for the maintenance of conservative and patriarchal value systems. There is plenty of validity in those critiques. However, the potential of sports to be a vehicle for resistance, empowerment and collective change deserves receive more scholarly attention.

The recent publishing of *What's My Name Fool* (Zirin, 2005) documents numerous examples of athletes using their notoriety as athletes to raise voices of resistance and social critique. Zirin's commitment to capturing moments of social resistance by athletes continues beyond his book. He also writes weekly articles that provide a critical analysis of society through the lens of sports (see www.edgeofsports.com). Such efforts are important because they draw attention to the fact that sports have been, and continue to be, a forum for raising social consciousness.

Unfortunately, Zirin's work is limited by the fact that most of the examples he provides are instances of individual resistance. Most of the cases he cites as examples of sports as a vehicle of social critique come about because individual athletes use their notoriety to bring their political views into public purview. It is true that some of the most memorable moments of resistance in sports are the results of athletes connecting their personal views with the views put forth by larger social movements (Tommie Smith and John Carlos in solidarity with the black Power movement and Muhammad Ali with the anti-war movement). However, it is not typical for the commentaries of these athletes to be deliberately linked to long-term organizing and resistance strategies of social change movements.

In relationship to their sport and their team, most acts of social resistance by athletes end up being individualized because they are not intentional outcomes of their athletic training. Such actions are not part of a collective team action, and they are not the result of a critical political agenda on the part of the team or the coach. But, what if they were? Could sports be used to develop a collective culture that aims to transform oppressive social norms? Can critical pedagogy help coaches to foster such a critical collective consciousness and agency with their teams? The upcoming chapters will discuss my use of three pillars of critical pedagogy (organic intellectualism, praxis and counter-hegemony) in the Lady Wildcat Basketball Program (LWBP) to develop a powerful counter-narrative to urban school failure. The success of the program suggests that there are fundamental principles of this work that can inform the development of similar cultures in other urban school programs and classrooms.

VEHICLES FOR ENGAGEMENT: PRACTICING WHAT WE PREACH

Reading the world always precedes reading the word, and reading the word implies continually reading the world (Freire and Macedo, 1987: 35).

Before I discuss the use of critical pedagogy in the LWBP, I want to briefly emphasize the importance of educators identifying a vehicle for delivering the tenets of critical pedagogy. The sad fact about critical pedagogy in U.S. urban schools is that many educators well versed in critical pedagogical theory are unable to bridge that theory into practice. There are many reasons for this failure. The most common reason is the inability of teachers to capture the minds and hearts of their students. An educator's ability to develop vehicles for engaging students is an essential ingredient for being an effective critical pedagogue. In the case of the LWBP, sport was the vehicle. However, in my previous work I have discussed other forms of popular culture (Duncan-Andrade, 2005; Duncan-Andrade & Morrell, 2005) and social science research methods (Duncan-Andrade, 2006) as equally effective vehicles for providing students a program that combines some of their own interests with a critical and consistent focus. In short, there must be a programmatic vision and it must be something that students can believe in; it must provide hope and a sense that their investment will be rewarded.

Ironically, aspiring critical pedagogues are quick to teach students to "read the world and the word," but they are less likely themselves to practice this element of critical pedagogy. If educators read the world of their students, they would find countless vehicles for moving forward their critical pedagogical agenda. Just such an opportunity presented itself to me as a high school teacher in Townville when my student asked me to fill the coaching vacancy in the basketball program. Given the level of personal investment students are asked to make as members of a sports team, I saw coaching as yet another opportunity to use the world of my students to deliver elements of critical pedagogy.

CRITICAL PEDAGOGY AND ORGANIC INTELLECTUALISM

Children do not all learn at the same pace or in the same ways, even though schools mostly operate as though they do. Far too many schools group students based on age, and frequently sort them even further using faulty measurements of ability[2] (Cone, 2003; Oakes, 1985). Once the sorting is done, students are taught from curriculum that essentially promotes the same pacing and instructional methods for everyone. Educators mostly ignore or explain away the fact that this approach to teaching produces achievement results that contradict our rhetoric that all children can learn. Even teachers deeply committed to the equity-oriented principles of critical pedagogy can end up reproducing trends of academic failure by reverting to time honored tradition of one-size-fits-all instruction and assessment.

Antonio Gramsci[3] (1971) contended that the inequitable outcomes of schooling that result from such pedagogical practices should be attributed to social design, rather than student inadequacies. For Gramsci, "all [people] are intellectuals…but not all [people] have in society the function of intellectuals" (Gramsci, 1971, p. 9). He believed that each person has an organic intellectualism that results from one's interaction with the world and that this interaction is almost always socially constrained by factors such as race, class, and gender. The fact that each person experiences the world differently means that each student comes to school with a unique form of intellectualism. However, schools are often ill equipped to identify and develop a person's organic intellectualism. Instead, they end up separating intellectuals from non-intellectuals through teaching methods that value the ability to acquire and reproduce information using specific formats within rigid timeframes. For this reason, much of what Gramsci saw as the organic intellectualism of humanity remains untapped in schools.

Gramsci's work suggests that many of the pedagogical practices in schools run counter to what we understand about cognitive development and educational psychology. It is widely agreed that students have considerable variations in their "zone of proximal development (ZPD)"[3] (Vygotsky, 1978), and that ignoring this fact virtually guarantees that students unable to receive considerable additional support are doomed to fail in school. Vygotsky's ZPD is particularly useful for educators because it explains that students have their own zone of development (social and academic) that they are capable of moving through if they are given support by someone that already understands the concepts in that ZPD. In the context of critical pedagogy, this tool is essential because it disrupts pedagogical trends that ignore our most basic sensibilities about teaching and learning.

For example, if Student A and Student B were in the same classroom learning about spelling we could graphically represent the basic idea of ZPD (see Figure 1 below). If the principles necessary for being a strong speller were represented linearly, then it would not be hard to imagine two students in the same classroom at different places on that line of expertise. So, Student A enters the classroom knowing some basics about spelling, but she has not built up practice strategies to fully develop the fundamentals of good spelling (see graphic below). Her zone of proximal development begins at the point on the line that represents the level of skills she has already mastered well enough to teach to someone else, and extends toward more advanced competencies in spelling. With assistance she can move through that zone (labeled in gray as ZPD) and become proficient at spelling. In that same class, we could have Student B who comes to the group already having had strong training in spelling. She might have already moved through some parts of the ZPD that Student A still needs to work through. To be fully effective, the classroom pedagogy would need to provide a different set of opportunities for Student B (also known as differentiated instruction).

In a classroom that begins instruction with the presumption that all students have proficiency in spelling, Student A is likely to fall even further behind her classmates. The outcome of that increasing gap is predictably

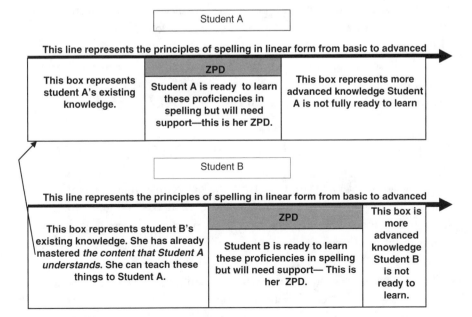

Fig 6.1 Graphic representation of ZPD

negative, and many issues of disengagement or classroom misbehavior can be attributed to a student's awareness of this widening gap.

Another scenario is that the instructor identifies large numbers of students who, like Student A, are below spelling proficiency and modifies the curriculum for the non-proficient speller. The outcome of this pedagogical adjustment is likely to be negative for Student B who will find the class unchallenging and begin disengaging or seeking other stimuli which will probably get her labeled as a behavior problem.

A third scenario, one that incorporates attention to the concept of the ZPD, could produce positive results for both Student A and Student B. In this scenario, Student B can be positioned to support Student A as she struggles to move through her ZPD. This would allow Student A to meet the challenges of the class while Student B could reinforce her excellent preparation and build pedagogical and leadership skills without feeling unchallenged in the class. This is an oversimplification. But, it raises the point that there are ways to conceptualize classroom env ironments that properly address the inevitable variance in zones of proximal development.

For each student there is a zone of material they are ready to learn if someone helps them, and there is also material outside of their ZPD that they are not yet in a position to learn. Educators using the concept of the ZPD understand that there will be variance in each student's ZPD, and that this variance is not neatly distributed based upon age. Therefore, being effective with all students requires educators to develop strategies for identifying a student's ZPD and then responding with the appropriate support for that student's particular needs. In most public schools, the only time this is formally required of educators is when students are referred to a Special Education program (known as Individualized Education Plans or IEPs).

IDENTIFYING STUDENTS' ORGANIC INTELLECTUALISM

In the case of the LWBP we used three reflective meetings per year, per student, to identify each student's ZPD, and their needs and goals for moving through that zone. The three meetings took place as follows: 1) at the start of each school year (September); 2) at the end of the basketball season (March); and 3) at the end of the school year (July). Before each meeting, students prepared responses to questions dealing with basketball, school and their future goals. The coaches also answered the questions based on their own evaluation and expectation of the student in each area. The questions were as follows:

Basketball

What are your strengths as a basketball player?

What are the areas you need to improve as a basketball player?

What are your strengths as a basketball player?

What are the areas you need to improve as a basketball player?

Academics

How would you describe yourself academically?

What are your strengths and weaknesses?

Why do you feel this way?

Future Goals

What do you want to accomplish this year as a player? How will you do it?

What do you want to accomplish this year as a team? How will you do it?

What do you want to accomplish this year as a student? How will you do it? What are your long-term goals (5 years, 10 years, 20 years)? How will you accomplish them?

The meetings where these questions were discussed provided opportunities for responses of both the players and the coaches to be discussed and amended based on dialogue. These discussions allowed us to identify areas where we underestimated students and/or places where students were undervaluing their own potential. It was important that this was a collaborative process because our experience as teachers and coaches allowed us to identify potential in students that they often did not see in themselves. The discussions also gave us important insight into student strengths that we had overlooked. Students and coaches alike left these meetings with clear goals and concrete steps to achieve those goals, a process that Ada pointed out was rare in her experience in urban schools.

> You got me to think about where my life was going and what I wanted out of it. I know that most of the kids I knew never even thought about that at all. When I'd ask them stuff, they would just say, "I dunno." But you got me to think about my future. …All the planning we do, it made me feel like I was together.

These meetings were part of a year long process of self-reflection and goal setting that helped participants focus their energies on specific goals. These evaluations were particularly helpful in providing us with a better of idea of what students expected from themselves. This powerful insight into the students' self-esteem allowed for the creation of individualized academic and athletic development plans. In turn, this meant more precise, personalized development catered to the needs of each individual. These individualized plans included workouts tailored to the individual athletic goals of the participant, and academic support geared toward the student's academic needs and goals.

The development of this structure for identifying zones of proximal development allowed us to more fully appreciate each student's organic intellectualism. We can take the cases of Ada and Lisa as examples. Both of these students came to the program at the same time, but with very different skill sets. Ada entered the 9th grade with the reputation as a top athlete and a marginal student. Lisa entered the 9th grade with limited athletic preparation and mediocre academic achievement.

Over their four years in the LWBP, we used the ZPD model to develop individual plans for both students which accomplished two primary goals of effective pedagogy: they were positioned to contribute to the program from their areas of strength and they received support relevant to their areas of highest academic, social, and athletic needs.

For Ada, we designed an athletic program that challenged her to grow into one of the top athletes in the city. Ada came to the program in 9th grade as a tall and gifted athlete. As her athletic excellence matured through her development of self-discipline, poise under pressure, and work ethic, she began to organically transfer these skills toward her academic growth. This process was organic because she was learning these habits of mind through her choice to participate in the sport. Students like Ada, who reflect habits of excellence in areas outside of the classroom, rarely encounter educators that help them bridge these skills into the realm of academia. In the case of the LWBP, we recognized that Ada came to our program having already begun the organic development of habits of mind that are demanded of excellent students. What was missing from the picture was a system for helping her build the bridge between athletic success and academic success. We helped her build that bridge by recognizing her organic intellectualism, identifying her academic zone of proximal development, and then providing the motivation and support for her to transfer the skills from sport to school. We provided Ada with daily academic support in the form of after-school and weekend tutoring from local college students, coaches, and teachers. We augmented this support with summer academic acceleration activities. As suggested in Ada's comments above, this support was all the more effective because it was coupled with on-going dialogue that helped her bridge her athletic and academic potential. Over our four years together, her low academic self-esteem never completely went away. However, by her junior year she was making the honor roll and had found the confidence to take multiple Advanced Placement courses.

Had we attempted to replicate the strategies we used with Ada for Lisa, we would surely have failed because Lisa did not experience similar success in athletics. Lisa, a second generation Chicana, had a rugged, self-assuredness that resulted in her being well liked and respected, but prior to joining the LWBP her charisma had not transferred into much athletic or academic success. For Lisa, we had to create opportunities for her to contribute as an emotional leader on the team because her athletic skills never developed to the same level as other members of the program. In most athletic programs, she would have been cut from the team because of her lack of athleticism. However, we saw in Lisa the organic intellectualism of leadership, which included other key elements for academic success (risk-taking, self-sacrifice, self-confidence). Lisa's self-confidence and tendency to be a risk taker allowed us to push her hard and fast academically. We quickly enrolled her in some of the most challenging courses at the school and made sure to provide her with the daily academic support so that she would experience success in those classes. Athletically, we remained patient with Lisa's slow gains, rewarding her for challenging others to work as hard as she did even though she did not receive the athletic notoriety that they received. Her rapid academic ascent made her one of the top students in the program and regularly placed her on the honor roll. Although we had other excellent students, we held her up as an example of academic growth, emphasizing that her achievements there were hard won. This position allowed her to take on a leadership role unique to most sports programs. Lisa became one of our most valuable tutors, particularly with younger students, because she understood the challenges of developing a new academic identity.

The application of critical pedagogy requires educators to challenge the existing one-size-fits-all pedagogical model. Critical pedagogues must develop practices that identify and utilize the organic intellectualism of students. This means having an understanding that students enter schools with different zones of proximal development across a spectrum of skills (social, cultural, academic, athletic, musical, etcetera[5]). These different levels of preparedness are tremendous opportunities for educators that are trained and willing to diversify the strategies they use for motivation, instructional pedagogy, and academic and social support.

CRITICAL PEDAGOGY AND CRITICAL PRAXIS

Successful sports programs are one of the best places to study the effective use of praxis. Praxis can be defined as a thorough process of reflection where ideas are tested and experienced in the real world, followed by reflection, revision, and reapplication of those ideas (Freire, 1970). Good coaches constantly reflect on their strategy, their performance and the performance of their players to find places for improvement. They video tape practices and games and review that video regularly and with scrutiny in hopes of uncovering areas for individual and team growth. Effective coaches regularly use these reflective tools to adjust their instructional methods to make sure that every player understands the team's strategy, and that each player receives maximum preparation to carry out that strategy. They also regularly check in with players to assess their health, their understanding of what is being taught, and to identify areas (social and athletic) where a player might need additional support. Finally, coaches regularly dialogue with other coaches, players and former players in search of critical feedback and advice for improvement. The teaching profession could greatly benefit from studying and adapting the way that the coaching profession uses praxis to improve their own instruction and performance.

Despite the proficiency of sports programs at using praxis for internal growth, they rarely engage in critical praxis. That requires engagement in, and reflection on, actions that aim to end injustice. In the LWBP we saw the challenge of critical praxis as the challenge to create a program that accomplished two things: 1) consistent and sustainable achievement for all our students; and 2) critical agency to respond to conditions of inequity that students saw in their immediate communities.

Morrel and I began with the understanding that we could not be effective if we asked students to do something we were not willing to do ourselves. We attempted to model critical praxis by being critically engaged as teachers in the school and as members of the Townville community (we both lived within 5 minutes of the school). Issues of racial, social, and educational inequality were always at the forefront of our agenda as teachers and as coaches. These types of issues were the mainstay of our discussions with students, whether in the classroom, on rides home from practice, or between summer league games. We expressed, in no uncertain terms, that we taught and coached because we saw it as the most likely path to supporting a movement for radical social change in our community.

Additionally, we modeled the reflective side of this critical praxis as students ourselves. We were both enrolled as graduate students at U.C. Berkeley, which allowed students to see us as lifelong learners, committed to the principles of social justice, but not having all the answers. Students saw us reading, writing and studying, challenging each other to think more deeply about issues of injustice. We shared with them our struggles as students, asked them for their advice and reflections, and brought them to our graduate classes as guests and presenters. Finally, we sought their opinion of our work as teachers and coaches in informal conversations throughout the year and with formal evaluations at the end of each semester. The importance of educators modeling critical praxis is under-emphasized in discussions on how to effectively implement critical pedagogy. In our case, modeling it illustrated the usefulness and impact of critical praxis and better positioned us to ask students to develop similar habits.

To help students in the LWBP develop critical praxis in their own lives, we developed a set of principles that each agreed to live by. These principles reflected habits of mind related to their desire to improve as students, athletes, and as a team. The principles were a modified version of Pat Summitt's "The Definite Dozen" (Summitt and Jenkins, 1998). Before a student could become a member of our program, they had to recite the Definite Dozen[6] (see Appendix B) from memory and agree to uphold them in their everyday lives. Before a student could become a member of our program, they had to recite the Definite Dozen[6] (see Appendix B) from memory and agree to uphold them in their everyday lives.

Students were reminded daily of the Definite Dozen, and were consistently asked to self-assess their commitment and actualization of them as they related to the team and to their broader lives. For most of the students, this was the first time they had been asked to commit to a set of principles that they could use as points of reflection for their personal and collective growth.

The Definite Dozen helped build three phases of self-development that DuBois (as cited in Kincheloe, 2004: 60) saw as essential components of a worthy education: self-respect, self-realization, and self-consciousness[7]. To participate in the LWBP meant embracing a commitment to ask for and utilize support to achieve intellectual, social, and athletic excellence. For our part, we had to be sure that we maintained high levels of expectation, motivation, and support for all the students. In contrast to the traditionally low expectations of the school, the LWBP raised the bar, demanded that everyone in the program struggle to reach that bar, and refused to let anyone in the program succumb to that struggle.

In one program evaluation survey at the end of the year, several parents pointed out strong gains in the self-respect of their students. The following are two examples:

Melinda (Ada's parent): I've seen my daughter's sense of herself and responsibility to others grow. In this program she has been

> provided with a second family. A group at school that
> I like her to spend time with. A real good group of friends
> that guide her right.
>
> **Linda (Mika's parent):** She has a place she feels she belongs.
> Academically she has never done better. She has friend-
> ships and seems to feel comfortable with herself. She seems
> more accessible than many teens—less rebellious and
> angry. The attention to team building has developed this.

As a young person's self-respect grows, so does their self-realization. The concept of self-realization is a translation of a Sanskrit expression referring to
knowledge based on experience, not mere intellectual knowledge. That is, the
more the students value themselves the more they are able to learn from their
experiences, successes, and failures. In most urban schools, students are taught
to undervalue, or worse, to devalue, their own experiences. Without a strong
sense of self-respect in the context of school and society, it is virtually impossible
for a person to engage in the praxis of self-realization. The process of self-respect
leading to self-realization is more likely to happen when students attain hard
to reach goals. It should be added that the perseverance necessary to achieve
hard-won success is more likely to happen when there are high doses of motivation (external and internal) and support.

During our end of the year program evaluation interviews, every student
referenced the fact that the adults in the program believed in their potential to
achieve excellence. Nancy's and Ada's comments below reflect the sentiments
expressed in those interviews:

> **Nancy:** When things started going bad for me last year, all I had was
> this (LWBP) program. Every day I wondered if I was
> going to turn out just like my older sister and brother. My
> sister was really smart, but she still dropped out and my
> brother was really good at baseball and he dropped out.
> But when I think about my teammates and this program
> and all…how much it means to me, I want to keep fight-
> ing. I know I would have dropped out if it wasn't for this
> program. I just know it.
>
> **Ada:** The most helpful part of this program was the conversations that
> you had with me. When we would meet and we would
> talk about what you thought I could do, I really started to
> believe in myself. Sometimes, it felt like you believed in

> me more than I believed in me. This was a dramatic
> change for me. Before I didn't even see a reason for com-
> ing to school. I think because I didn't have any goals.

When students have self-respect and are allowed to value the self-realizations that emerge through their lived experiences, their self-consciousness is heightened. This self-awareness has the potential to develop into critical consciousness, particularly for students that have felt the sting of being denied access to quality educational programs. Sadly, this potential remains largely untapped because successful urban students are often encouraged to leverage their success to escape their communities and the problems associated with living there. Schools tend to teach that agency is about an individual's ability to pull themselves up by their bootstraps. Schools should focus instead on the development of critical self-consciousness to develop the students' confidence that they can use their agency to challenge and change inequities in their communities.

The LWBP gave attention to developing students' sense of critical self-consciousness by reading excerpts from books such as *Savage Inequalities*, *Hagakure*, and *The Art of War*. We had formal and informal discussions about the readings and their relationship to the conditions in Townville schools, their communities and the global society. These opportunities helped students understand that they, together with other youth in their community, could be agents of change. Along these lines, the students in the LWBP developed a free basketball camp for elementary and middle school students[8]. To spread the word about the camp, students distributed flyers in the community and returned to their elementary and middle schools to make presentations in the classrooms of their former teachers. Over three years the camp served more than 100 students for two full days, focusing largely on building self-confidence and strategies for coping with the challenges of adolescent life.

After the first camp, students decided that there needed to be more workshops in the camp that addressed the challenges of urban adolescence. They identified two particular areas that would have eased their transition into young adulthood, but that their schooling had mostly ignored. First, they felt that they would have benefited from a crash course about the ins and outs of high school life. They called this workshop "The Secrets to High School Success." They also thought that they would have benefited from advice from other teens about nutrition, physical conditioning, sleep, drugs, alcohol, and sex. They called this workshop "Healthy Lifestyles." Students developed curriculum for those two sessions by anticipating some of the challenges that the campers were already facing as young women of color in an urban center, and gave strategies for overcoming those challenges and coping with defeats. They sought out advice and information from parents, teachers, other students, and the Alameda County Public Health Department so that their sessions would be informative and accurate. They also went through multiple drafts of the curriculum for the workshops using each other and the adults in the program to fine-tune their plans. It is worth noting that these two sessions, not the sessions focused on basketball skills, always received the highest ratings from young people attending the camp.

This work with young people in the community became a key element of the critical praxis in the program. Each year students would make improvements to the camp based on their experiences as teachers and in response to critical feedback they received from campers and parents. They also found ways to expand the impact of their work with youth by working at the YMCA summer camps, volunteering as coaches for youth basketball leagues, and speaking in classes at their former elementary and middle schools. Two other students started flag football and basketball teams on their blocks with elementary age youngsters in their apartment complexes "so they can play outside and be safe instead of just sitting on their couch."

CRITICAL PEDAGOGY AND COUNTER-HEGEMONY

If hegemony includes the process by which mainstream social, economic and political inequalities are made to appear normal, then counter-hegemony should include critique of those inequities and actions to improve them. For Gramsci (1971), this requires a dual platform made up of a "war of position" and a "war of movement" (238–239). The war of position is waged through efforts to gain access to voice and power in social institutions (education, law, government, health care) in order to normalize discussions of social and economic inequities that inspire revolutionary acts to change structural inequities. The war of movement occurs when victories in the war of position develop a widespread shift in social consciousness that leads to collective public action against inequity.

In the LWBP we engaged in the war of position by using our institutional capital (as teachers, coaches, and graduate students) to develop a counter-hegemonic education program that normalized self-respect, self-realization, and critical self-consciousness. We implemented this program by using the aforementioned academic and social support structures that relied on the concepts of organic intellectualism (Gramsci, 1971) and the zone of proximal development (Vygotsky, 1978). These structures were victories in the war of position in that they used the institutional resources of school to provide equitable educational opportunity for our students. However, in urban schools, it is not hard to find instances of individual success, but these should not necessarily be considered counter-hegemonic or victories in the war of position. Success as defined by the achievement of outstanding individuals that use their success to escape the severe structural inequalities of poverty should not be considered counter-hegemonic. These isolated cases reinforce the dominant hegemony, which suggests that only an exceptional few can find success in urban schools and that success is partially defined by their ability to leave their community to join a more "successful" one.

This is where the concept of the war of movement is helpful because the traditional individualized model of success does not prioritize shifts in social consciousness that lead to collective public action against inequity. Quite the contrary, it contributes to social reproduction by reinforcing a survival of the fittest paradigm that legitimizes inequitable opportunities and outcomes. To counter this traditional paradigm of success in urban schools, the LWBP emphasized the development of structures that supported success and collective consciousness for all its participants, rather than a select few.

There are two ways to think about the approach we used as counter-hegemonic. First, the program's consistently high achievement rate was counter-hegemonic to school and district cultures that normalized low achievement for most students. We ran the LWBP for six years (1996–2002), conducting a formal study of its impact over the four middle years (1997–2001). Over those four years, the team had a grade point average of 3.4, compared to a 2001 school-wide average of 1.6 for African Americans, 1.7 for Latin@s, and 2.4 for Asian Americans. The most significant points of comparison for this measurement of achievement are the school-wide grade point averages of African American females (1.75) and our team grade point average of 3.4 because 10 of the 12 participants were African American females (the program also had 1 Chicana and 1 Cambodian student). At the end of the four-year period of study, the program had 100% graduation and four-year college enrollment rates for all 6 of the participants that entered the program as 9th graders in 1997.[9] During that same period, the school had graduation rates of 53%, 47%, and 72%, and college eligibility rates of 9%, 9%, and 31% for African Americans, Latinos, and Asian Americans respectively[10] (California Department of Education, 2006).

We can also think about the methods used to achieve these results as counter-hegemonic. We worked hard to develop a counter-culture in the program, one that normalized excellence and collective achievement. We did this, in part, by raising students' awareness of the critical "double-consciousness" demanded of them if they were to become successful in school and the larger society. Du Bois (1903) explained the idea of double-consciousness as the effect black people in the United States experience by having to struggle with two "warring ideals." Many urban youth of color experience this effect. On the one hand they are "American," but never fully accepted as a group in a society that often portrays them as pathological and non-intellectual. They are also aware that they are connected to distinctive cultures (Pan-African, Pan-Latino, Pan-Asian), but that living in the United States means that they might never fully realize that identity. A critical double-consciousness occurs when a person faced with this internal battle is able to develop a critically conscious response to these conditions. Such a person is able to acquire the mechanical skills necessary to navigate oppressive social conditions and institutions, and the critical skills to analyze and resist the hostility they endure there while developing a strong sense of self and community.

We sought to develop this critical double-consciousness in our students by helping them acquire the "master's tools" (Lorde, 1984) and the tools of "transformative resistance" (Solórzano and Delgado-Bernal, 2001). We paid special attention to providing academic support to students all year. Part of this support meant having explicit conversations with them about how to navigate the hostile dispositions and low expectations of some adults in the school. In Lorde's concept of the master's tools, she argues that the master's tools are the tools of oppression. She makes the point that oppressed people will not dismantle oppression by acquiring the tools of oppression and then using them to oppress others. Instead, the master's tools must be put to use for the purposes of dismantling oppression. This message was explicit in our program. We insisted that students learn to effectively negotiate their school environment. However, there was also the expectation that as students acquired tools to effectively navigate the institution of school they would share that knowledge with their peers.

We considered this sharing of their knowledge the application of Solórzano's and Delgado-Bernal's concept of transformative resistance. They distinguish between forms of resistance that are conformist (self-serving) or self-defeating (self-destructive) and those that are transformative. Transformative resistance is the concept of a collective resistance that results in positive and transformational change for the individual and the community (Solórzano and

Delgado-Bernal, 2001: 319–320). Our students were able to resist the temptations of the model of individual achievement often promoted in schools and sports programs by finding ways to redistribute the knowledge they were acquiring. Part of this happened informally as the older students would naturally develop mentoring relationships with younger students. It also happened formally through the program's year-round academic support program that we called study table (see Chapter 8 for a fuller description). In short, study table was a mandatory tutorial session three times per week for two hours. In study table, students that displayed the skills to be successful students were assigned younger players to mentor to ensure that they learned the habits and skills to succeed at Townville High. Students also shared their strategies for academic success in less formal ways with peers that were not in the program, and formally with younger children in the community through their development of the summer mini-camps.

Team sports are well positioned to develop young people's sense of collectivity and community when coaches emphasize the relationship between the individual and the team. In the LWBP, each student was responsible for personal growth (social, academic, and athletic) and for contributing to the growth of the team in those same areas. They had, in effect, a double-duty in that they had to develop their own skills while also finding ways to use that growth to contribute to the growth of the team. A simple example of this might be if one player worked hard to shoot the basketball better. The development of that skill would not necessarily benefit the team if there was not someone to screen their defender so that they could get open, and someone to pass them the ball at the right time so that they could get their shot off. We often used these lessons about complementing each other for successful team play to challenge the individual achievement model promoted in school and the larger society. We also regularly talked with students about extending these principles of interdependency beyond the goal of athletic success and into other aspects of their lives (relationships, academic achievement, and community responsibility).

The impact of our emphasis on teamwork over individual achievement was reflected in the deep sense of community that students came to associate with the program. Lisa, like many of the students, described the program as an extension of her family.

> **Lisa:** This isn't really like a team to me. It's more like a family. You know if you ever need anything you can ask your teammates or your coach. They always have your back. If you

are ever really in need or you're really down, someone is there. It's just like a real good support system, especially if you don't have any siblings or if you're not too close with your family. You have someone to lean on and support you which most people don't have throughout high school. People say all the time to us that they wish they had friends like we have in this program. They ask me how we do it. I tell them we work hard at it.

Similarly, Sandra equated her teammates to her sisters, saying that the program was the most significant part of her high school experience.

Sandra: I had a team. This was the best thing that ever happened to me. If you go around the team, you have so many people you can talk to. They are like my sisters.

Like most tight-knit communities, we had our share of disagreements and conflicts. However, unlike many adolescent relationships that flame out in petty jealousy, the program's attention to the cultivation of community turned conflicts into opportunities for deeper friendships. It is counter-hegemonic to have that kind of closeness in an environment that rewards individual achievement and generally promotes a hostile culture that discourages positive emotional investment—the presence of bars on windows and doors, overcrowded social spaces, and intense police presence are a few of the ways that schools create these unhealthy conditions. Most high school students find a way to make friends anyway, and some of those friendships are lasting. What is rare is to have a school program that helps them cultivate those friendships and connects the power of those relationships to academic achievement and community consciousness.

WHAT A COACH CAN TEACH A TEACHER

As a teacher-educator, the story of the structure we used in the LWBP is chock full of pedagogical lessons that I would want students of teaching to understand. A section similar to this one concludes each of the chapters where the program is discussed so that teachers that read this book have a specific reference section that translates what I did as a coach to lessons for the classroom.

You need a vehicle

The first takeaway from this chapter is the importance of teachers having a vehicle for delivering their pedagogical strategy. It is not enough to say that you are a believer in critical pedagogy, direct instruction, or cooperative learning. In order for your pedagogical strategies to work, you must have a vehicle, a "hook," for delivering your pedagogy. Over 20 years ago, Willis (1981) warned that schools were rapidly becoming obsolete in the lives of young people because they had failed to keep up with their everyday cultural experiences and interests. Before Willis, Dewey (1902) argued the same thing, saying that effective teachers put the child at the "center of the curriculum" by drawing from students' needs, experiences, and interests to build curriculum. In short, this means developing pedagogical strategies that emanate from things that your students are interested in. In those things you can almost always find the content and concepts you want/need to teach.

Additionally, we it is our responsibility to build the scaffolds from where our students are (their interests) to the place where we want them to go (standards based outcomes). Too many of us wind up expecting students to build that bridge for themselves. I refer to this as the business as usual approach to instruction (back to basics, textbooks and tests, paper and pencil, drill and kill, etcetera). Just as Willis predicted, these approaches have made school virtually irrelevant in the lives of countless youth. A few still enjoy these "time honored" practices, others remain willing to tolerate them, but growing numbers are checking out because of them. We all know where these patterns of disengagement are the most intense and the most costly. We all also know that those classrooms are the ones that are the least likely to engage students with culturally and socially appropriate pedagogies *and* the most likely to be handcuffed with methods and curriculum whose only tradition is failure for most.

Have you played a Playstation 3 game, surfed the internet, sent a video to your friend using your phone, or had a text message "dialogue" lately? Until our pedagogical vehicles catch up, we're behind, and we will continue to lose the hearts and minds of our young people to things that we all know are more engaging to them than what we offer them in most of our classrooms.

See your students as organically intellectual

The creation of a classroom culture where all students can learn requires us to develop strategies for identifying areas where each of our students is already skilled, and then incorporating space for them to use those skills in the classroom. There is not one-way to meet this challenge. A strategy that works for one student may not be effective for the next. So, we must develop a toolbox full of ways to identify and understand our students' interests. Some of the approaches that I have used with relative success include: student journals, individual and group conversations, participating in social activities with students, attending events that students are participating in, and letting them play their CDs (now iPod tracks) or favorite radio stations during rides home. In short, we should always listen, take notes, pay attention, and think strategically about how to bring their skills and interests into our teaching.

Identify and utilize the ZPD

As a refresher, a student's zone of proximal development is the zone of development (social and academic) that they are capable of moving through if they are supported by someone that already understands the concepts being taught in that zone. To create the conditions for this to happen educators should: 1) know the skills we want to teach; 2) know the level each student has attained in those skills (their ZPD); and 3) deliver dynamic lessons that allow multiple skill levels to feel challenged *and* successful while advancing their mastery of the skill(s) being taught. In a classroom of 30+ students, this can be very challenging because there is likely to be a range of zones of proximal development. If you have over 160 students, as I did for most of my career, the complexity of the issue grows. One strategy I have found useful in meeting this challenge is to identify students' approximate ZPD on the skills I am teaching. This can be done using combinations of test scores, conversations with previous teachers, conversations with the student and their family, and previous work from the class. Then, using project-based learning, students of all skill levels are evenly distributed into groups. Explicit directions are given to those with higher skill mastery to *teach* the skill, rather than just doing all the work for the group to insure a good grade—this means that part of my assessment is how well all group members reflect growth on the focal skills at the end of the group activity or project. I also make sure to build in a range of skill elements into the group project and assessment so that all students can be positioned to shine at various moments in the project.

This approach to grouping students can be dangerous if you allow it to spiral into lowered expectations, or if students feel they are being tracked. This is where building a critical collective classroom culture becomes essential to success. Well-meaning teachers that act as though all children come to class at the same skill level are disingenuous, rarely respected, and even more rarely successful. The truth is that long before we assert our teacher judgments onto a new group of students, the institution has already ascribed their position and that of their peers on the skills hierarchy. I am convinced that students do not take issue with teachers that acknowledge their skill level, even if it may be low. What they take umbrage with is having their value attached to that acknowledgement, lowered expectations or high expectations without support, and failure to recognize the other skills they do possess. When I do group students, I try to do it in ways that avoid these four pitfalls, while recognizing and responding to the fact that my students arrive with different zones of proximal development and therefore they will need different kinds of support to be successful.

Critical praxis—using video to reflect on our teaching successes and struggles

One of the most beneficial tools for improving our classroom practice is the use of video lesson study. I regularly videotape my teaching. I look at these tapes, often painfully, by myself. When I do this, I typically have specific things I am looking for, such as the delivery of a key idea or an interaction with a particular student I'm struggling to reach. I might also be looking for insight into the organization of the group activities that I discussed in the previous section on ZPD.

In addition to this individual strategy, I also frequently meet with close friends that are teachers to discuss our practice. It is not uncommon for us to watch video of each other's teaching. These collective video study lessons might only happen a couple of times a year, unless I am participating in a formal teacher inquiry group in which case it happens weekly. Particularly in the former scenario, it is important to me that I am receiving feedback from people that I have developed close friendships with over the years because they are more likely to be aware of my teaching philosophy and to be openly critical of places where my teaching does not live up to it. It is also important for me to say here that the critiques I receive from colleagues are sometimes accompanied with solutions to my challenges. Sometimes, they are not. In either case they are accompanied with a clear and caring commitment to supporting me for the long haul, so that I might find solutions and keep getting better as a teacher.

Countering the hegemony without being counter productive

Hegemony is the control over prevailing ideas and norms by using culture bearing institutions like schools to create consensus for those ideas and norms (i.e. the largely unquestioned belief that large numbers of urban students will not succeed in education). To act counter-hegemonically as a teacher, developing a counter-culture inside of a cultural institution like school, is no small task. While engaging in this project, we should always be aware that even when we act to disrupt the negative elements of schooling, we are sometimes complicit with the very system we are critiquing—for starters, if we are teachers then we are taking a salary check from the school. Nevertheless, it is our duty to establish a counter-culture when we are teaching in schools where mediocrity and low expectations have been normalized.

This project is initiated in our classroom, beginning with our being explicit with students about the hegemonic elements of school that we are trying to interrupt (i.e. rugged individualism, social reproduction, racism, misogyny, etc). We should also be explicit with our students about the difficulty of such an effort because of the deeply entrenched role school occupies in this country as the primary social sorting institution in our society (Duncan-Andrade and Morrell, 2008). However, a critique without solutions will do very little for your students. Cornel West refers to such efforts as attempts to achieve "affirmation through negation," which may actually end up being counter-productive for some students by exacerbating their frustrations without offering them relief.

Instead, our critiques should begin by deepening students' understanding about *what* is happening to them in school and *why* it is happening. This process of demystifying school lends itself to a second level of discussion where we can speak explicitly with students about how to bend the system to their advantage—how to win at the game of school. Indeed, if school is a game with rules and norms, we have to teach our students to understand those things if we expect them to win. These strategies might include ways to deal with dysfunctional classroom learning environments or effective ways to make up credits (explicit examples of my use of these strategies in the LWBP are discussed in greater detail in upcoming chapters). In many schools, especially those serving poor children, these kinds of explicit conversations rarely happen and this makes it all the more difficult for students to understand an experience that frequently strikes them as unjust and illogical. Is it any mystery why our students get so frustrated with school?

I often wish that I could offer my students a totally different type of school. I'm working on that, but right now I cannot. In the meantime, it would hypocritical of me to only critique the negative elements of school—especially given that, at some level, I found ways to make the system work for me. Instead, my aim is to teach students to understand the ways in which school can be unfair, how to navigate those injustices, and how to take advantage of the places where school can offer them opportunity. This is what I mean when I talk about helping students develop a critical double-consciousness.

One half of the double-consciousness nurtures students' resiliency. This begins with open and honest conversation with our students that school, like society, can be hostile and unjust. Many of our students are instinctively and acutely aware of these injustices, but have been conditioned to normalize them by blaming themselves and/or their communities for conditions they did not create. Any such recognition must also be accompanied with the honest assessment that these conditions are not going to change tomorrow. And so, while these conditions are not their fault, it is their responsibility to learn to sail those stormy seas. In this first case, students must be encouraged to persevere through moments of strife when conditions simply do not present the opportunity for immediate change (i.e. a parent loses their job). In short, they must be resilient enough to handle setbacks in their life.

However, we must also nurture the second half of critical double-consciousness, which develops students' sense of agency. This half of students' consciousness is developed by fostering their ability and responsibility to transform unjust conditions when there are opportunities for action. This is accomplished by helping students develop a set of pragmatic skills that allow them to confront, and/or negotiate around, perpetrators of institutional injustice. In the short-term, we can also expect our students to share those skills with their peers. In the long-term, we should insist that our students gain access to power and use those positions to fundamentally transform institutional injustices.

War of position—war of movement

Gramsci's concept of the war of position and the war of movement has usefulness for classroom teachers on two levels. For those readers that are put off by the metaphor of war, I'd encourage you to think of our work in the classroom as a battle for the hearts and minds of our students. This should not be thought of as a battle *against* our students, but a battle with them and on their behalf. This is the inescapable challenge before us as urban educators, and it is often misunderstood. Too many of us try to create classroom spaces that are safe from righteous rage or, worse, we design plans to weed out children that display it. The question we should be grappling with is not how to manage students with these emotions, but how we will help students channel them. This is the war of position—the battle to win the trust of each of our students, particularly those students that are manifesting their personal pain in the form of self-defeating behaviors.

In the context of the classroom, the war of movement is the beautiful struggle to create collective consensus in your class such that it functions as a healthy and cohesive unit. If you have taught long enough, you know that the first step often requires you to win the trust of key personalities in the class. If we win these micro-battles, we begin to win the war of movement.

Although common sense might dictate that students make their evaluations of our trustworthiness based on how we treat them as individuals, this is only partly true. Numerous students have told me that they came to trust me because of how they saw me treating other students, particularly peers that other teachers consistently disregarded. My willingness to be firm and fair, while clearly conveying my love and compassion for students that were not necessarily reflecting those same feelings back to me, helped other students come to believe that I would never give up on them, even when they screwed up.

We can also think of the war of position and war of movement as connected to our larger project as educators. If we think of ourselves as change agents for society, then winning the hearts and minds of our students is the war of position. If enough us are able to create students that have a different and more just vision for the world, then we will shift the collective consciousness of our society, and in so doing, we can win the war of movement. I can think of few groups in our society that are better positioned to do this than teachers.

This belief that we are in a war for the hearts and minds of our children guides my outlook on the importance of our work in the classroom and it is why I take my calling as a teacher so seriously and so personally. In my lectures on this topic, people often refer to me as "passionate," but I feel that my lectures about teaching reflect my fear that I am not doing enough, my desperation over feelings that we are losing ground with our youth, and my indignation over our collective failures as a society. However, my lectures also reflect my audacious hope that results from being around young people everyday—hope is the gift that they keep on giving to me.

Finally, this idea that our work as educators is part of a battle over the future direction of our society helps contextualize guidance given to me by two of my mentors. The first piece of advice comes from Joan Cone, a remarkable teacher of over 30 years, who told me once that "schools have to *better* than society if society is ever going to improve." The second pearl of wisdom comes from an interview with Tupac Shakur where he said, "I don't believe that I will change the world. But, I do believe I can influence the mind that does." To connect our teaching to a project that is bigger than us, our students, and our classrooms is an essential ingredient for understanding the value of our work in a society that rarely acknowledges it.

NOTES

1   This chapter borrows heavily from Chapter 4 in my book with Ernest Morrell, *The Art of Critical Pedagogy*, printed by Peter Lang (2008).

2   This process is known as tracking. See the work of Jeannie Oakes (1985) for an analysis of how this structure operates. See the work of Joan Cone (2003) for an example of how teachers can actively combat tracking in their schools.

3   Antonio Gramsci (1891–1937) was an Italian critical philosopher that was jailed by Benito Mussolini for his ideas. At this trial, his prosecutor stated, "For twenty years we must stop this brain from functioning" (Gramsci, 1971, p. lxxxix). His most comprehensive work, composed while he was in prison, *The Prison Notebooks*, articulates his belief that all people are naturally intellectuals.

4   Simply put, a person's ZPD is a zone of information (ideas, theories, principles, strategies, etc) of on any particular subject that an individual is ready to learn with support from someone that has already mastered that zone.

5   Howard Gardner has referred to these as multiple intelligences.

6   See Chapter 3 for a discussion of the origins of the Definite Dozen and its evolution as a framework that I now use as the philosophical centerpiece of my classroom teaching.

7   Psychologists distinguish between private self-consciousness and public self-consciousness. The former leads one to be acutely self-aware and introspective such that one is examining their inner feelings and emotions. The latter bears more negative connotations as it refers to a preoccupation with how others view you. DuBois' refers to the development of private self-consciousness as a means to empowerment.

8   The camp is discussed in greater detail in Chapter 10.

9   This was the first graduating class from the LWBP that was in the program for the full 4 years of high school. The following year, the program's 100% college enrollment continued with another 2 seniors moving on to universities.

10   I am not ignorant of the importance of the small size of the LWBP on these outcomes. Rather, this comparative data is a suggestion that something different and special was going on inside the program, and that when we find these pockets of success we should spend time working to understand it. For what it's worth, in my work as a classroom teacher, I have never had a cohort meet this mark of 100% 4-year college admissions. But, I have consistently been at or above 70 percent.

11   In some of my other work, I have referred to this explicitness as having a "critically conscious purpose" (see Duncan-Andrade, 2006 & 2009).

12   See the work of John Taylor Gatto (2007, 2009) as good examples of these kinds of critiques. Gatto's work is light on discussions of race, but they do capture some elements of the counter-hegemonic discourse I am suggesting and they are from the perspective of an accomplished veteran classroom teacher.

13   Of course, I am capitalizing on the current popularity of this term as a result of Barack Obama's borrowing it from Reverend Wright as the key slogan for his 2008 presidential campaign. But, it is a term I have been using to talk about teaching for quite some time. In a recent article (Duncan-Andrade, 2009) I discuss the various kinds of hope that I see as dangerous ("false hope") and useful ("critical hope") for educators.

CHAPTER SEVEN

SUMMER SEASON (JUNE TO AUGUST)

Each summer, the students in the LWBP traveled up and down the west coast competing in basketball tournaments. During the focal students' four years in the program, the team traveled to tournaments in Canada, Seattle, Portland, Los Angeles, and San Diego. These tournaments served as an excellent opportunity for the development of a team culture. The primary objective of the summer travel was to develop a critical community of practice. According to Wenger (1999) a community of practice has three basic tenets: 1) it is a *joint enterprise* as understood and continually renegotiated by its members, 2) it functions through *mutual engagement* that binds members together into a social entity, and 3) it produces a *shared repertoire* of communal resources (routines, sensibilities, art ifacts, vocabulary, styles, etc.) that members develop over time.

I use the term 'critical'[1] as a modifier for our community of practice because it was designed with the intent of developing a viable counter-culture to Townville High School's culture of low expectations. The critical elements of our community of practice were premised upon the formation of a peer group driven by a "pedagogy of hope" (Freire, 1995). Freire describes hope as an "ontological need" that enables people to struggle against fatalism to "muster the strength we absolutely need for a fierce struggle that will re-create the world" (8). Further, he argues that hope must be anchored in our day-to-day practices so that it can be developed as a critical response to the material conditions of our lives, rather than as the naïve notion that hope alone will produce change. He goes on to explain:

> The idea that hope alone will transform the world, and action under-taken in that kind of naiveté, is an excellent route to hopelessness, pessimism, and fatalism. But the attempt to do without hope, in the struggle to improve the world, as if that struggle could be reduced to calculated facts alone, or a purely scientific approach, is a frivolous illusion. …Without a minimum of hope, we cannot so much as start the struggle. But without the struggle, hope, as an ontological need, dissipates, loses its bearings, and turns into hopelessness. And hope-lessness can become tragic despair. Hence the need for a kind of edu-cation in hope…One of the tasks of the progressive educator, through a serious, correct political analysis, is to unveil opportunities for hope, no matter what the obstacles may be. After all, without hope there is little we can do (8–9).

I have argued that hope grows as a young person develops a sense of control over their life and that educators can play a fundamentally important role in that process (Duncan-Andrade, 2009). To cultivate hope in our students in the LWBP, it was important that they saw their participation as something beyond a typical school program, something different than the up by your bootstraps survival of the fittest model that Townville schools promoted. Our time together in the summer was critically important in this process on three levels. Firstly, it allowed us to be the first sphere of high school influence on new students because we started working with them before their formal high school experience began. Secondly, it allowed us to maintain our existing influence on the lives of our current students, avoiding some of the slippage that can occur over the summer months if students do not have access to a critical and supportive educational community. Thirdly, the summer provided the oppor-tunity for more intensive social and educational development because we were the primary program of influence. Our intention was to use these three advan-tages to deepen our students' sense of community, reinforcing the critical and collective strategies that would be used in the school year by creating oppor-tunities for them to former deeper relationships with each other and with the program. The program's commitment to advancing this collectivity in the summer was central to developing our students' hope, showing them that they were really part of a community of practice that would work together to chal-lenge and overcome the obstacles in their lives. The opportunity to be connected to something bigger than themselves disrupts the isolating petty individualism students experience in most high schools, and this sense that you are not alone is an important component for cultivating hope in young people.

DEVELOPING OUR COMMUNITY OF PRACTICE

This process of developing a community of practice focused on creating a set of common goals around which the group could unify. The three primary goals were: 1) increased social and academic expectations with support to meet those expectations; 2) developing a program culture where each student felt belonging and responsibility for our community of practice; and 3) the cultivation of individual and collective agency to respond to challenging conditions in their lives and in the Townville community. The summer portion of the program provided retreat like settings where the seeds could be planted so that these three expectations could take root by the time the school year started. Each of these goals was pursued using the tenets of critical pedagogy mentioned in Chapter 6 (organic intellectualism, critical praxis, and counter-hegemony).

The first programmatic goal (increased expectations and support) pulled from the concept of counter-hegemony by developing a social and academic culture that challenged a Townville High culture that normalized mediocrity and tolerated failure. This goal also pulled from the principle of organic intellectualism, building skills and confidence by supporting students through their respective zones of proximal development. The second and third programmatic goals relied on the principles of counter-hegemony and critical praxis, helping normalize the counter-culture of our program such that students felt ownership over it (agency), and a sense of responsibility for advancing it once they returned to a less supportive environment at Townville High.

ON THE ROAD AGAIN: TRAVELING AS A BUILDING BLOCK OF THE COMMUNITY OF PRACTICE

The examples provided in the remainder of this chapter come from the summer of 2000. I am sharing some of the events from that summer because in many ways it represents the most thorough summer program we offered. It was a milestone period for us because this was the summer preceding the senior year of our first 4-year cohort of students. It was also the first time we had ever left the country together, and the longest we had been away from home as a group.

We spent two weeks on the road, leaving Townville on July 2nd, traveling to Canada, Seattle, and Portland, before returning on July 16th. For most of the players, this was the longest they had ever been away from the city of Townville, and for all of them it was the longest they had been away from their families. As Nancy put it:

> That first trip to Canada was scary and exciting to me. I had never been away so long and my mom was kinda trippin' at first. You know we had never really been apart like that and I am her baby (smiling). But, once we got on that plane and got there, it was like I was still with my family. I mean we just got closer from those trips. We had to 'cause we were spending all our time together.

As Nancy points out, summers together created a family-like space, one where the concept of the program as a community gained credibility. Outside the comforts of their daily routines, players were forced to rely upon each other for support and social development.

In our efforts to establish a counter-culture to the social norms of the school, we ran the risk of our students feeling marginalized from peer groups outside the program. To offset this, we knew our program's culture had to be viewed as something desirable—something non-participants would want if it were offered in other places at the school. This was partially achieved by making sure that students had memorable experiences in the program, which developed most prominently during the summer because we made traveling together fun, making sure that most activities were social and collective. Part of this happened because they were teammates. However, our students frequently commented on the fact that their friends in other sports programs did not experience the same closeness because they did not travel together and after games they did not eat and socialize as a group. Our goal was to travel together, compete together, relax together, and think together.

On our trip to Canada we flew into Seattle and then drove rental vans across the U.S.-Canadian border. During the drive, a few girls commented about the fact that we were allowed to drive right into Canada without any hassles. This opened a conversation between Adriana and a couple of other players, including Ada. Adriana, one of two Chicanas in the program, started in on a social commentary comparing the US-Mexican border to the one we were crossing:

> Adriana: This is fucked up. How come people can just go in and out of
>   Canada and nobody's trippin? But if you try to go to

México, or come and visit your family in the US you get
stopped and it takes forever. It's like they don't want people
coming in and out of there, but here they aint trippin.

Ada: That's because they're white.

Adriana: Who's white? We're not white. Oh...in Canada?

Ada: Yep. You know that if they (Mexicans) was white wouldn't
nobody be trippin'.

Adriana: That's so ghetto. That's just like how they do us in [Townville].
If you're white nobody's trippin', but if you aint you know
you gonna get stopped hella times for nothin'.

Adriana's frustration with unequal border policies, and her willingness to raise
the racialized politics of that issue among her teammates is reflective of the
heightened sensitivity to social and political issues in the team's culture. In your
typical prep summer sports program, you would not likely hear this kind of
politicized conversation in the team van. In the case of the LWBP, critical conversations about racial and social justice had become a normal part of team culture.
Our students were critically aware of differential treatment in society, and were
beginning to apply that awareness to their reading of the world. Although none
of the younger players engaged in the dialogue with Adriana and Ada, their
exposure to these types of conversations emanating from their older peers helped
them to see critical thinking as a part of our community of practice.

Traveling together also created regular opportunities outside of basketball to construct communal relationships across age, race and background
(going to the movies, eating together, going to the mall, hanging out at the
hotel). For a majority of the students, this opportunity to travel with the team
was their first chance to leave Townville since their birth. The time spent
driving and flying to places such as Seattle and San Diego often resulted in
bonding through lengthy conversations among players, the sharing of music
and books while in the van or on the plane, or the use of a teammate's
shoulder to sleep on.

ROOMING ASSIGNMENTS AS COMMUNITY BUILDING

Once we arrived in Canada, the bonding deepened as teammates were placed
into hotel rooms based upon my assessment of their need to develop stronger
bonds. Sometimes this meant pairing younger players with older players who
were instructed to mentor them. At other times, this meant the pairing of

people within their age group so that bonds developed among players facing similar age-based issues. The team participated in an average of five tournaments per summer, all of which resulted in them staying in hotels with their teammates.

Players sometimes disliked the fact that they did not always get to choose their own roommates. Had they been able to choose all the time, they probably would have stayed with the same group of friends. This would certainly not have facilitated the feelings of community outside of the social cliques within the team. As Mika commented, although unpopular at times, our rooming assignments ultimately came to be understood by the older players.

> **Mika:** Sometimes I used to get really pissed off at you for making me stay with people on the team I didn't really like. I mean you knew who we were closest with and then you would split us up. But, after we would switch hotels...I mean, you know, after a tournament, I knew why you did it. We were so much closer with the people we had to stay with. We didn't always like each other, but we knew each other, that's for sure.

This point by Mika is a critical one for educators to understand. While we aim to teach young people about community and how to work with a variety of different people, we rarely create opportunities for that to happen. It is far too rare that students are allowed to work as groups in schools or programs, and it is even more rare that educators challenge students across age groups to work together and mentor each other. We also can make the mistake of wanting all students to like each other, when we know from our own relationships that that is highly unlikely. What Mika acknowledges is that students in the program learned that they did not have to like everyone to be able to respect and work with everyone toward a common goal.

We approached even the seemingly mundane details of our program (such as rooming assignments) with intentional planning. Each action was treated as a teachable moment. Students did not always ask for an explanation of our thinking, but when they did I was prepared to help them understand the deeper purpose behind decisions. We wanted them to be clear that every decision was backed by a reason so that they understood why we did, what we did, when we did it.

Too many educators overlook the truism of the adage "the devil is in the details" when they are attempting to build a program or classroom culture that fosters excellence. The importance of clear planning for program structure and activities is obvious, but explicitly connecting everyday activities to the program structure is indispensable for success. The devil is in the details because the actualization of grand ideas is rarely about the ideas themselves. It is about the attention we pay to the small steps that make up the journey we must take to actualize those ideas.

We wanted students to approach their lives with great care and planning. In order for us to demand this from them, we had to model that approach to each of the decisions we made that impacted the program. The more our students understood that each thing we did was connected to the larger program goals, the more they bought into approaching their own lives with a deeper sense of the value of planning and goal setting.

For example, when we were in Canada the girls were placed in rooms together based on the number of years they had been in the program. The primary reason for this was because we wanted the younger students in rooms together because it was their first trip with us. This allowed us to focus on their rooms because we anticipated they would need extra attention to develop the self-discipline we expected from our students when we traveled. We also wanted to give the older girls the independence they had earned over their time in the program. We knew we would not have to check up on those rooms as much because after two or three years on the road with us they had become very self-disciplined.

When we returned from Canada to our hotel in Portland, most of the older students knew that room assignments would probably be changed from Canada. The younger girls, however, presumed their roommates from Canada were their rooming partners for the entire summer and so they gathered around each other in the hotel lobby. After checking the team in at the front desk, we gathered the girls together and announced their rooming assignments. This time, students were put in rooms based on the positions that they played on the team. This meant that there were veterans and rookies sharing rooms. The older girls were the only ones that were allowed to have keys. This was a clear message about who was in charge in each room, and we also met with our older students that night to explain that we expected more mentorship from them at this tournament. This meant tending to things like curfew and making sure that everyone in their room made it to team meetings on time. If somebody in their room was not ready for bed check, was late for a team meeting, or unprepared for the vocabulary quizzes, the veterans in the room would always be the ones that faced the most severe consequences. This helped to develop a sense of responsibility and urgency among the older students for bringing the younger ones up to speed. Among younger students, it helped to build a sense of collective responsibility since their actions would have direct consequences for people other than themselves—I am quite certain that veterans reinforced this point in private conversations as well.

As students matured, they noticed the differences in the room pairings and came to understand the reasons for changing things up. Erika pointed out that in her early years in the program room pairings with older girls helped her to understand program expectations.

> **Erika:** I remember the first time I went out on the road and I just wanted to stay up and talk with everybody. I would wake up in the morning and I was so tired and then we would always have to answer those questions for SAT words and it seemed like I could never make it to our meetings on time. Then I got in the room with Sandra and Mika. And things sure did change. I remember they came back to the room after the captain's meeting and a bunch of us were in there talking and watching t.v. and it was like[2] minutes 'til lights out. They came in and they were like, "what do you think you are doing?" They went off on us because we weren't already in bed. I knew right then that they weren't playing. They didn't want 'dawn patrol'[2] for something I did. I went right to bed that night. Now, I know that I might have to do that with younger players too so they understand that I'm serious.

Traveling together provided numerous opportunities for students to learn to lead, and to learn to be led by their peers. With only each other to count on while we were away from home, students learned to value the communal discipline and responsibility. This helped to foster opportunities for mentoring and created a peer culture that was largely self-regulating toward discipline and excellence. The fact that expectations were equally as high off the basketball court helped players understand that the LWBP community of practice extended beyond sports.

SUMMER TIME FOR PARENTS

Our time on the road, although difficult for parents, was also celebrated by many of them. Just as this was the first time away from home for many of the students, it was also the first time that many of our parents had been separated from their children for any extended period of time. For many of the parents, this meant accepting that their daughters were growing up and establishing new levels of freedom. For younger students, this frequently meant having to convince their families that they were ready for that independence. Once they were on the road, they were often required to check in with their families several times a day to assure them that they were safe. As Nancy noted, it took several summer seasons for the process of leaving home for the summer to become normalized for her and her Mom.

> **Nancy:** At first my mom used to get really upset about us leaving for so long…especially when I was a sophomore. She couldn't understand why we couldn't just play games around here. But, now, I think she understands it…and she probably likes it because she knows what happened to my brother and sister when they just stayed around and didn't do nothing. Now, I think she's used to it where before she would get pissed 'cause she'd say I was putting the program before the family. Now, it seems like it has brought my family closer together…they can all come to games, but before we never did anything together as a family. Now we do.

Despite concerns about being separated from the family, many parents expressed that they were actually less worried about their children when we were traveling than when they were in Townville. When traveling, students were away from some of the dangers of their neighborhoods, which can be heightened in the summer because students are out of school but parents still have to work. Although parents might want students to stay in the safety of the house while they are at work, as students get older they are more likely to spend the idle time of summer on the streets. Programs that offer urban youth the opportunity to spend their summer days engaged in activities that are directed and supported by adults are few and far between. For this reason, many of our parents welcomed the summer travel because their children were off the streets, surrounded by positive peer influences, and engaged in meaningful activities for their physical, social, and academic development.

In the summer months, Townville is like most urban centers in that it has far more youth than its youth programs can accommodate. As Lisa, Mika's mother, explained, extended activities such as our program's summer travel were virtually impossible to access in Townville. This left many parents with few, if any, meaningful options to choose from during the summer months.

> **Lisa:** Undoubtedly, the travel was important to me. I never knew what to do with Mika in the summers because I still had to work. Summer school still didn't keep her busy all day. When she traveled I knew that she was safe. And I knew that she was doing something positive. For her brother and sisters, they never had that, and you can see the difference.

However, as Melinda, Ada's mother noted, it took time to earn the trust of the parents.

> **Melinda:** When Ada first went out with the team I was so nervous. She had never been away from me for that long and certainly not with a group of her friends. It was very hard. But, I got used to it, sort of (laughing). Even now it's hard for me to let her go away to college. I just always worry about her. Even though the summer travel was hard and expensive, I was also glad that she was getting the opportunity.

The summer component of the program provided parents a viable solution to the persistent dilemma of how to support their children over the summer. The major hurdles for parents to overcome were the anxiety over being separated from their child and the cost of travel. The first hurdle was addressed through family potluck meetings where parents could receive all the details of our trips and have concerns addressed. Additionally, we asked veteran parents to actively seek out new parents during these community events to discuss their strategies for utilizing the summer program. We also made sure to schedule time every day during our travels so that students could call their families.

The financial burden of traveling was partially offset by a variety of fundraising opportunities made available to families over the course of the year. Although finances were tight for many of the families, these fundraisers helped to ease some of the burden. It is important to note, however, that the lack of financial resources was a constant struggle for the program. As is too often the case with programs that are providing direct service to urban youth, our program received no funding from the school or outside sources during the summer. We operated from the finances we were able to generate through nickel and dime fundraisers (candy sales, car washes, donations), and through the generosity of the coaches' credit cards. However, no student was ever denied the opportunity to travel because of a lack of money. When students were short on money, which was always the case for at least a third of the team, coaches would come out of their pockets to make up for the shortfall. Very little was made of this publicly because we did not want any of the players to feel like they were a financial burden to us. However, this was a major strain on the program, and challenged our sustainability over time because all the coaches were volunteers.

Most of the other sports programs in the city traveled very little, or not at all, in part because of the lack of resources. Meanwhile, wealthier suburban schools often had full summer programs on the strength of their parent booster clubs, which are often made possible by the extra time and income available to middle class and wealthy communities. This not so hidden inequity of time and money, contributes heavily to the opportunity gap between rich and poor children (Alexander, Entwisle & Olson, 2001). The gap is less obvious during the school year because at least every child has access to a school (school to school inequities notwithstanding). However, during the summer months, children from families with disposable incomes have numerous programs available for their enrichment. For children from families without that disposable income, funded programs are so rare that they over-enroll, and programs like ours are mostly financed on credit and sweat equity. If we really want to close this opportunity gap, it is worth considering the policy implications of the funding challenges our program faced every year.

NORMALIZING COMMUNITY CONSCIOUSNESS

Extended conversations about the team's responsibility to the larger community of Townville were quite normal throughout the year. But, summer travel provided an excellent opportunity to press these types of dialogues with players because there was more time and space available for them to reflect. Without the incessant hustle of the school day bearing down on them, they could have meaningful dialogues about issues facing them and our community.

One activity we used to facilitate these dialogues was to have students read the same text so that we could discuss it as a group. During the summer of 2000, players were given copies of Chapter One from Jonathon Kozol's *Savage Inequalities* to read as we traveled from Portland to Seattle. They read the chapter while we drove and we met that night in the hotel to discuss their feelings about it. The reading activity started out with volunteers reading a couple of paragraphs aloud during the van ride. After four or five readers, they were on their own to finish the chapter. Typically, the van was bursting with conversations and music, but this time it was completely silent with everyone reading.

I had used this same text as part of the first unit in my 12th grade English classes at Townville High School. In my English classes, it was very common for students to express their dismay that schools such as those in East St. Louis were even allowed to exist. It was not until I pointed out that most of the injustices that appalled them were prevalent right there at Townville High that they would begin to see their own relationship to the text—they were in utter denial. The girls in the LWBP, however, immediately picked up on the similarities. In our team conversation that night, Adriana identified several comparable conditions from her own experiences in *Savage Inequalities*.

Adriana: They (teachers) see us and they think that they don't have to teach. They think, what's the point? I mean, we only have four counselors for our whole school...but it's more than two thousand [students]. And I have at least one sub a day, sometimes more, especially on Fridays. I mean, my [Honors] English teacher has us watch these senseless movies and so people just go to sleep. In [Honors] English! They should show movies that have some relevance to our lives. It's just a lot of stuff wrong. So much stuff. I can't even say it all.

The consistent access to a critical community helped the LWBP students develop high levels of critical awareness about their schooling conditions. Many of them could articulate the presence of those injustices more readily than their peers at Townville High. Identifying the problems was not much of an issue for them. However, the creation of these kinds of critical dialogue spaces was only the first part of the challenge. The next level was creating opportunities for them to respond to the conditions so that they also saw themselves as agents of social change.

CRITICAL PRAXIS: WHEN STUDENTS SEE THEMSELVES AS AGENTS OF CHANGE

Our commitment to raising our students' critical double-consciousness (awareness of inequities, resiliency to overcome, and agency to respond) was connected to specific group activities. Once such activity was group readings and dialogues, using passages from texts such as *Savage Inequalities*. These challenged players to consider the problems facing our school and community. However, we insisted that our students move beyond critique, using their individual and collective successes to impact the larger community. In places like Townville, it is not uncommon for successful students to be told that they are role models, but the implicit expectation there is that "good" students should lead by example and that others will learn through observing them. We did subscribe to this idea to the degree that we expected our students to understand the sign in their locker room that read: "Character is who you are when no one else is looking. Reputation is who other people say you are." In other words, we expected our students to always represent themselves, their families, and our program with the utmost integrity. However, we also insisted that leaders must be active agents in the lives of others by sharing the resources and the knowledge that have allowed them to become successful.

This happened through unstructured and structured activities. An example of the former is revealed in the numerous times our students brought peers from their classes to study table, sharing the resources provided there rather than using them to get ahead of their classmates. An example of more structured efforts to impact the community is evident in the students' development and implementation of the Lady Wildcat Basketball Camp (discussed in greater detail in Chapters 6 and Chapter 10) which became an annual tradition offered free to elementary and middle school children in Townville. After the camp had been running for a couple of years, five students in the program, including Erika and Mika, were motivated by the discussion of Kozol's work over the summer to extend their impact beyond the mini-camps. Erika, a junior at the time, explains:

> I never really thought about how fucked up our schools are. When you had us read from *Savage Inequalities*, it really made me think about some stuff. I mean I always knew that Townville schools are bad, but the more you talked to us about inequality and things like what happens at P- High[3], the more I thought about doing something. I mean for M- (Erika's younger sister), she's gonna have to go through these same fucked up schools. And maybe I can do something about that, to maybe help out or change some stuff. So, that's why I went to my old elementary school, just to let kids know that they can make it too, since nobody ever really came and told me about that. I mean teachers used to come with that "you can be president one day if you really want

it." But kids think that that don't happen for nobody from Townville. So, I went back to let them kids know that it can happen because I did it, and if I did it then they could do it too.

Erika refers here to her decision to return to her elementary school in Townville to speak to her former first grade teacher's class. This came about when the teacher contacted Erika because she had been reading about her so frequently in the newspaper's sports section. Erika decided to take it as an opportunity to impact the community. She set up a day to go to the school and speak to the class and was an instant success. In the six months following her talk, I received six more phone calls from elementary and middle school teachers and principals about having students speak in classes. Each of those engagements produced similar positive results, and resulted in several of those schools bringing their basketball teams to our home games.[4] Schools would do well to develop this tradition of bringing recent graduates back to work with students, rather than paying for "motivational" speakers that are much older than the students and often less connected to the community.

For Mika, her growing sense of responsibility to the community resulted in her spending weekends with a local YMCA basketball program to run skills clinics for elementary school players.

> **Mika:** When I first went, it was as a favor to L- (a program supporter). But, then I started to think about how these kids were looking up to me and I thought about how we're always talking about doing more than just getting good grades and winning games. Every time I would go, those kids would get so excited and jump around, like it was the greatest place in the world to them. It kinda made me want to go because I knew *they* [emphasis in her speech] wanted me to go. Then when I got Kendra and Adriana to go too, then it was even better because it was all of us doing something together.

Ultimately, Mika managed to bring along three of her teammates to work with the youth at the YMCA. Adriana graduated with Mika, but the other two continued to work in the youth program for the next two years after Mika and Adriana had left for college. Those students then recruited some of their younger teammates. This passing of the baton from one generation of players to the next made service to the community a common theme in the LWBP.

SUMMERTIME ACADEMICS AS COUNTER-HEGEMONY

A key element of the program's counter-hegemonic community of practice was the commitment to a culture of continuous academic growth. Many students are conditioned by urban schools to think that unless school is in session there is no learning going on. For many students in Townville, the s ummer signified one of two things with respect to academics: the end of studying for two and a half months, or summer school remediation. The LWBP aimed to counter this mis-education by insisting on conscious participation in the cycle of teaching and learning every day.

Field Note Vignette
Seattle, WA
July 13th. Gymnasium. 5:00 p.m.
Our team stayed at the gym after our semi-final victory to scout the team we will face in tomorrow's championship game. The scene is hardly conducive for studying...whistles blowing and sneakers squeaking provide the gym's soundtrack. The smell of burning rubber mixed with the funk of sweat, filters into your nose before you even reach the gym door. As I scan the gym, watching young people from around the world playing basketball, I notice Erika and Mika tucked away in one corner of the bleachers. They are both reading their books and seem oblivious to all the games going on around them. Just below them, stretched out on the bleachers are Sandra and Nancy, quizzing each other with flashcards on the vocabulary words that they have to recite in the morning to play in tomorrow's championship game. I can hardly be disappointed that the girls are less interested in tomorrow's opponent than in their academic growth.

The summer component of the program worked to develop this counter-hegemonic approach to urban education with a steady diet of literacy development. This included vocabulary development and college entrance exam training through daily vocabulary words, as well as reading and writing assignments. Each night that we were on the road in the summer there was a vocabulary assignment. After the day's games were over and students returned to their hotel rooms, a list of five common SAT words and one Greek root were slipped under their doors. Every one was assigned the same words. They were required to write the words and the root on separate flashcards, putting the part of speech and definition on the back. They were then expected to quiz each other in preparation for a quiz from the coaches.

The following morning at breakfast, students would approach one of the coaches with their vocabulary flashcards in hand and recite the definitions, parts of speech, and three words using the Greek root. The coach would then choose one of the assigned five words and ask for it to be used properly in a sentence. If they could not complete this series of tasks, they would not be allowed to participate in games on that day. When students struggled with words, they could meet with coaches in the evening to get help understanding how to use them in context. It was not uncommon that coaches themselves would have to learn the words along with the students, which was important for the program's community culture because it modeled commitment to life-long learning.

The program's commitment to developing strategic, disciplined study patterns was yearlong, but received particular emphasis in the summer because we were together for weeks at a time. Erika pointed out that the summer's nightly routine allowed her to develop an intellectual discipline that she applied to her English class the following year.

All those words you made us memorize in the summer, at first I hated it. But, I knew I had to do it to play, so I did it. After a while it got easier when you showed us to use flashcards and quiz each other. That's why I got so good on Ms. F-'s tests the next year. They were so easy because I just studied like it was the summer.

Ada echoed Erika's sentiments.

When I first came to Townville High, all I wanted to do was graduate. I never even really thought of college. I had no real goals. I really didn't care. If you asked me what I wanted to do in the future I would have just said, "I don't know." But, this program put me around people who had bigger goals than me. It gave me a different view on everything. Even during the summer, I was always learning, like with the SAT words and the essays. I never would have even thought about the SAT if you didn't make us study those words. And you *know* (emphasis in her speech) I would never have just studied those things on my own.

The development of an academic culture was possible, in part, because most of the coaches in our program were teachers or teachers in training. This is increasingly uncommon, particularly in urban schools, where many teachers are no longer willing to take on the extra duties of coaching. However, our experience as classroom educators made us all the more aware of the value of extending intellectual discipline into the summer. This also gave us valuable insight into the needs and skills of our students, and prepared us with strategies to build on their strengths and address their academic weaknesses. The truth of the matter is that many of our students had never received the necessary support from school to develop a structured method for studying. This lack of attention to the rigor and discipline necessary for developing effective study patterns contributed heavily to inconsistent achievement patterns. To disrupt these trends, we used the time and space provided by summer travel to help students transfer the discipline of athletic training to their academic identities.

In addition to these language development activities, we also helped students work on their writing during the summer. At the end of the school year in mid-June, we gave the players the Advanced Placement (AP) book list and a list of essay prompts to guide their written discussion of the book (see Appendix E). A few weeks later, we went to a bookstore together so they could purchase a book off the list. During the next month, they read the book and wrote a 5–7 page literary analysis of it. With students that were new to the program, we explained the process of tracking[5] and the significance of Advanced Placement in that context. Included in this explanation was a critique of tracking as a process that sorts students in ways that can have negative consequences for their academic futures. Most of our players would have been on the negative end of the tracking process, as they would not have been considered "AP material" by the school.

The second part of our explanation of the summer reading assignment was the issuance of a challenge to rise above the low expectations of the school and teachers that might have doubted their abilities. This challenge came with the promise of support from the adults in the program and access to a peer community that was taking on the same challenge—they would not be the lone newcomers to the AP culture. Finally, they were encouraged to partner with at least one other student to read the same book so that they could work together to analyze and write about the text[6].

In mid-July, the team would be back in Townville for close to two weeks before the second set of summer tournaments in Southern California. During this time, students were expected to finish their books and to meet with their partners to complete the essay assignment. For most of our new students, this was the first time they had been asked to write an essay of any considerable length. To support them, we used a high school classroom to conduct two writing seminars and met with students individually to workshop drafts of their essays.

The writing workshops were designed to help students at all writing levels practice the structure of literary analysis. During these seminars, students were provided with writing techniques and strategies and given access to college writing tutors that had already been working with our students during the school year. Students were also given access to former students' essays, which proved useful as examples of the type of writing we were looking for, but also as positive reinforcement that their peers had successfully cleared this hurdle in the past. The provision of this kind of additional support is an often overlooked element of success when raising expectations of students.

A commitment to high expectations and academic rigor is a promise made in many programs and classrooms. If we had not provided support to match our expectations, we would have created a false rigor. That is what happens in most cases when urban schools raise their academic expectations without attention to greater academic support. I call this false rigor because to ask more of someone (particularly a young person) without providing them the motivation and support to reach that higher standard does not increase the level of rigor, rather, it increases the failure rate. To truly raise the level of rigor requires educators to accept the added responsibility of providing students a system of motivation and support that matches the new expectations.

The added motivation and support consistently worked. Year to year, every student placed their typed essays in my manila folder as they boarded the team van headed for our second set of tournaments in Southern California. My evenings on those trips were spent reading and commenting on the essays, which were returned at the end of the trip with extensive commentary and hearty congratulations. The feedback on the essay was another place where the concept of the zone of proximal development was applied. The students showed a range of writing ability and our goal was to nurture them from where they were to the next level of writing. I never put a letter grade on the essays, but instead encouraged students to use my comments to revise and resubmit their work in their respective English courses during the school year.

Although not every student picked a book that they would be required to read in the upcoming school year, many of them knew their next year's English teacher's reading list because teammates, friends, or family members had been in their class previously. Others asked their next year's English teacher before selecting their summer book. In Mika's case, the summer reading assignment proved advantageous almost every year.

Mika: That was one of the cool parts about the summer. I mean, writing the essay was hard, especially since it was supposed to be the summer. But when school started and I knew I already had one essay done, and it was already pretty good, and I knew what to change to make it better. That kinda made it worth it. Sometimes, I felt like I was cheating because it was so easy to use that essay, but I guess I was just working smarter [laughing].

ADDITIONAL ASSIGNMENTS FOR SENIORS

After we finished our summer tournaments, seniors in the program were given two additional tasks to complete by the end of August. First, they were asked to make a list of 10 colleges that they were interested in attending[7]. Four of those schools were schools to which they were highly confident that they would be admitted. Five of the schools were schools where they felt they had at least some chance to be admitted. The tenth school was called the "pie in the sky"— this was their dream school, a school they would positively attend if they were admitted. They were instructed to pick one dream school, no matter whether they were academically qualified to apply or not. We wanted them to go through the process of applying to the best schools in the country, even if they felt they could not be admitted. The intention was to build a sense of entitlement, so that they knew that they had the right to apply anywhere they desired. Also, it was crucial for them to understand that being told 'no' was part of the process of moving forward—nothing ventured, nothing gained.

Seniors were asked to use answers to the following questions to guide their research into their colleges of interest.

What type of climate (weather) do you want to live in?
What size of school do you want to attend (small college is under 8,000 students, medium is under 15,000 students, and large is over 20,000 students)?
What state do you want to be in?
Are you willing to live away from home? How far?

How big do you want your classes to be?

How important is racial and class diversity on campus?

How much financial aid will you need? Are you willing to take out loans? Are you willing to work?

The team's locker room had dozens of college catalogs and the coaches were readily available to share their knowledge of various colleges. The team had also visited and stayed on numerous college campuses during our summer travel. As an additional resource, seniors were given copies of the U. S. News and World Report College Rankings Guide so that they could look up schools that interested them.

When a senior's list was narrowed to ten, they either drafted a form letter to those schools requesting an application, or obtained one via email or website. All our students were eligible for application fee waivers, which made it possible for them to apply to multiple schools at little to no cost to them. If the high school's counseling department ran out of fee waivers, or limited the number available, the students or I would call the universities directly and advocate that the fee be waived. On the occasions where we were unable to secure waivers and the family could not afford the fee, we paid the application fees for students out of our pockets.

In addition to their list of 10 schools, seniors were also expected to use the last few weeks of summer to prepare a draft of their personal essay. To facilitate this process, we met with seniors as a group to discuss strategies for writing effective essays and helped them begin brainstorming their essays. One thing I've learned over the years is that our students are often encouraged to write a "woe is me" story about how hard their life has been. These narratives often end up pathologizing our students, families, and communities while mostly ignoring the assets that students acquire by emerging triumphantly from struggle. Our tact was to encourage students to write stories of resiliency and perseverance that capture their struggles while highlighting the strength of their character and the skills they developed that will help them be successful in college. These drafts were turned into me at the beginning of the school year for revisions. Over the first few months of their senior school year, these drafts underwent multiple revisions until they were ready for each of their 10 applications.

This process was not always well received by seniors. They frequently questioned why they had to do more than everyone else, but also seemed grateful that they were being pushed and encouraged to think about college before their peers.

Mika: It all seemed like way too much at first. No one I had ever known had done this much work in the summer. But, then I saw all these students scrambling around trying to finish their essays and looking for this and that and stressing, and mine was already done...I see why you made us do it.

This kind of discontent with the process dissipated over time, as returning players saw the previous group go through the process and get positive results. Eventually, the grumbling was replaced by a sense of tradition, as college preparation became a normal expectation for the girls in the program. Erika, who was in the graduating class after Mika's group explained.

Erika: I never really thought much about [the workload] because everyone had done it before me. When it was my turn, I wasn't really surprised because it was just what we had to do. I guess seeing all them before me kind of helped because when it was my turn I was expecting to have to do it.

INDIVIDUAL MEETINGS AS CRITICAL PRAXIS

Our summer travel concluded in early August, which left a month before school restarted. During this final month of summer, the program continued to use sports participation to counter potentially negative elements of our students' school and social environments. This was accomplished with regular athletic training sessions to ensure that students were interacting with each other and the coaching staff on a consistent basis. During this time, students scheduled individual meetings with me and were asked to prepare responses to the following three questions: 1) Who have you been in the past?; 2) Who do you want to be in the future?; and 3) Why do you want those changes for yourself? The students were asked to prepare written responses to these questions, which they read and discussed with me when we met. At the end of our meeting, I stored their responses in a binder so that we could revisit them at the end of the following school year. In that follow-up meeting, we would use the responses to reflect on their progress in the areas of their lives they most wanted to improve upon and make revisions based on their new goals. During these meetings, I would also discuss my evaluation of the student's growth as a member of the LWBP community during the summer, and share my expectations of them for the upcoming school year.

When I interviewed our students about the program, all four of the students focused on in this book commented that this reflexive evaluation process helped them learn how to establish clear goals for themselves. The following comments from Ada are generally reflective of each of their sentiments.

> The most helpful part of this program were the conversations that you had with me. When we would meet and we would talk about what you thought I could do, I really started to believe in myself. Sometimes, it felt like you believed in me more than I believed in me. …This was a dramatic change for me. Before I didn't even see a reason for coming to school. I think because I didn't have any goals. All the planning we do, it made me feel like I was together. I knew that I worked harder than the other kids and that I was doing it for a reason.

These end-of-summer meetings began a yearlong process of self-reflection and goal setting that helped participants focus their energies and have meaningful areas for self-evaluation. They also proved helpful in providing the adults in the program a better idea of what each young person expected of herself. This insight allowed for personalized development plans that catered to their athletic and academic goals. As Ada mentioned above, the combination of goal setting and support provided through these types of conversations were instrumental in the development of students' self-confidence and self-awareness. But, perhaps most importantly, these meetings were a chance to fill students with hope by teaching them to design their own visions for growth and then supporting them to achieve that vision.

PRE-SEMESTER COUNSELING AS COUNTER-HEGEMONY

The team bonding and academic development that took place during the summer led the girls into the start of the school year. As the school year approached the need for academic counseling increased because players had to finalize their class schedules. Sadly, outside of a select few high achieving students, academic counseling at Townville High was rare. This was due in part to a counselor to student ratio of around 400:1. To make up for the lack of academic counseling, we worked with a few of the more supportive counselors to make sure that new and returning students in the LWBP had appropriate college-bound class schedules before the school started.

Townville High designed its registration process around grade levels. On the day assigned to their grade level, the LWBP participants registered for school, received their schedules and promptly met individually with me. I reviewed their course schedules and with remarkable frequency, students did not receive the schedules that they requested from their counselors at the end of the previous semester. The mistakes in their schedules ranged from: being scheduled into inappropriate classes (i.e. scheduled into an art class instead of a Physics class); not receiving a full schedule of classes; or being scheduled into a class that had no teacher assigned to it. For older students, the scheduling errors often meant that they did not receive a course they needed for college admission. In each of these cases, I worked with supportive counselors to provide students advice on which classes to shuffle so that they could take college preparatory classes from the most talented teachers, or most manageable in cases where strong teachers were not available. Teacher recommendations were made largely upon my experience as a teacher at the school for six years and upon recommendations from prior program participants.

Part of this pre-semester counseling involved encouraging students to take advanced courses that they were not tracked into. In some cases, students had the desire to take these courses but felt that they would be out of place there or that they would not receive the support they need to be successful. Both Ada and Nancy made comments to this effect.

Ada: I didn't have any direction when I came to Townville. I had no plan. If you hadn't guided me on which classes to take, I would never have known. But, I started to think that if it mattered to you then it must be important. Plus, I started wanting to be in the "good" classes because everyone was in them, and I started wanting to go to college. Other kids at the school just take whatever the school gives to them. Nobody ever tells them any different so they just take it and think that it's ok.

Nancy: I always wanted to be in the high level classes, but I didn't think I could be. I thought that they were just for the smarter kids. None of the people I kicked it with in junior high were in any of those classes, so I just figured I couldn't ever get in. But, then you got me into advanced math and it wasn't that hard and so I just kept on going like that.

As Ada and Nancy point out, students welcome the opportunity to be academically challenged. Part of what made our program successful was our commitment to supporting students to meet the challenges that we encouraged them to take. This support system included pre-semester academic counseling about why it was important for students to take advanced courses. It also included the cultivation of a program culture that normalized taking college prep courses to reduce the amount of isolation students felt in those classes. Finally, we provided immediate and consistent academic support so students succeeded in those courses. By doing these things, we avoided the all too common mistake of raising expectations of students without providing the support structures for students to meet those expectations. As the following chapters will reveal, the strong culture of academic, social, and athletic excellence cultivated during the summer carried over to the school year.

WHAT A COACH CAN TEACH A TEACHER

Make your classroom a special community

One of the most consistent messages you will receive in this book is that the students in our program felt they belonged to a special community. When we work in schools that struggle to consistently help students achieve, we need to make it clear that our classroom will be offering them something different. We cannot afford to have them see our class like all the other classes they have attended. If we want different results for our students, we need to speak and act differently than the norm. When we took over the LWBP in 1996, the team was one of least successful sports programs in the city—they were mostly losing on the basketball court and in the classroom. We knew that countering a team and school culture that had normalized these patterns of failure meant developing a counter-culture, one where habits of excellence became the norm. To accomplish this, we focused on the various things I discuss in this book. But, all these efforts began with us stating very explicitly that we would not allow them to fail any longer and that from that moment forward things were going to be very different. In my classroom, I convey similar sentiments on the first day of class by telling my students that I do not care what they have done as a student in the past. I promise them that I will help them improve from wherever they are and that each student will only be measured against their self, not against their classmates. I also convey that our classroom is a community, which means that each person's challenge is everyone's challenge, just as each person's success is everyone's success. Together we succeed or we fail, but it has to be together. This is the easy part. Words are cheap. The real challenge comes in the day-to-day grind of trying to grow this community of practice.

The value of retreat settings

When you coach a team, run a school club, or direct a school program, it makes sense to have retreats that allow the group to step outside of daily routines and focus on a collective organizational culture. In the LWBP, our summer travelling served this important purpose. However, this would be much more difficult for a classroom teacher to do with all her classes and for an elementary school teacher because of the age of his students. However, the value of travelling with students is undeniable. When we have the opportunity to travel with students, it disrupts the teacher-student routine. This gives us a chance to see our students in a different light and it allows them to see us as something other than just their teacher. The chance to participate in the day to day routines (cooking, eating, riding in the car) together is a humanizing process that helps to build trust between the student and the teacher. There are, of course, no guarantees but I have made it a habit to create these opportunities to connect with students that I am struggling with and have found great success with it. You do not need to organize the activities yourself. Most schools have clubs and programs that already have trips organized and they are always looking for adult chaperones. If my student is already in that club, then the decision is made for me. If they are not, then I'll use all my powers to encourage them to go on the trip. This might include asking them directly, having a teacher that they do connect with asking them, or having some of their peers push the trip. The point is that sometimes the best medicine is a change of scenery, and there are a number of ways that we can create this opportunity for strengthening our relationships with our students.

Set common and individual goals

Throughout this chapter I have discussed the centrality of goal setting (collective and individual) for the success of the LWBP. The common goals of a program or classroom community are the foundation of its collective culture. However, one should not mistake "rules" with goals. In the case of classroom rules, for example, the language almost always frames things in the negative, as absolutes, and/or using an implied deficit framework. That is, classroom rules typically tell students what they *cannot* do (no gum chewing), establish one absolute "right" way of doing things (raise your hand and wait to be called on to speak), or focus on simplistic preconditions (bring your supplies), rather than on outcomes.

This is not an exact science and the development, delivery, and direction of common goals should regularly be revisited and rethought. A review of my versions of the Definite Dozen shows how they dramatically changed over the years and how different they were for the LWBP and for my classroom. However, the intention of establishing common goals is to establish a set of principles that will give reason to the mundane, daily activities of a program. Common goals establish the core culture and common language, laying the foundation for measuring collective success.

Although I have always asked for input on the common goals of my classroom from students and colleagues, they are rarely up for negotiation at the school year. The opportunity for students to set individual goals within the more didactic structure of the common goals is important in that it gives students a sense of ownership over their place inside that collective culture. This opportunity to goal set based on their self-evaluation provides added layers of accountability (I can always say to them, "you set that goal") and authentic assessment (students can be measured against their own growth goals).

Inspire critical awareness without paralysis

As mentioned in Chapter 6, the development of critical awareness among our students is essential, but it brings with it the added responsibility of developing students' critical double-consciousness. If we create a critical culture where it is acceptable to challenge injustices then we must be prepared for students to speak candidly about their experiences. Sometimes this will be raw, as we saw with Adriana. We must be careful not to judge that rawness, or shut it down. It is also our responsibility to help them transform that raw perspective into more developed analyses that do not lose that sense of indignation over injustice. With Adriana, her passion over the mistreatment of people in our community by state authority figures, led her to partner with one of her peers to write a grant that funded a youth magazine where they reported on the inequalities they experienced on a daily basis. As students critical consciousness is encouraged, there will also be moments where they are seeing and experiencing things that they cannot resolve. In those moments, it is our duty to be a stabilizing agent in their lives so that their growing awareness and voice with regard to issues of injustice does not become paralyzing. We should never stop working with them to identify actions they can take to respond, but sometimes they just need to speak on things and know that we are willing to listen without judgment.

Youth collectivity through group learning

A team sport seems to naturally lend itself to students developing a sense of accountability to one another. Structurally speaking this is true, but it's easier said than done. The success of our team on the basketball court was the result of deliberate efforts, on and off the court, to design effective group activities that allowed students to practice being accountable to each other. This is also possible in the classroom, but it requires us to structure effective and meaningful group activities where students are truly inter-dependent on one another. Like anything, learning how to work effectively in a group takes practice, so we have to be patient with group learning because it is not a skill that is normally taught with much rigor in classrooms.

Early in my career when I put students in groups, I just expected they knew how to work together—this expectation was certainly not based on any research, personal experience as a student, or logic. Things usually went badly and this sometimes led me to abandon group work with the conclusion that this student group lacked the maturity to handle it. After a few years of reaching this same conclusion, it dawned on me that I was expecting students to have mastered something that they were rarely given time to practice. Working collectively is a skill and we need to teach it and give students time to practice it.

Now, I am prepared for the inevitability that group projects at the beginning of the year will leave much to be desire. But, if I teach the process well and stick with it, end of the year projects will run more smoothly and produce better outcomes. In the cases where I loop with students, the growth is even greater. Each time we do group work I am evaluating their process as much as the product it produces. This allows me to give individual and group feedback on areas where I will be looking for improvement on the next project. This focus on process over product is an essential tool of effective coaches. Successful coaches rarely worry about the final score because they know it can be deceiving. That is, sometimes you win a game, but you move backwards as a team because you make mistakes you were not previously making. The inverse of this scenario can also be true—losing while showing improvement as a team. What teachers can learn from this is to pay attention to the process students' use in group work, in addition to the product it generates. If the group process is constantly improving, then better work is sure to follow.

There are many advantages to group work, but the one I want to emphasize here is the development of youth collectivity and accountability. Together, students can produce amazing projects that they could not accomplish by themselves. Along the way, they can also learn to value each other's individual skills and the impact of bringing those together in a focused way. These efforts can be particularly impactful when students are given the opportunity to work with students that are outside of their typical circle of friends. Without group work structures it is less likely that students will leave their social comfort zones.

Students as their sister's/brother's keeper

There are a number of places in this chapter where I explain the opportunities our students had to mentor their younger peers, both in the program and in the broader community. However, outside of sports teams and clubs, schools rarely present students with formal opportunities to work across age groups. This is unfortunate because the chance for a student to be accountable for teaching and mentoring a younger peer is an invaluable learning experience. I have seen teachers at a variety of grade levels create this opportunity for their students with great success, many times with students that struggled to find success in the regular class environment. One way that I have used this strategy in my classroom teacher connects back to my use of school clubs and programs. Through these mixed age programs, I have been able to create opportunities for current and former students to form peer mentoring relationships. I typically encourage these partnerships when I have a student that is struggling with things that a former student has been able to overcome. This might be a personal or an academic challenge, but I have found that advice from a peer that has recently confronted the same challenge is more useful to a student than the advice I can offer. My ability to effectively urge former students to step up to the challenge of mentoring a student that they might not even know is largely an outcome of establishing a classroom culture that normalizes community responsibility. These pairings do not always work out. In those times when they do not, I can learn more about each of the students so that future endeavors to set up mentoring relationships are a better match.

There are any number of ways to set these opportunities up for students. Others include forming partnerships with lower grade teachers in your school or in a neighboring school. You can also set up after-school, weekend, and summer opportunities for your former students to come back and work with your current set of students. There is no one best way, but opportunities to be our brother's/sister's keeper helps to foment a sense of self-worth and community responsibility that is impossible to teach out of a textbook.

Form partnerships—Parents, families, and food

This chapter touches on a few of the strategies we used to engage families in support of our program. It should go without saying that our effectiveness as educators improves when we form partnerships with parents and families. As with many of the other teacher takeaways in this book, there is no one way to accomplish this goal. As someone that started teaching at the age of 21, I recognize that one major hurdle can be the awkwardness of being perceived as an authority figure in a child's life when the guardians are older than you. Regardless of whether an age difference exists or not, there are some things that you have to contribute to the partnerships and there are things that you need to learn from the family to be more effective. If you can remain true to your role as a partner in your students' growth then it is much more likely that you will be able to help the family better support their student and, in the process, learn lessons from the family that make you a better teacher.

A few strategies that I have used as a teacher and a coach to build these relationships with parents include home visits, potlucks, and barbeques at my house. When I have done home visits in the past, it is usually because a parent has invited me to come. This invitation has almost always been offered when I drove a student home. When I give students a ride home, I will often take the student I am most concerned about home last so that we can have a chance to talk. When I feel like there has been some trust built up, I will ask if I can come up and meet their family when I drop them off (sometimes the student will ask me first). These introductions to their home and their family often result in an invitation to return for a meal, which I always accept.

The visit for a meal creates a number of opportunities for me as a teacher. First, I can some insight into their home life, including whether or not they have a good place to do their studying. A visit to their room tells me a lot about their interests, which have obvious value for getting them engaged in class. Observations and conversations with family can reveal a student's strengths that I have not recognized in class, such as their maturity with a younger sibling, an older sibling that has a strong mentorship presence in their life, or home responsibilities that reflect a strong work ethic. Each of these becomes a tool that I can use to motivate and support the student in future. In addition to the amazing home cooked meal that I get to eat, home visits also personalize my relationship with the family in ways that make it easier for me to support them, for them to support me, and for the student to understand our relationship as members of a shared community that extends beyond the walls of the school.

Sports participation lends itself to public performance. In my teaching, I work to create similar opportunities for students to share their work a public venue. These often come in the form of group presentations of their projects in the evenings or on the weekends. Any time I have these kinds of community gatherings I prepare food and invite parents to participate potluck-style as well. These gatherings create opportunities for parents to interact, and share challenges and solutions with one another. It is not uncommon for me to ask certain families to reach out to others based on resources they have or challenges they are facing. The effectiveness of these events grows when I am able to loop with students because my relationship with families is more developed and they feel a greater sense of connectedness to the work in our class, to me, and to the other families with whom they have interacted with on other occasions.

Finally, I often host a couple of celebratory events at my house each year. These activities give families a chance to meet my family and share our space. This helps to humanize me in their eyes, and helps to make them more comfortable with group study sessions at our house during the school year. It also gives me a chance to honor their efforts in making our community stronger by cooking a meal for them. I'm not a great cook, but they humor me, and usually supplement my barbeque with food that actually tastes good.

Are you a student too?

Earlier in this chapter I mentioned that we sometimes had to learn the words that we were asking students to learn in preparation for their SAT exam. Of course we are all always learning, but it is important that students have the opportunity to see us in that light. First of all, it humanizes us. Second of all, if they see us as learners, they are that much more likely to be willing to sometimes teach us too. If I don't know something in my class, I will just flat out say, "I don't know. Do any of you?" If no one knows the answer we are looking for, I typically follow up by saying that I will find out and report back while asking them to do to the same.

It is also common for me to assignments with my students and to let them give me critical feedback on it. As one example, I will sometimes begin my class by having students do a timed reflective journal piece on some philosophical statement. When we do these assignments, I often pull out my laptop and write my own response in an electronic journal that I keep. At the end of the writing period I ask for volunteers to read their writing and receive feedback from the class. Every once in a while, students will ask me to share what I have written and I am always willing to do that and accept their feedback. Sometimes, this will just be an exercise in content feedback. At other times, I will use the LCD projector to put my writing on the overheard screen and we will actually workshop my sentence structure together to practice some of the writing conventions we are learning. In either scenario, I am positioned as someone that is still learning ways to make his writing better, even while I am a teacher of writing.

Provide students with structured study methods

One of the first things we gave our students in the LWBP was a structured method for studying because over the years we found that most of them came to the program without any clear plan for studying. The basics of our formula were about helping them develop consistency (place and time), organization, and positive peer influences. I often find that my students already employ these strategies in other parts of their lives and when I am able to point that out to them they are more confident they can learn to study in those ways. With students whose work reflects inconsistent study habits (i.e. inconsistent quality or assignment completion) I will meet with them to discuss things that they feel they do well (i.e. video games, music, dancing, fashion). As we talk about what they like to do, I'll start exploring their own understanding about how they got good at those things. Inevitably, the key factors for effective studying emerge as they talk about commitments to places where they practice, heavy investments of time and effort, organization of their materials (magazines, game guides, websites) and supportive peers. Once they know that they know the techniques of effective study, then we begin to map out strategies for them to make similar commitments to their school work. An effective study plan is not the whole battle, but it is an important first step.

Show students what you are looking for

When I mentioned that we provided students with samples of strong essays, I was highlighting the all-important teaching practice of modeling. Sometimes, we think we have given clear directions when we really have not. I learned this lesson again recently while teaching one of my graduate seminars at the university. I thought I had clearly explained the required writing structure, but a number of my students struggled with the paper and stated that they did not understand the requirements. I tried to explain it again by using examples and one-on-one tutoring. Towards the end of the semester, a student said, "I think I might understand it better if you showed me another student's paper where they are getting it right." This was my first time teaching this class and I had rationalized to myself that I could not provide a model paper until I taught the class a second time. If I had been better prepared, however, I would have anticipated the students wanting an example and prepared one from another class or written one up myself.

In short, students at all levels benefit when we provide them with concrete examples of our expectations. That I had to relearn this lesson shows that good teaching means we not only have to be clear with our students, but we also must be clear with ourselves—sometimes we will get it wrong and we have to be willing to humble ourselves and correct it.

Be a motivator

To teachers, it might seem that being a motivator is easier for coaches because students are participating in the sport by choice. In the example given earlier in this chapter, we had our students complete unsavory tasks (vocabulary quizzes and essays) in order to play in games. However, if this stick and carrot strategy were the only motivational technique we used to get our students to study, we would not have been nearly as successful as we were—especially given that there were games where some players did not get to play very much, if at all. The coaches that are most effective at sustaining their players' motivation understand that the best motivational strategy is to develop strong relationships with their players. Weaker coaches rely primarily on stick and carrot strategies, believing that fear of consequences is an effective motivational strategy. If you are still wondering whether it is better to be feared or loved, just ask yourself whether you would push yourself further for someone you fear or someone you love.

In the LWBP, we employed a number of motivational strategies rooted in caring relationships that challenged students to test their limits. I find similar strategies are effective in the classroom. One of these strategies is the use of storytelling to convey the importance of meeting the challenge at hand. Stories connect the challenges students are facing to other people's life experiences. Sometimes the stories I use are about some of my own failures and the lessons that I have learned from them. Whether the theme of the story is success or failure, the point is to alleviate students' feelings that they are alone in their experiences. The real life connections provided by storytelling allow students to visualize themselves on the other side of the challenge, having grown stronger as a result of going through it. Numerous students have come back to me years after they left my class and thanked me for sharing those stories, but I remain unconvinced of their effectiveness in the moment.

In my estimation, the motivational tool with the most immediate impact is a strong relationship with students. Students do not want to disappoint people that believe in them. When a student is struggling in my class, I have found that increased investments of time and care (rather than punishments) are the most effective ways to motivate them to try harder. The deeper the investments of time and care, the more willingly students respond positively to my cajoling and challenges that they can do better.

Talking to students about college is not the same as having a plan to get them there

The LWBP placed a heavy emphasis on preparing all of our students to enroll and attend four-year universities. Thus far, this book has only discussed the summer component of those efforts, but the remaining chapters reveal the complete strategy. The larger point I would like to make here is that we must have a plan for getting our students into college. Talking to students about college, taking them on college tours, and surrounding them with college information books helps, but it is not be enough for many students. Teachers should have a comprehensive plan for their students and it is never too early to start. This plan should include self-educating on the deadlines and requirements for admission and financial aid, so that you can be a resource to the students and their families. Recent college graduates are especially good sources of information. Whenever possible, have them come and talk to high school seniors to help them navigate college life and avoid mistakes.

It is never too early to start this planning with students. Laurence Tan is an elementary school teacher in Los Angeles who begins the college discussion with students in his 4th and 5th grade classes. He stays in contact with many of his students throughout middle school and high school. Over the years, he has done all of the aforementioned college-going culture activities. This year, his first class of students are graduating seniors. He has worked with several of them and their families to navigate the complexities of the admissions and financial aid process. He tells me that the process is much more difficult than when he applied for college; that he does not have all the answers, but that the parents look to him for support in navigating the process because most of the high schools no longer have college counselors available. Not all teachers will develop this kind of long-term plan to help their students get into college, but some exceptional teachers do and their efforts matter.

Better to be loved

Mika's comment that "it all seemed like way too much" is an indicator that sometimes I received resistance (and resentment) from students. This comes with the territory if we challenge students to move beyond their comfort zones. Our ability to handle this resistance with compassion and understanding, without lowering our expectations, is often the dividing line between being liked and being loved by our students.

Educators that are liked, but not loved, have an overly simplistic interpretation of student resistance as evidence that they are ineffective. It is not uncommon for these educators to choose the path of least resistance with their students out of fear that challenging their students will result in them being labeled as racists, classists, or otherwise insensitive to the challenges facing their students. The irony of this response is that it is rooted in the prejudicial expectation that their students are less capable because of the social inequities in their lives. Students often end up "liking" these teachers because they are not out to get them or making their lives arbitrarily difficult, and these teachers can end up feeling like they have done the best they can given the circumstances.

I like to reference my mother when I describe teachers that are loved. When I was growing up, my Mom made me do things I did not want to do—like studying and washing the dishes. She did not care if I liked her in those moments when I gave her static about having to do those things. I can recall numerous occasions when she would say to me, "I don't care if you like it or not. Someday you'll understand that I love you." My Mom knew that the world would be tough on me and that part of her job was to teach me that I could handle it. I did not always like my Mom for these lessons, but I always loved her for them. Teachers that are loved take a similar approach with their students. They set their standards so high that 'it all seems like too much," and then they set about pushing and supporting their students to reach those limits, using the inevitable failures and triumphs along the way to teach students the lessons they need to learn to be successful in life.

No one does it alone

Throughout this book, I often use collective pronouns to describe the work of the LWBP. The reason for this is that the success we had as a program was the result of supportive efforts on the part of a range of people—custodians, coaches, tutors, teachers, and bus drivers. The list goes on and it is long. These collaborative relationships, such as the one with the counselors mentioned in this chapter, allowed us to provide students with comprehensive rather than compartmentalized services. In my classroom practice, I make it a point to identify allies on campus because I know that inevitably my students will present me with problems that I cannot help them resolve by myself. Earlier in my career, I did not always understand the importance of collaborating with supportive colleagues and it was my students that lost out because I failed to connect them to a network of resources that would have made their lives easier.

As I learned the importance of collaborating with my colleagues, I also came to understand the importance of acknowledging their supportive efforts. If you build a successful program or classroom practice, you will be the primary recipient of public praise, and criticism when mistakes are made, perhaps rightfully so. But, the people working behind the scenes to support your students, the ones that rarely get recognition, are invaluable for the long-term sustainability of our work with students. We should make a concerted effort to acknowledge their efforts and we should make sure that our students do the same.

NOTES

1   Critical, as it is typically used in social theory, refers to efforts that are committed to challenging all forms of inequality.

2   Dawn patrol was the nickname for the discipline players would receive for breaking a team rule. If players violated a team rule, they would have to meet me in the lobby at 5 a.m. to join me for my morning run and workout. This was not a popular event.

3   P- High is a high performing high school in a wealthy community very close to Townville.

4   The activities we designed when elementary schools visited our games are discussed in Chapter 9.

5   Tracking is the process by which students are sorted based on their perceived academic ability (see Oakes, 1985). This process remains prevalent in schools, despite the fact that research indicates it has significant negative social and academic impacts on students. The negative impacts are most prominent among low tracked students, but tracking also has deleterious effects on high tracked students.

6   I toyed with several ways of structuring this component. One year, I had students in each grade level choose a book that they would all read. Another year, I had the entire team choose one book that they would all read. Another year, the same book was assigned to

everyone. However, the most commonly used approach was the one where students could choose their own book. This remained the most common because I wanted to preserve the student's right to choose the book that most interested them.

7   Each year, one or two of our seniors was seriously recruited as a scholarship athlete, but most were not. If a scholarship was being offered that was great and we welcomed the additional support during the application process. But we wanted all our students, regardless of their athletic standing, to be exposed to the application process.

FALL SEASON (SEPTEMBER-OCTOBER 15TH)

The school year began in September, but the school's basketball season did not begin until October 15th. To build on the momentum gained in the summer and to avoid any drop off in commitment, the Lady Wildcat Basketball Program continued to have regularly scheduled activities during this period. To continue their athletic development, the team participated in the Townville Parks and Recreation Fall League, comprised of the stronger girls' basketball teams in the area and engaged in an intense weight training and conditioning program on school days that we did not have games. The continuation of the summer's basketball activities into the Fall season maintained sport as a vehicle for pursuing our other pedagogical agendas. For example, participation in the Fall league and the weights and conditioning program was contingent on a player's investment in our after-school academic development component called "study table."

STUDY TABLE—CREATING A STUDIOUS CULTURE

On my first visit to the campus library during my freshman year in college, I was taken aback by the sophistication of my peers' study strategies. The intensity with which they approached their work was unlike anything I had ever experienced in the public schools where I had formed my study habits. When I started teaching in the Townville schools, I recognized the same lack of attention to helping students develop effective methods for studying that I had experienced in school. I vowed that when my students went to college they would not be caught off guard like I was. This was the origin of study table, a disciplined and rigorous study environment designed to teach students *how* to study effectively.

Study table took place three days a week after school in a classroom for two hours. During this time, players would do their homework, receiving assistance from teachers at the school, the coaching staff, their peers, and undergraduate student tutors from the University of California, Berkeley. The impact of something as simple as having our students around university students three times per week should not be underestimated. In a school where almost 50% of the students were dropping out, and the cumulative grade point averages for African American and Latino students were both below 1.8, it was critical that students consistently saw other possibilities for themselves. Exposing students to other young people that were already immersed in university culture was a crucial to our cultivation of a college-going climate.[1]

In their reflections on the program, people with various levels of involvement referenced study table as the most important program structure for our academic success. Both teachers and students involved with the program acknowledged the impact of "intertwining of sport and school" by using the rigors and collective nature of the basketball program to develop similar approaches to studying.

> **Wyatt (Townville High math and science teacher):** The kind of support that the girls in this program receive is unprecedented in any sports program that I have ever heard of. In fact, they get more academic support than most academic programs are able to provide. But, having that support and creating a system whereby they are accountable for using it are two separate issues. This program seems to have been able to do both by intertwining sport and school. I see the two as being equally important in the girls' eyes. They seem convinced that one depends upon the other and that is key.
>
> **Ada:** The structure of study table helped me to be motivated to do well in school. I knew that I could take tough classes because I knew that I would get help. Plus, it taught me how to

focus and pay attention for long times. It also gave me a place to go and study. If I had to just wait around school for practice to start, I know I wouldn't have studied because there's nowhere to do that here. I liked it that my time was occupied and that I was around people with the same goals when I was studying.

It is not uncommon for dedicated teachers to open their classrooms as informal places for after-school tutoring and studying. Some schools will even sponsor after-school study halls in places like the school library. However, the absence of formal training for the students on how to use those spaces typically results in it becoming unproductive and/or a place that is reserved for students that already have strong study skills.

To avoid those outcomes, study table had a specific design and operating logic that would provide students the training and support to develop study habits that supported their personal academic growth and that of their peers. Students and tutors that were new to our program received separate introductory explanations before they entered the space so that they could better understand how to maximize their participation. Our most experienced tutors (typically students that had been with us for at least two years) were asked to conduct this conversation, explaining the logic of the physical space (group study spaces versus individual study spaces), as well as the cultural norms of study table.

We hosted study table on Mondays, Wednesdays and Fridays to allow for consistency, and to be sure to start and end each week with students feeling added support. It began in the first week of school so that it was programmed it our students' weekly routines and continued throughout the year to avoid the mistake made by many athletic teams of only providing seasonal academic support. Nancy saw the effect of this kind of temporary academic support with the boy's basketball team at Townville High after they decided to adopt the study table concept for their program, but chose to only employ it during the basketball season.

Nancy: Having study table all year was the best thing for me. Without that, I know that I would have played too much when it was not basketball season. That's what happens to everybody else. Like the boys, they have study table right? But, then when they don't because basketball is over, most of them just go back to wandering the halls. Especially after school, they aint' really doing nothing at all except just wasting their time. If they always had to be in study table, then it wouldn't happen.

As Nancy points out, if we had waited until the season started some of our would likely begun the basketball season playing catch up in their classes and would need to relearn the academic discipline we had worked on over the summer. Also, if we were going to back up our promise to love our students, we would have to care deeply about them all year, not just when they were competing for a league championship. The hope of this year-round commitment was that they would consistently be involved with a peer community where academic intensity and success was the norm. The consistency of the message that the LWBP was a community of learners also made it much easier to stabilize a counter-culture to the failures of the school. It also made it clear that the people involved with the program were committed to the development of the students as whole people, not just as athletes.

This dedication to our students' lives outside of basketball built trust, which allowed us to push them harder in their athletic training. This resulted in more success. Their success as a basketball team, in turn, allowed for a bigger push in the classroom, leading to increased achievement. This positive cycle where hard won success brings affirmation and self-esteem, is one of the most powerful breeding grounds for generating deep commitments from young people, and was essential to convincing our students that we were a community rather than just a team.

An interview with Courtney, a tutor and UC Berkeley student, reveals the fact that you did not have to be a student or a coach in the program to see our community building agenda.

Courtney: This isn't just a basketball team. That was so obvious to me from day one. These girls are so close to each other it's amazing. I know they must disagree sometimes, but I just don't see it.

JDA: What do you think creates that closeness?

Courtney: Well, I think it's the amount of time and the type of time they spend together. I mean, they're always together because you encourage that and I think they like each other. Just the way the program is set up, I mean, they are going to be together for at least five days every week. So, they learn about each other and the fact that they are on a team together means that they have to sort of depend on each other too. But, a lot of that comes from all the off the court stuff, like study table. I mean they are constantly helping each other with school stuff, so that it's not just about basketball, it's about how they inter-relate.

THE ROLE OF STUDY TABLE IN NORMALIZING HABITS OF EXCELLENCE

The purpose of study table, and the discipline that was demanded from them while they were there, was a regular topic of discussion between the students and I. I wanted them to understand that we were deliberately challenging them as students because in so many ways the odds had been stacked against them. As athletes, they were frequently asked to rise to challenges such as these, to make come backs against all odds, or to upset teams that were ranked higher than them. If they could be successful at such feats of the body, then I insisted to them that they could meet similar challenges as students.

Our students noted that sometimes they needed motivational and affirming "talks" that explicitly challenged them to rise above low academic and social expectations and to take advantage of structures like study table to support them in that effort.

Nancy: I needed your talks. Sometimes I would forget that school is like sports and that if you stop working hard you'll get beat. Like those times [in study table] when you would stop us, and just start talking to us about that stuff for no reason. But, it seemed like you knew we needed it. You never really let us slip like some people would. I know I thought it was too much sometimes but I know I needed that.

Ada: Your talks were the most helpful thing to me. They motivated me. I mean nobody ever really told me I should get straight A's before, until you. And then you were really serious about it, like I was supposed to do it. Usually, you know, people say, oh a "B" that's really good, or a "C," oh that's not bad. You know as long as you're not flunking. But you made me want to get better than that and you actually helped me do it with study table and tutors and making that part of practice. You made it seem like it was just another game we had to win.

In short, study table exposed students to structured study time. Most students came to our program with no real plan for studying from night to night. Some would study inconsistently at best, and would get their homework done whenever and wherever they could. This lack of a patterned approach to studying often resulted in students at Townville High being dragged down into the academic mediocrity and inconsistent achievement patterns that abound in urban schools. Study table counteracted these trends by providing a positive peer community, injected with consistent support, positive role models, and a clearly articulated set of academic expectations for our students.

FALL FOR SENIORS

In addition to making sure that our seniors were off on the right foot with their classes and study habits, this time of year was also used to move their college application process forward. The applications they requested in the summer and early Fall were now in their hands, and our focus turned to filling these out and revising the personal statements that they worked on over the summer (see Chapter 7). This was the most labor intensive portion of the application process because it required us to work through drafts line by line with students to make sure they truly captured their abilities and their life stories. There are no shortcuts to this part of the process. Most of the work is one on one with students, although we did do some group sessions where we went over the basics of common applications such as those for the University of California, California State University, and elite private school systems. Most of the heavy lifting for this was done by Wyatt, myself, other supportive faculty members at the school, and a select few tutors that we felt had a strong understanding of the process.

WHAT A COACH CAN TEACH A TEACHER

Teach the student, not the subject

Throughout this book, I make the case that our program's capacity for building a sense of community was at core of our success. Our ability to do this was directly connected to our willingness to meet each of our students where they were as individuals. These same principles apply in the classroom. We do not teach academic subjects, we teach young people. The subjects we are required to teach should be thought of as a means to an end, and that end is the development of more complete young person. Our success in the classroom is no less dependent on long-term investments in students' lives, than was the success of the LWBP. Cliché or not, the teacher's adage is true: students don't care what we know until they know that we care. There is no getting around this challenge, and the more quickly we own up to it by developing practices that reflect a desire to build supportive and caring relationships with students, the more quickly our students will invest in the lessons we aim to teach them.

Avoid aesthetic caring

Valenzuela (1999) describes teacher care that is not supported by consistent actions as creating the aesthetic of care. All the right words are coming out of our mouths, but students do not actually feel cared for which is the real test of our caring. Had I just given motivational speeches to our students, they would have eventually found those words hollow. You can see in their comments that they want to be motivated, but they also want to know that we are going to support them to step up to the challenges we are placing in front of them. This support is the line that divides aesthetic care from Valenzuela's "authentic care."

One of the most common places I see this play out is around teachers that want hold students to high standards. When those raised expectations are unmatched with support, they end up only providing an aesthetic of care. The teacher is released from being complicit with "the soft racism of low expectations," but very little changes in terms of student outcomes. Any success that I have had with holding my students to high standards can be attributed to my ability to match those expectations with high levels of support. I have never met this challenge by myself and I do not think I ever could. In under-resourced schools, our ability to support our students is dependent upon great personal efforts and the creativity to supplement the meager resources made available to us through the school.

Colleges and universities are one place where you can garner some additional support for your students. Set up a meeting with locally active professors to discuss opportunities for some of their students to get additional units for volunteering in your class or as after-school tutors. Keep banging on doors. I promise you that there is someone on your local college campus that is interested in connecting their students with classroom teachers. You may need to develop screening criteria and maybe even do some training with those students, but the impact these young people can have on your students will make it worth it. Colleges are not the only places where you can generate additional resources to show your students that you care, but they are a great place to supplement the human capital side of those efforts. The short of it is that there are always more resources in the community than we know about, and caring about our students means seeking those resources out, bringing them into our space whenever possible, and connecting students to them externally when it's not.

Teach students how to study, not just what to study

Our program did things outside of study table during the six week period that is the focus of this chapter. However, the majority of this chapter is focused on describing study table because I believe it was the single most important structure in our program for building academic success. Coaches understand that great players have a mastery of the fundamentals of the game. In most cases great players end up violating some of those fundamentals on their way to accomplishing feats that even the coach did not believe was possible. But, as with great writers that also violate standard writing conventions, this bending of the rules works for them because they have such mastery over the rules that they know when and where they can be manipulated for maximum positive effect. Then there are those without mastery of the fundamentals that break from them with ill effect—these young people are solely responsible for the "highlights" in my hair. The difference between these two groups is not in their will to break the rules. That appears to be a genetic rule for adolescents. It is in the preparation they have had for breaking the rules so that they end up refining the rule for themselves, rather than falling victim to its limits.

The lesson here for teachers is that successful students have learned how to study successfully. The operative word there is "learned," because study skills are not passed along genetically, they are taught. Young people need our support to develop good study habits and not enough of us are teaching that as part of our classroom instruction. This is not to say that every student has to study in the exact same way, but if we aim to create strong students we had better be prepared to teach them the fundamentals of good study habits. There is no scientific agreement on any one set of principles for good studying, just like there is no agreement on how to execute most of the fundamental skills in most team sports. What *is* agreed upon is that students that develop a system for studying tend to do much better than those that do not.

If we want students to believe that we are serious about them studying, then we have to be serious about teaching them how to do it. In my practice, I emphasize three fundamental areas with students: organization, discipline, and strategy. I ask students to purchase academic planners and we all work out our daily schedules in the first week of school. I also make using the planners a part of class everyday. Some students ask to use the calendars on their phones as their planners (that's what I do), which I am okay with as long as they are willing to learn how to back up the information in case something happens to their phone—if you spend time with teenagers you know this *never* happens. With students that cannot afford planners, we will take a trip to the local university bookstore where I will purchase one for them in exchange for their promise to use it dutifully.

Structured study sessions like study table give me a chance to teach students the discipline of dedicated study time. With students that cannot attend study table, I work with them to identify consistent times and places where they can productively study, as well as study partners when appropriate. I also give students strategies that they are expected to master by using them consistently in their study spaces. Those include a range of tips like how to use lecture notes and textbooks, how to annotate when you read, and how to use flashcards and pneumonic devices to memorize material.

Most of my students welcome direct instruction on how to be more organized and study more effectively, and some of them are already pretty good at it. In the event that they already have good study habits, I just work on helping them refine those skills even further so that they are that much more effective. When they do not have those habits, I work with them to break the old habits by creating new and more productive ones.

Ultimately, the teacher takeaway here is that simply asking students to be more committed to studying will never be as effective as designing a strategy to help them make that happen. If you can couple a clear strategy for effective studying with a consistent structure that allows them to practice that strategy, your students will experience even more success.

It is easiest to help students develop a system that works for them if you can also create a structured place where they can practice that system and get feedback from you on that practice. So, whether a teacher runs an after-school study table, hosts office hours at a local café or bookstore, or makes home visits to help families set up study routines, there must be a consistent structure where students can practice their fundamentals.

NOTES

1   Much of the prevailing logic about bringing involving university students with high school students emphasizes the importance of a shared racial and social background. I acknowledge the advantages of shared experience. However, I will add that some of our best tutors come from backgrounds that are very different from those of our students. In the end, our best tutors were always young people with a deep commitment to the youth. I have yet to be convinced that there is a background (racial, social, or otherwise) that predisposes one to this kind of persona.

CHAPTER NINE

REGULAR SEASON
(OCTOBER 15TH–MARCH)

Nancy: Being in this program gave people a different image of me.
When I was in junior high I mostly hung out with people
that didn't do too good in school. Now people see me and
they think that I must be smart because I'm on this team.
They know that you have to do good in school to play for
us. They just assume that I'm going to college because I'm
in the program.

We often see ourselves through the mirror that reflects the impressions others have of us. When we believe others judge us as smart and capable, we
often fulfill those expectations; of course, the opposite is true as well.
Rosenthal and Jacobson (1992/1968) revealed the manifestation of this in
schools with what they called the "Pygmalion effect in classrooms." In their
study, they randomly selected 20 students from an elementary and dubbed
them gifted, telling their teachers that they showed "unusual potential for
intellectual growth" (vii). They then tracked the academic achievement of
these students in comparison with the rest of their peers in the school. Over
the course of the year, these 20 students outperformed their peers and
Rosenthal and Jacobson attribute this primarily to what they call "interper-
sonal self-fulfilling prophecy" (ix).

Nancy's sense that people's perceptions of her were changing is important in that it suggests that she was also changing how she saw herself. This commitment to building our students' academic esteem was an essential part of countering the hegemony that normalized academic failure at Townville High School. The self-fulfilling prophecy is an interplay between DuBois's three phases of self-development (self-respect, self-realization, and self-consciousness—see Chapter 6 for more explanation) and the affirmation of others that you are capable. In a perfect perpetual cycle of this process, external affirmation raises self-esteem, buoyed by higher self-esteem a person performs successfully again, resulting in additional external praise, and so on. However, urban students do not typically operate in consistently supportive environments where their "unusual potential for intellectual growth" is regularly affirmed. Instead, they often find themselves in schooling environments with adults that are hostile to their potential, which makes attention to building self-esteem all the more important for combating the hegemony of urban schools.

Despite Nancy's statement that people acknowledged her academic potential when they were aware of her participation in the LWBP, not all her teachers saw her as capable. On one occasion, Nancy's Pre-Calculus teacher stopped to talk to me in the school's front office. She smiled and asked me if Nancy still played for the team.

"Yes," I responded.

"Well, you know," she said with a smile. "She is the nicest girl. But, she's just not all that smart." Then, she just walked out of the office like she had paid Nancy and me, as her coach, a compliment.

Nancy succeeded in the class despite numerous battles with the teacher over her potential to handle the demands of an advanced math class. She ended up being one of three black students in another teacher's AP Calculus the following year—the other two were also members of our program, Mika and our team scorekeeper. I never shared this conversation with Nancy, but her perceptiveness about the feelings of other people toward her, and the treatment she received in the class, lead me to believe she probably knew how that teacher felt. Her achievement, in spite of the potential for a negative self-fulfilling prophecy, suggests that attention to DuBois's three elements of self-development and proper academic support can help our children combat the potentially negative effects of our adult colleagues that do not believe in the academic potential of all their students.

BUILDING A SENSE OF BELONGING TO A COUNTER-CULTURE

For some of our students, their sense of belonging grew through the wearing of "gear." Players were given t-shirts, sweat suits, and bags, all labeled with the program's name. Each year, new t-shirts were printed with the program's most recent athletic accomplishments (i.e. league championships, 20 win seasons, Northern California championship tournament appearances). Gear was so popular that it was not uncommon for non-participant students to ask me if they could buy a t-shirt or a sweat suit to wear around the school. As the team's success grew, so did the social and cultural capital behind wearing gear that represented belonging to the program's culture of success.

As the team continued winning, and seniors continued to matriculate to college, the media began to pay more attention to the team. This meant regular coverage in the area's two major newspapers. The press would wait outside the team's locker room after big games to interview our players. Weekly polls would rank the teams in the area, and our students would regularly field questions from teachers and peers about their current ranking. Could they rise in the polls? Could they upset teams ranked above them? No matter what their position on the team might have been, all of the girls were considered experts in this activity that genuinely mattered to the school and neighborhood communities. Erika commented on the impact of these changes for herself and many of her teammates.

> **Erika:** A big group of us likes to kick it at lunch and almost everyday somebody is asking us about the games for this week. Well, it's more like they want to see if we agree with their predictions. They'll tell us how much we'll win by and things like that. It makes us feel like people care about what's gonna happen and then you'll probably see some of the same people at the games and you want to make their predictions about us winning come true. I know it makes us feel like what we do matters. But, I still feel like we play more for each other than for what other people will say about us.

This attention from the school and the surrounding community helped our students feel a sense of importance behind the activity of basketball. For many of them, this level of recognition made the high levels of expectations outside of basketball worth the effort. But, as Erika mentioned at the end of her comments, most of the girls ended up valuing their membership in the community more than the outside praise.

Belonging to this culturally and socially significant activity also allowed our students to renegotiate their roles at home. Although some parents saw the program as taking their children away from responsibilities at home, they also recognized that the program kept them away from the negative influences that often cut lives and opportunities short for Townville youth.

> **Nancy:** At first, all the time away from my mom and my family made things hard at home, especially in my first couple of years in the program. I would leave from home in the morning and not come back until 9 at night. No one really understood why it had to take so much time and they always wanted me to baby-sit my nephew and I couldn't do it anymore cause we had practice or something for the team. In the end, I actually think it brought us closer together because everybody would come to the games and cheer for us and they felt like they were part of something too.
>
> **Melinda (Ada's mother):** I know that I used to go easy on Ada when she would come home because she was working so hard in the program. Lots of time she wouldn't get her chores done and I wouldn't say anything because I knew she was tired. It would have been different if she just wasn't doing anything. But she would come home and just be exhausted and so I wouldn't be upset with her. I still expected her to do her chores, but when she didn't I wasn't as angry as I might have been.

As both Nancy and Melinda point out, the schedule for our students during the season was very demanding. On a typical day students arrived at school in time for their 8 a.m. classes. When school let out at 3:30 p.m., the formal activities of the LWBP would kick in. They would either have a game or study table/ practice, both of which would not end until 7:30 p.m. If the game was away from Townville High, students might not get home until after 10 p.m., and for tournaments they may be gone from home for three to four days. Practice, weight lifting, and film sessions were held on Saturdays when we didn't have a game, and these sessions typically lasted four hours. When all was said and done, our students had little time available for babysitting younger siblings, taking part-time jobs, or doing household chores. This meant that the students' lives were often quite different than their peers and older siblings who were frequently asked to pick up the slack in homes where all the adults, often only a single parent, were working. The intensity of this schedule did produce tension for some students, but the success of the program often meant that the issues at home were resolved in their favor. The power to ask and receive reduced loads at home was sometimes a powerful reason for them to invest large amounts of time in the program's various events, including the academic components.

It is important to note that the renegotiation of roles was something we worked on directly with parents and students. This advocacy included meetings with parents as a group to explain the program's expectations of the students and to describe ways that parents could support their students in the program. Many of our parents had never had access to a year-round program for their students and were interested in strategies for how to make the most of it. There were also times when we met with parents individually, at school or on home visits, to talk about issues specific to their child. Finally, we also worked directly with students on how they could become better advocates for themselves. These conversations were typically focused on giving students negotiation skills so that they could become better communicators with the adults in their lives.

GOAL SETTING AND THE ZONE OF PROXIMAL DEVELOPMENT

Although the regular season period was focused on developing the team, there were still components focused on the individual. The purpose of this individual attention was to create the habit of self-evaluation and goal setting. With so little attention paid to teaching students the process of creating habits of success at Townville High, the use of individual goal setting meetings helped students to envision their own pathways to success (personal, academic, and athletic). This process was formally revisited three times each year and was a central component in the development of a culture of critical praxis.

Individual meetings were held at the beginning of the regular season, at the beginning of the Spring season, and at the end of the summer. Their purpose was to communicate the coach's expectations to the student, to evaluate the student's growth, and to have the student discuss their goals and expectations. Just before the season began, students were given the following three questions and asked to answer them based on self-evaluation.

1. What are your expectations for yourself as a player this basketball season? Be specific! Discuss how many minutes you expect to play, how many points you want to score, rebounds, steals, assists, position...etc.
2. What are your expectations for the team? Be specific! How many games do you expect us to win? How will we do in league? Playoffs? State? What will be our team GPA?
3. What are your personal academic goals? Be specific! What will be your GPA? What will you do to achieve that? SENIORS: Which college do you want to attend?

I would also answer these three questions based on my expectations of each student for the upcoming season. The first of these meetings took place in October and served as an opportunity for each student and myself to privately compare our expectations, making sure that everyone was on the same page before the season started. This helped to reduce issues that might arise from players expecting more or less from themselves than we did. It also helped tailor the program's support system to meet individual's needs based on the goals they identified as most important—this is what we refer to when we talk about the use of the zone of proximal development (see Chapter 6 for a fuller description of the term).

These individual meetings did not allow us to anticipate every individual need or problem, but they did consistently produce three positive outcomes: 1) a goal setting culture; 2) a pedagogy of hope; and 3) clearly defined role development. The school culture at Townville High tended to ignore the relationship between goal setting and hope. To develop a counter-culture it was critical that students were asked to visualize the future that they hoped to achieve. I wanted to hear them articulate their hopes, and then to develop a plan for making those visions a reality. To simply tell our students to dream big would have been irresponsible—although it is a frequent part of what Haberman (1991) calls the pedagogy of poverty. Rather than promising pipedreams, we wanted our students to have access to a pedagogy of hope where planning, rather than dreaming, was the focus. Erika pointed out that the coupling of high expectations with structured planning helped her to map out realistic and meaningful goals:

I like all the planning we have to do. It's helped me to get a real picture about my future. I don't just think about going to college. I know what I need to do to get there and that makes it a whole lot easier for me.

The creation of a community of practice where goal setting and hope were staples was also helpful for students to establish their roles as athletes on the team. When we would meet to compare our answers to the three questions, students would often over-estimate their role on the basketball team and under-estimate their potential as students.

This pre-season discussion of roles was essential for an open and healthy team culture. Classrooms and programs alike can have an otherwise positive culture disrupted when students and adults are unclear about their roles and expectations of each other. However, when there is a structure that establishes consistent and open dialogue about these issues, the program culture stands a greater chance of being healthy. This does not mean that the strength of the collective will not be tested at times. Rather, as the following excerpt from my notes suggests, the question is not *if* the test will happen, but whether the program's culture has the strength to make it through that challenge.

Field notes excerpt

December 12, 2000
It finally boiled over today and I am glad for the individual meetings. Adriana has become increasingly less satisfied with her lack of playing time. She has been in the program for three years and feels like she should play more. Today, she acted more like a cancer than a teammate. She was sabotaging virtually every drill and even her closest friends were at a loss for how to motivate her. I got so angry with her that I asked her to step out of practice. I left the team with Gina and David and went outside to talk to her.
I asked her why she was being so destructive and she just gave me the silent stare. I knew she was frustrated with not playing, but I was not going to give in to her temper tantrum tactics. I reminded her about the pre-season individual meeting. I asked her to recite the role that we had laid out for her in that meeting. She did, articulating that she would not play very much and sometimes not at all if the game was very close. She also acknowledged the fact that she had agreed to accepting and fulfilling that role. This helped to calm her temper, and I couldn't help but laugh when she commented, "Yeah, but I never agreed that I wouldn't get upset about it sometimes."
I agreed to give her the space she needed to work through her temporary insanity. Within a couple of minutes she was back on the basketball floor, back into her old routine of cheering everyone else on and flying all over the floor banging bodies with people.

The discussion of roles ahead of time helped to defuse Adriana's discontent over playing time, a concern that undermines many sports teams. This level of honesty with students helped to reduce issues of jealousy or unhealthy competition. If they were not clear on their roles before the season started, they might become increasingly frustrated with playing time. However, by addressing it before the first game, and helping students to understand why decisions were being made, we could re-adjust their individual basketball goals to make them attainable. If these expectations, or the team's needs, changed over the course of the season, then we would meet privately with individuals whose goals would be affected by these changes. This level of clarity on individual roles allowed students to settle into a team culture where honesty and candor presided. These two elements are frequently absent in sports programs, and this can lead to increases in jealousy and back biting which ultimately destroy the sense of community.

While setting the basketball goals for individual students and the team were critical to maintaining a healthy team culture, they were some of the least labor intensive elements of the program for me. The development of students' academic expectations was another story. Most of our students understood that the "right" thing to say was that they were going to make honor roll and go to college. But, the younger the student the less likely they had any concept of how to achieve such lofty goals. Many of our students figured they would just do what they had done in the past, and with a little more effort they would magically jump from a 2.0 grade point average (g.p.a.) to a 3.5 g.p.a. The individual meetings became a place where real planning to achieve these goals could take place.

> **Erika:** If we hadn't met and talked about my classes and what colleges I could go to, I never would have done this good. I never would have taken AP Physics if it wasn't for this program. And I would have always been happy with like a 2.5 because I know I was [happy with that] in junior high. But, when we would meet and you'd make us have those goals written out, I really wanted to try to go higher every year and I had a specific goal that I was trying for. Most of the time I didn't get it all the way, but I knew what I was trying for and the next year I would try even harder.
>
> **Ada:** The individual meetings… well, like I said, your talks really helped me. But, I never would have taken those hard classes, like AP Physics, if you hadn't told us we should and then had all my teammates in there with me. I think that's probably true of a lot of the classes that I took here [at Townville]. I

think everybody knows how much I changed as a student. I got so much confidence from just being encouraged to expect more from myself as a student. All the things like study table, and helping us plan our schedules and then the goals that I would set, those really helped me.

The opportunity to formulate goals collaboratively with students also gave me greater awareness of each student's objectives, which made it easier to help them achieve those goals. This was particularly important for students like Erika and Ada because of their success as ball players. When preparing individual goals, they typically had clear visions about increasing expectations of themselves as athletes. However, they were reluctant to stretch themselves in similar ways academically because they did not feel the same sense of confidence and accomplishment in the classroom.

The use of the zone of proximal development (see Chapter 6) in the program allowed me to respond to the individual needs of students in goal setting meetings, pushing students like Erika and Ada to raise the bar on themselves. Unlike the situation with their athletic goals, if they over-reached on their academic goals, it was very rare for me to tell them to lower their expectations. Some would argue that allowing students that were behind academically to stretch themselves in AP courses would just set them up for failure. In some cases those people would be correct, particularly in those instances where young people do not have a peer group, supportive adults, and proper academic support. But, the absence of these elements in a child's life are not the sole responsibility of the child. If educators understand these things as a formula for academic success, especially in the lives of struggling students, then we must work to build those support systems for our most needy students, rather than using the absence of them as an excuse for low expectations. In the case of students that lacked academic self-confidence, the goal setting meeting served as a safe place to articulate a vision of themselves as successful students. Once they found the courage to speak of themselves in that light, it was my responsibility to make sure our program could properly support them to achieve those dreams.

The use of the zone of proximal development in goal setting meetings was also important for students like Mika who already had academic self-confidence. In Mika's pre-season individual meeting during her senior year, she was encouraged to consider ways to expand her academic role in the program. She reworked her goals to include a definition of academic success that included responsibility for the academic success of her teammates. During that year she had the toughest class schedule on the team, which included four AP classes.

Still, she managed to help her teammates almost every day in study table. Even though we had two or three teachers from Townville High and four or five tutors from UC Berkeley at almost every study table, some students preferred to get help from Mika. In effect, she took on the role of a preferred tutor, especially in math and science. Some of the younger girls even began to model their academic identities after Mika's, copying the ways she used her academic planner, her organization of her notebooks, and her note taking techniques.

This mentorship was particularly evident in Mika's relationship with Adriana, a sophomore during Mika's senior year. Adriana came to the program an exceptionally gifted basketball player, but was extremely introverted and faced serious challenges with her social and academic self-confidence. After rooming together during a couple of the summer tournaments, Mika became a trusted confidante and mentor for Adriana. At the end of that summer, Mika helped Adriana choose her class schedule for her upcoming sophomore year, making sure she registered for the most challenging courses offered so that she would be on the college track. Mika even went to a former teacher to advocate for Adriana (as well some other students) to be admitted to the 10th grade advanced English literature class. Although the two did not take any classes together because of their age difference, Adriana began to model her academic strategies after Mika's. Mika helped Adriana arrange her academic planner, take notes, annotate her readings, and gave Adriana numerous study and test taking strategies. The result was a major shift in Adriana's academic achievement and self-confidence, as well as numerous social-personal gains that came from having an older peer committed to seeing her be successful.

COACH AS PEDAGOGUE: CULTIVATING STUDENTS' ORGANIC INTELLECTUALISM

People that go through intense experiences together tend to emerge with levels of trust and care for each other that are hard to replicate without those kinds of experiences. Coaches are provided the opportunity to build these kinds of bonds with young people because of the emotional roller coaster involved with team competition. In this scenario, the coach is pedagogue, the person entrusted with the responsibility to prepare the community to successfully navigate the ensuing challenges of those competitions.

Researchers have argued that one of the most important places for the coach to act as a pedagogue in prep sports is in helping athletes see the similarities between sport and school (American Sports Institute, 1995; Snyder,

1985; Tharp & Gallimore, 1976). This can be achieved by facilitating a scaffold between athletic skills and academic skills. This includes explicit discussions about the similarities between the school and sport to help student-athletes see that through sport they are already displaying many of the same skills that are needed to be a successful student (i.e. self-discipline, intensity, focus, repetition, organization, and performance under pressure).

In the LWBP these connections were regularly emphasized. We would remind students of the transferable skills they were developing by memorizing our playbook, recording and reading statistics, and analyzing practice and game performances through film study. The skills required in these activities mirrored classroom skills which students were expected to perform, such as keeping a notebook, calculating percentages, and examining cause and effect in science or literature. Nancy recounted the importance of the explicit nature by which we helped students make these connections.

> **Nancy:** You taught us that school is like sports and sports is like life. All those talks you used to have with us after games and after practices and in the summers, they made me think a lot. I started to understand that everything is not going to go your way and that that doesn't mean you can quit. If you practice hard and you keep on practicing, then you'll get it. But if you quit after one loss, well…what's the point? That's just like most things, like school too. You can't just do an assignment sloppy and expect a good grade…just like you can't practice sloppy and expect to win against a good team. They're just the same.

Conversations that helped students scaffold their existing skills to new challenges were an important part of our efforts to raise students' sense of agency and esteem. They gave students a clearer understanding that they already possessed many of the skills they thought they lacked in the classroom. Similar to the explanation Nancy gave during her interview, Erika also expressed the importance of these conversations for helping her transfer lessons learned from basketball to the classroom.

> **Erika:** I used to think basketball was just fun. You taught me that it was work…I learned to love to work. Plus I knew if I could make it through our practices, I could do anything that a teacher told me to do.

The lessons from sport also became scaffolds to academic skills through sports-related readings that we gave to our students. Their desire to constantly improve their playing abilities opened the opportunity for suggesting books that would allow them to learn more about the game they loved. For some of our students, the basketball books we gave them were the first books they had ever read cover to cover. Like with most things, the first time is the hardest. But, once they saw they did have the discipline to read a book in its entirety, they saw themselves in a different light as readers. Their willingness to read basketball-oriented material opened the space for conversations about reading more generally, which allowed us to nurture in them a belief that they could also do the readings they were assigned for school.

The process of offering books or passages to players was an informal one, but became a regular part of each student's experience in some form. There were essentially three ways they were given access to these readings: 1) students could ask me to purchase a book for them; 2) I would recommend a book to them; or 3) the entire team would be given a passage to read and discuss. The first of these was the most common. This option for students was part of a promise that I made to them. During our talks about schooling inequalities (see Chapter 7) and the higher standards they would be held to in college, students would wonder out loud about why their high school was not preparing them to do things like annotate their books if this would be standard practice at the university.

In my English literature classes at Townville High, I did teach students how to annotate in their books by creating a program where students were able to buy the books assigned in our class at a heavy discount.[1] This helped increase the academic culture of our classes by giving students literal ownership of the texts they were reading. It also helped to encourage students to interact with the text through annotations in the margins—a basic skill expectation in any college literature course. In my first year as a coach, I extended a similar proposition to one of the players in the program who had heard about this practice in my English classes. I told her that I would buy her any book that she needed to read for her English class since she was not in my class. She consistently took me up on the offer and over the years it became a regular part of team culture.

For students like Ada who struggled with their reading self-confidence, it was less likely that they would approach me to request a book. In those situations, I was more proactive. I was constantly on the lookout for books that

I thought might interest them. As one example, on several occasions Ada saw me reading a book by Pat Summitt, the head women's basketball coach at the University of Tennessee.[2] One evening while I was reading it in the stands before a game, Ada asked me what the book was about. After a brief conversation about it, she said she would be interested in reading it and so I bought her a copy later that week. In an interview with her a year later, Ada recalled that as the first book she had completed since her days in elementary school.

> **Ada:** I remember that book by Pat Summitt that you suggested for me to read. That was the first time I really got into reading a book since I was younger. I read it cover to cover and I hadn't done that in a while.

Ada ended up recommending the Summitt book to one of the younger players who also completed it. Ada followed that reading up with Cynthia Cooper's[3] autobiography, which she recommended to another of the students. Chain reactions such as Ada's sharing of books or Mika's sharing of effective study habits were made possible by identifying and nurturing each student's organic intellectualism (see Chapter 6 for Gramsci's description of this concept). This belief in our students as intellectuals empowered me to play the role of pedagogue each time teachable moments presented themselves. It also normalized the role of student as pedagogue as they came to see themselves as teachers in the program, rather than just as athletes on a team.

Another strategy for growing the program's culture of intellectualism was the use of quotations from prominent thinkers and texts. Many pre-practice and pre-game talks that were given to the students were opened with one of these quotes. The relevance to the athletic task at hand was usually quite obvious, but when students heard the name of the writer or text they often expressed surprise. Some of these were the same names that they found boring and irrelevant in their classes during the day, and yet in this context the message suddenly seemed relevant to their lives. This is what scholars mean when they talk about culturally relevant pedagogy (Ladson-Billings, 1994).

A good example of this is the Maya Angelou poem, "Phenomenal Woman," that I read to them during our pre-game talk at Arco Arena when we played for the Division I NorCal Championship.[4] This was arguably the biggest girls' basketball in school history and I wanted to make it clear to them that it was their strength as phenomenal young women that had brought them to the title game. Several weeks later, one of the students commented to me that she had heard the poem in her English class but had not seen its relevance until that night.

> **Tameka:** I had heard that poem before in Ms. W-'s class. I never really thought much about it until that night you used it. I like that poem now. I copied it down and I like to read it. It's weird though, I heard it before and didn't really get it until that night at Arco.

On more than one occasion, this strategy of using literature in the context of our condition as a team led students to rethink texts from which they otherwise might have felt disconnected. On other occasions, motivational passages were used with individuals to inspire them to overcome difficulties in school or life. It is important to note that the selections were often taken from women of color[5] both for their poignancy in the moment, but also for the lasting impact of exposing our students to women like themselves that had excelled, not in spite of struggle, but because of it.

THE DEFINITE DOZEN—THE IMPORTANCE OF RITES OF PASSAGE AND COMMON LANGUAGE

My primary role as a pedagogue, however, was to build a collective reservoir of resiliency and hope that could be drawn upon during difficult times. Sport certainly lends itself to this, as dialogues about overcoming the odds and pushing one's limits are normal. The impetus for these sports-related talks varied from motivating the team to defeat a more talented opponent, to inspiring the team to pursue excellence despite facing an inferior opponent, to calls for team pride through increased work ethic in the classroom. No matter what the occasion, there was a common language and set of core program values around which all these talks centered. We called this the "Definite Dozen".[6] We borrowed the name and some of the principles from Pat Summitt's program at the University of Tennessee. The general outline of our Definite Dozen was similar to Summitt's, with small adjustments to suit our particular circumstances at Townville High (see Appendix B).

During the Fall period, students were given a copy of the Definite Dozen and were told that they would need to memorize all of it. At the beginning of the regular season, every student (returning and new) was required to recite the following dozen principles from memory in front of the team in order to receive their uniform and their practice gear. After they were done, each member of the program (self-included) voted as to whether the student had met the expectations of the community and was ready to become an official member. In order to pass, a student had to receive a unanimous vote in their favor. If anyone from the program voted in the negative, then they were asked to give constructive feedback to explain their vote.

Virtually any challenge a student, or the team, was facing, on or off the court, could be addressed by drawing from these principles. They provided a common language for students and adults alike to develop concrete strategies for confronting difficulties in our lives. The following are examples of exchanges I had with students where concepts from the Definite Dozen were used to guide them through difficult times. The first is an email exchange that I had with Erika during a tough stretch in her senior season. Erika wrote:

> What happened to us tonight? Is it that they [the other team] wanted it more? This shit is new to me so how am I supposed to react? At times I'm fuck-in pissed off but then there's a side that says let it go. What should I do to help better this team and become a better leader? I know it will be another long night for you also. I don't want this to be the downfall for the team so help me help this team. Your team captain, -Erika-

I responded with a lengthy discussion of many of the principles that had been emphasized to her as a member of the program and as a team captain, particularly her role as a leader of a very young team. I have included the entire response, despite its length, to reveal the level of engagement I was having with Erika about our program and her role as a leader in it.

> Dear Erika,
>
> Hopefully you will get this message before practice today. We have to do a better job of leading this team. This WILL determine how far we go in March. I think you don't really understand what I am trying to accomplish with this team and so you are unnecessarily concerned and frustrated.
>
> This is not last year's team. This is a new team that is VERY young. Generally the biggest problem with young teams is to get them to play hard and to be consistent. We are playing VERY hard. When I look at our game tapes, we are really getting after it defensively. We are better defensively right now than we were in March last year. I am very pleased about this.

This will pay off in March because we will just get better and better. Offensively we are struggling. This is normal at this time of year, particularly with a young team. That team we played last night had 8 seniors. 8! Three of them have already signed with Div. I schools. We held them to 35% shooting and 48 total pts. That is a monster defensive effort. We just didn't score. Pure and simple. This is nothing to panic about. I am very happy with where we are and I am enjoying coaching this team because I am getting to do so much teaching. That is what I love about coaching, not winning...although winning is cool too.

Listen, what I need from you is for you to understand what we are trying to accomplish here. I know it's your senior year and that you want to go out with a bang. OK, well if that's what you want then you'd better listen up. This team believes in you. They believe everything that you say and they hang on your words. We've talked about this. They aren't really sure whether they are any good right now and that is why I spend so much time telling them that we are going to be fine. They don't understand the purpose of the tough schedule. When they look at you after tough losses, this is where they figure out if they need to panic or not. If you appear disappointed but still supremely confident in our mission, then they will believe that we will be there in March. If you look like you have after the Mitty and MC games, then they will wonder. If they wonder, you won't go out with a bang in your senior year. I am telling you that this team is better than last year's team. No bullshit. But, it's going to take time, several months before they can peak. You need to keep them going until then. The only time they should be getting negativity from you is if they aren't putting out effort. That's it. If they miss a shot, hollering at them won't help. They didn't miss the shot on purpose. Who would do that? They just missed. If you want them to take that shot in March and make it, you'd better make them feel like you believe in them. Tell them you are going to keep giving it to them because you know that they can make it. Now, if they aren't working hard, you can let them know that by getting on their asses. But, anything else they need you to support them and let them know that you have confidence in them. This doesn't mean that you pass up on shots that you can take and make so that they get shots. It means that you continue your play on the court and get them to believe in the system. Do you remember last year how we would get 2 or 3 different people in double digits all the time? No one knew who to key on against us because we had so many that could hurt you. We will get there again if your teammates believe in your confidence in them.

Right now they just think that they are letting you down. That makes them feel like you feel if I tell you that you let me down. That will not produce a championship team.

The key to this is practice. You must learn to lead like this in practice. You must get more people (Kendra, P-, H-, T-) to be vocal and positive in practice. You need to talk to Kendra about that. She gets really negative when mistakes are made and that is going to hurt us this year and next year when you are gone. Help her to get better as a leader and that will help this year as well. Explain to her what I am teaching you. P- too. She is really struggling. Two straight games without a single point. She is doubting. You need to boost her confidence. Get T- to lead that bench. She is our Adriana, except she'll play more. Maybe A- could fill that role too. Empower H- to run the show with confidence not panic. Teach her how to be calm and still intense. Big jobs all of them, but these are as important as anything you can do in a game.

Lastly, I don't want to hear anything else about UCSB around our team. I want the UCSB taken off your shoes today. Wipe it out. You don't play for them, you play for Townville High. If our team sees you looking toward next year, they will think that you have given up on this year. They listen to everything you say, even when you think no one is there to listen. They will start to doubt your allegiance to them and your commitment to us. You are a Wildcat, not a Gaucho. How would you have felt last year if Ada was talking about USF when we were 6–7 and Nancy talking about Cal? Would you have believed that they bled blue and white? Would you have believed that they would die a Wildcat? NO! Well then, learn from them! We're in great shape right now as a ball club. Trust me. But we will only stay that way if you can get everybody to believe that you believe that. Confidence breeds confidence. Remember the Definite Dozen…loyalty and team before yourself!

Each team is different, which means you must adjust as a leader. You must learn how to read each situation, find out what is needed, and deliver it. UCSB may need you to be hard nosed and get in people's butts. We don't need that right now, unless you see a lack of effort. Stay intense, stay yourself, learn and get better. I learned a lot last year about coaching. When we were 6–7 I questioned my choice to put together such a tough schedule. I kept my faith in my seniors though. I believed in you. In March, I became a seasoned coach. I learned my lessons about the value of tough competition. You want to be the best, you'd better play the best. Otherwise you get a false sense of security. Did you learn this lesson last year as well? OK then. Understand that of all those tough teams we played last year, none of them had multiple seniors...except us. All those kids are back this year. It is so early, of course they were more ready than us. The real question is, will they improve as much as we will? I don't think so. I love to teach and teaching produces growth. If I can get some help, that growth will help us to close the gap. If you want that, then become a better teacher starting today. —J

The educators reading this book may not understand the basketball lingo in the email, but the point here is to show the passion that I had for our program. When we are passionate about our work with students, it is easier for them to rationalize taking the leap of faith that is required for someone to make an intense investment. If we are not willing to put ourselves at risk *first* with significant investments of time and emotion, it is not fair for us to ask our students to make those investments.

Erika responded wonderfully to the email, shifting her leadership style that day in practice to a more supportive one. Later in the week, she called a players only meeting where she encouraged the younger players to believe in themselves. Later, she commented to me about the lengthy email:

Erika: How long did it take you to write that thing? I read it all though and I understand what you were saying. It's the same stuff we talked about during the summer...shoot it's the same stuff you've been teaching me since I got here [as a freshman]. We talked about it as a team...we'll be OK.

Erika was right. The team was okay. They ran off a string of victories to end the season, won their third straight league title, and made their third straight Northern California Sweet 16 playoff appearance.

It is not often that young people find something in school that they care as deeply and passionately about as Erika did about the fate of the team. It is equally as rare that students are able to develop meaningful relationships with adult mentors in school such that they can candidly express their passion and seek meaningful advice as Erika was doing. It is almost impossible to find educational environments where these two come together such that students and educators share an equally passionate commitment to a set of outcomes. However, we know as educators, that creating conditions where students and teachers share a stake in the outcomes of their work, while developing meaningful relationships of mentoring and shared leadership, are essential to raising levels of engagement, achievement, and hope.

The guiding principles of the Definite Dozen were just as powerful in producing critical thinking and self-exploration off the court, as reflected in this email that Adriana sent to me.

> I was so mad in 2nd period today because senora L[sic] wouldn't teach, and she is gonna go preach about how we shouldn't quit and keep on learning and all this other stuff...it's all talk. I was so mad I didn't even want to see her face. This morning when I was walking to class and seeing all the things written on our walls I thought to myself that this is the kind of messed up school you see in movies and that I can't believe I'm attending one of those schools. I want so much more that sometimes I feel like I'm being greedy. I never feel like what I'm doing is enough and then I get so upset that I just shut everyone out.
>
> Since I was little, you know what I wanted to do? I wanna go to Africa and help the children there. That's been what I have been wanting to do since I was little. I wanna help them out and all this time all I thought about was make money and then I can help them. Now it's not just all money. Yeah, I know I'll need money to help them but it's not even that anymore. I have been thinking about it all the time and even during class I think about it. I wonder and wonder how it's gonna be like...how is it gonna work out? I'm afraid that I will fail in helping my teammates out in school and stuff. —Adriana

This email came as a response to a lengthy conversation I had with Adriana about her responsibility to her younger teammates. Adriana and I met the next day to discuss her email and her dreams of working with youth in the future. We talked about her anger at the substandard educational conditions at Townville High and the importance of sharing her critical awareness with her peers. But, we also discussed the importance of her going beyond her critique of these conditions to strategizing ways that these conditions can be overcome in the short term and changed in the long term. Adriana reiterated that she did not resent her responsibility to do those things and to provide academic support for her peers. Instead, she worried that she would fail them in those efforts. We revisited numbers three and number twelve in the Definite Dozen: be honest (leaders don't make excuses, they make improvements) and be a competitor (never, ever give up). I shared some of my struggles as a teacher and told her that I believed each failure I had as a teacher was preparation for a future moment where I would be given the opportunity to show that I learned from that mistake. We laughed and cried together for over an hour and in the end she agreed that she could use her role as a leader on the team as a training ground for her future work with young people. True to her word, she actively pursued peer tutoring relationships with young students in the program during study table and joined Mika as one of the most sought after tutors and mentors. Later that year she also wrote and received a grant with another student to publish a magazine that highlighted youth exposés highlighting inequalities and positing solutions.

The conversations with Erika and Adriana that I've shared here reveal our potential as educators to build up the individual student while also connecting that individual student's capacity to effect change among their peers. This collectivity was critical for nurturing a programmatic culture of collective hope, one that privileged the success of the collective over the success of any one individual. This responsibility to the larger community is emphasized throughout the Definite Dozen, including "be responsible" and "treat others the way you want to be treated." However, it's worth noting that both of these appear in the first section of the document, and therefore are characteristics required just "To Stay in the Program."[7]

The lesson for educators here is not about the Definite Dozen per se, but about the importance of creating scaffolding tools for young people. The lessons that students learn, whether those come from issues they face as athletes or from challenges confronting them as urban students of color, present invaluable opportunities for savvy educators. For our program, helping students turn their struggles into solutions was about developing their sense of individual and collective agency to create positive change. If they could accomplish lofty goals as individual athletes and as a team, then they could certainly find similar success as students and citizens. However, on the court or in their life, the successes that would mean the most would be hard-won and would almost certainly require them to endure pain and sacrifice. The key was getting them to believe that the trade-off would be worth it in all aspects of their life, like it was for them on the court.

EMPHASIZING ACADEMICS OVER SPORTS

One of the most difficult parts of developing a counter-culture to Townville High was negotiating the value our students gave to sport in their lives. I wanted to tap into the cultural capital of sport as a source of empowerment, but I did not want basketball to become the sole defining characteristic of the program. Rather, basketball was supposed to be the catalyst for creating successful students and citizens.

For this reason, study table during the season was considered a part of the team's practice. When the practice schedule was distributed at the beginning of the season, study table was written into that schedule three times per week. This helped to develop the academic culture of team. It emphasized to students that studying was also a team activity, and as such was as critical to our success as having good basketball practices. The interviews with key stakeholders in the program suggest that for students, parents, and tutors alike, the incorporation of study time into the practice schedule provided much needed structure to the students' academic lives.

> **Mika:** I think I am just as smart as I was before I came here, but the whole way I looked at things changed. I understand how hard I have to work to be successful, and I understand how important structure is to doing that. The structure of things like study table helped me to expect more, and it made my Mom expect more too...
>
> **Adriana (Mika's Mom):** The advising and support have been the most beneficial parts of the program for Mika...individual attention in academics and the team building. The structure of the program has raised her self-esteem. She is proud of her accomplishments because she knows she has worked for them. She sees the work in front of her every day because of the structure. She has learned the value of working hard to succeed. It [program structure] has also taught her to balance her time well.
>
> **Kat (tutor):** The time requirements made by the program build in very high expectations. This sets a standard for the kids and eliminates complaining because they know right from the start that this is serious and that everyone is held to these standards. With things like the progress reports, study table and all the other team activities, they learn that these are people that they can trust and depend on and their teammates are too. It also motivates parents to be more involved because there is an end game here...they are seeing kids graduate and go off to college.

For many school sports coaches and after-school program coordinators, comments to their students about grades are made in passing or in the context of scolding a student for her failures. To avoid this type of passive or reactionary intervention in students' academic lives, weekly progress reports (see Appendix F and G—"Weekly Progress Report Sample 1 and 2) were made mandatory year round.[8] We explained to students that the progress report was a support mechanism, not a piece of busy work or a way for us to hyper-monitor their lives. One of the most common mistakes I see being made with academic support systems in urban schools is that the interventions come too late. My colleague David Stovall at the University of Illinois (Chicago) refers to this trend as "search and rescue" because its reactionary design does not deploy support until students are already drowning. Our academic support model was designed so that we would know immediately when students were having trouble in their classes, or when negative attendance patterns were developing. Rather than waiting until the report card period when patterns of academic identity and relationships with teachers were already established, we aimed to address issues before they affected a grade.

The use of progress reports in urban schools is not rare, but I would guess that not too many programs take them as seriously as we did. There were no exemptions from progress reports. I contend that our team culture was effective, in part, because successful students were held to the same standards as struggling students. When academic support structures such as progress reports and study table are only for struggling students, stronger students are removed from structures where they can act as role models, tutors, and leaders. To have excused our best students from the academic support network would have been akin to exempting my best players from practice because they already displayed the basketball skills we were teaching. By avoiding this mistake, we circumvented the perception that academic support was just coded language for remediation. These structures built the team's sense of community and created shared responsibility, which is common sense in team sports. However, coaches rarely develop students' responsibility for their teammates with respect to academic performance. In classrooms, particularly in the upper grades, the type of team building seen in sports is rare, despite its potential to create a healthy classroom culture and raise achievement for all students.

It is also important to note that I did not presume that students with high grade point averages had no academic needs. For this reason, study table was not treated as a remedial activity. Instead, it was a place where strong students grew stronger and were expected to help their teammates in any way that they could, and struggling students were supported with the expectation that they grow into success and, eventually, into a supportive role for their peers.

This support mechanism was welcomed by most teachers at the school, and often resulted in raised expectations by virtue of a student's participation in the program. The intensity with which teachers used the progress reports varied (see Appendix F and G), but for the most part they provided excellent feedback, particularly for students that were struggling in classes. As Erika noted in her interview, the progress reports were a consistent form of contact between the teachers, students, parents, and myself and became a valuable part of the students' support and accountability network.

> **Erika:** Things like the weekly progress reports made a big difference for me. They kept me honest I guess you could say. I knew you would know pretty much anything that I did because I couldn't play without my progress report. Plus, once teachers know you're on the team, they just change up their whole attitude with you. I mean they just know that you're serious about school and that you're gonna be going to college so then they start expecting that kinda stuff from you too.

The whole of our academic support structure was designed to expose our students to a peer culture where a high level academic work ethic was normalized. Studying and team dialogues about grades and schoolwork were a regular part of the program's culture. Students that entered the program as academically marginal students were constantly exposed to the study habits of successful students. This created a culture of mentoring in study table where students tutoring students was as common as students being helped by tutors from the university. Being a good student placed you in a position of power and responsibility within our program culture. In short, studying became cool (or at least tolerable) because everybody else was doing it and it could extend your peer influence (which translates to making you "popular").

DEVELOPING TRADITIONS TO ESTABLISH COUNTER-CULTURE

Field Notes Vignette

June 2001
The orange door labeled "Custodian" opens up to reveal a hidden refuge of athletic and academic excellence and tradition. What was once a room filled wall to wall and floor to ceiling with janitorial supplies, dated gymnastics equipment, and school records dating back to the 1970s is now the only per-

manent "team room" on the entire campus. The donated royal blue carpet on the floor is clearly a throw rug more than a custom carpeting job as it leaves gaps revealing the linoleum beneath it. The royal blue walls blend into white and orange ceiling pipes and air ducts that run through the room.

Created solely to engender tradition, each item in the room has been selected to impart its own daily reminder to all those who cross into this sanctuary. From left to right the walls are covered with posters of ball players, mostly women, and banners of college teams from around the country. On one wall, a poster of Michael Jordan stares at those that peer in…a headshot only, his arms completely outstretched, the caption citing William Blake: "No bird soars too high if he soars with his own wings." Sitting below Jordan on top of a set of makeshift wooden lockers is the massive league championship trophy, a golden ball resting on a wooden block. Next to it rests the most prestigious individual award in the program, the only trophy in the room with individual player's names on it—the Valencia Award for Courage and Commitment. Below these two trophies, and also against the adjacent wall are the players' lockers. The adjacent set of lockers partially conceals hundreds of boxed school records dating into the early 1990s. These randomly stacked cardboard boxes clutter the back third of the room, despite a four-year-old promise that they would be moved elsewhere.

Each individual locker, a converted wooden bookshelf, dons a magnetized individual name strip with a jersey number on it. In the corner, an extension of the team's lockers, is the "Roadmap to College" bookshelf, holding dozens of college guides from around the country.

Next to the door is the wall of motivation, a wall covered with mantras like, "Above all Else Character Matters" and Vince Lombardi's famous remarks: "Winning is not a sometime thing; it's an all the time thing. You don't win once in a while; you don't do things right once in a while; you do them right all the time. Winning is a habit." To leave the room, one has to pass under a sign, slapped by every player, every time they walk out of the room, that reads "Play like a champion today."

On the wall adjacent to the wall of motivation is the "Wall of Fame," the only other place (besides the Valencia Award) where individual accomplishments are recognized in the room. There are no press clippings to be found anywhere on this wall, no mention of individual sports accomplishments… just names of graduated seniors with the colleges they are attending, sitting below a simple sign which reads, "Tradition Never Graduates."

Perhaps the most critical element in the establishment of the LWBP's counter-culture was the building of tradition. This meant creating markers of our success and developing a space where those indicators, along with ideological tenets of our program, could be displayed for our students. This space became known as the "team room." The markers of success were what we referred to as our "perpetual awards." The term comes from a local trophy shop owner, who designed what she called "perpetual trophies" for these awards. They were not designed to be given to the recipient. Rather they remained on display with the program, commemorating the recipient by etching their name on the award. Three such awards were established, all of them commemorating excellence in aspects of participant's lives that would lead to them going on to college.

The first of these awards was the "Valencia Award for Courage and Commitment." This was the only perpetual award that was given to an individual and was considered the most prestigious award in the program. The award is named after Jolynn Valencia, the point guard from the 1996–97 team. Jolynn was the most outstanding female athlete in the school and was an equally outstanding student. At the end of the 1996–97 season, she was diagnosed with a pulmonary condition which ended her days of playing basketball. The award was created to honor the commitment she showed to her teammates and the program. She was also the first recipient of the award. Each subsequent season the award went to the student that most exemplified Jolynn's commitment and courage. Although commitment to development as a basketball player was taken into account, the award was given to the student that best balanced the challenges of sport, school, and leadership. The award is the largest trophy in the team room and is the only trophy that has an individual's name engraved on it. It is also the final award given out at the season ending awards banquet.

The second perpetual award was the "Team GPA Award." This award was placed on the "Tradition Wall" and is a calculation of the varsity team's grade point average at the end of each semester. Our older students frequently made it clear to the younger girls that they did not want their senior year to be the year when the team g.p.a. went down. This kind of positive peer pressure to perform academically has kept the overall team grades well over a 3.0 since the inception of the award in 1997 (see Table 5). The award provides a daily visual reminder about the level of consistent academic success that is expected of the team. It also serves as notice that the program doesn't measure its success on the back of individuals, but on the performance of the team as a unit.

The third perpetual award was the "Wall of Fame." "Making the Wall of Fame" (this was how students referred to it) was the only way for an individual student to get their picture on the team room wall. This "wall of fame" was reserved for players that moved on to a 4-year college after they graduated from the program. If they successfully met that program expectation, they had their picture framed with a caption noting their name, their year of graduation, and the college they attended. For six consecutive years, every senior that participated in the program for their entire high school career made the Wall of Fame. When I left the program, we were a perfect 11 for 11. Erika, who was a senior in the last year I ran the program, commented on the tradition and positive pressure this brought to her life.

> I feel the pressure of being a senior. Nobody wants to break the streak…
> not me for sure. My whole career, I wanted my face up on that wall
> and I knew the only way I could do it was to get into college.

This level of academic success inside of a program at Townville High was unparalleled. Each of the strategies discussed in this chapter contributed at different times in different ways to student success. Each by itself (goal setting, academic support, collective accountability, high expectations, tradition) would likely not have produced the program wide success that we experienced. As is often the case in successful urban school programs, it is a combination of strategies that establish a viable counter-culture to urban schools as "factories for failure" (Rist, 1973).

WHAT A COACH CAN TEACH A TEACHER

Creating self-fulfilling prophecies

Early on in this chapter, I discussed the impact of the Pygmalion effect in the classroom. Teachers should be mindful not to overvalue the student's agency or undervalue the teacher's role in their understanding of the Pygmalion effect. It is wrong to presume that students will succeed if we just tell them they are smart. What the Rosenthal and Jacobson study revealed was that teachers changed how they treated students when they believed the students were high achievers; the teachers' perspectives changed the students' achievement. There is plenty of research evidence that supports this conclusion about the importance of teacher expectations. It should be made explicit, however, that high expectations for students are as much, if not more, about what we do as what we say. What teachers can learn from the positive impact of the LWBP's high expectations is the importance of connecting our positive words of encouragement to actions of direct support.

Being critically conscious and cool

Style is an important part of youth culture. This chapter discussed our use of clothing "gear" to tap into this part of our students' youth culture, deepening their positive associations with being a part of the LWBP community. I have continued to use this approach with classroom-based programs I have developed. The key here is to make sure that the gear (shirts, hats, bags, hoodies) you design can pass for cool with your students. My best advice is to have your students help you design the gear so that it meets their style interests, but also includes the positive message you are aiming to promote. This way, it can promote their leadership and initiative, substantiate the message of primary program goals, while giving students a sense that they belong to a collective that is both cool and conscious. As an added benefit, designing gear for your students can allow to develop relationships with local entrepreneurs and artists while supporting their businesses—if you do not know who does that work in the community, ask your students.

Demanding more requires family support

Throughout this book, I purposefully reveal the significant time commitment we required from our students. This would not have been without our concerted effort to clearly communicate those expectations to the families, anticipate their concerns, and show some flexibility and understanding to alleviate them. This formula was not always successful. There were times when families pulled their students from our program. This, usually happened early on in their participation and often because the requirements were too demanding for the family to meet at the time, or because of poor communication on my part or the part of the student.

The takeaway for teachers is that we will need to make demands of our students that may seem extreme in comparison to the expectations of our colleagues that preceded us. It is logical for families to be cautious of this sudden shift in their child's school life. Our job is to be proactive in helping families understand who we are and why we are asking for this change. This requires us to be good communicators early in the program and have consistent dialogue with the families.

The standard communication strategy is to send written information home in a timely manner. This is important but insufficient. We should coach our students on the importance of communicating the information to their family and give them strategies for how to actually accomplish that goal. Then, we follow up with the families to make sure that they have received the information, talked to their children about it, and feel welcomed to ask us any questions. One of my favorite times to do these queries is when families come to pick their student up or when I am dropping the student off at their house. A little bit of face time with parents to talk with them about their concerns or questions goes a long way to building the home support that students need to be fully committed to intense regiments.

In the LWBP, when we communicated directly with families they often understood more clearly *why* (this is the key) we were demanding so much and that our mission was much bigger than basketball. Students are not always the best people to do this because they get frustrated with hearing 'no' from parents and they cannot always fully articulate the larger mission of the program. It is also important that we help our young people learn how to communicate better with their families. I frequently insist that my students tell their families 'thank you' for being supportive and for making extra sacrifices so they can participate in our program.

Finally, I also work in partnership with families so that in moments when students do something wrong and need to face consequences, the families can act with our full support. On these rare occasions, peers follow up with students to explain the impact that they were having on them by not being there. At times, this positive peer pressure has resolved issues when adult pressures could not. Sometimes the cause of the problem was something that the student did not want to share with me or other adults in our program, but once they were able to talk through it with another peer in the program that they trusted, the issue was resolved.

Shared experiences deepen bonds

Young people that get the opportunity to participate in collective struggle (team sports, debate teams, school band, drama productions, etcetera) often reflect fondly on the depth of the relationships they formed as a result of their collective struggle. Classroom teachers should aspire to foster similarly meaningful relationships for their students. We can accomplish this by designing our classroom pedagogy around a meta-event that only happens once or twice a year. In some of my other work, I have given examples of my use of yearlong group research projects in my English classroom that crescendo in community presentations and participation in national research conferences. Other teachers I know use science fair type events, gallery showings of student work, poetry performances, and any other number of public displays of student work. The point is to make students' work matter beyond the walls of our classroom.

There is a risk here if we do not invest the time and effort to prepare our students for these moments of public display. So, I am adding this caveat because I have seen no small number of public displays of student work that were embarrassing because the students had not been rigorously prepared. We must have a clear standard that we set for our students before we put them in a position to publicly display their work. The bar should be high enough that both the student and teacher feel the student is prepared and displaying work that reflects hard earned growth and achievement. Students should be clear of what is expected of them and they should be given multiple opportunities to rehearse under close scrutiny of the teacher so that their public presentation is polished.

When we guide students through these endeavors of public intellectualism, their relationships with us and their peers grow deeper. It bolsters their sense of accomplishment in ways that test scores cannot, and it creates a set of memories that are much longer lasting than grades. These are the transformative experiences that transfer to other parts of their lives because the intensity of these opportunities validates that what they do matters and that the struggle and sacrifice required to learn is not arbitrary.

Being culturally relevant

Chapter 4 revealed common misinterpretations of culturally relevant teaching. In this chapter, you can see the effects of those misinterpretations with the example of Maya Angelou's "Phenomenal Woman." It is important that we change our curriculum so that it is more reflective of the students that we teach. However, as Tameka points out, this will not be sufficient for connecting our students to the things we teach. What we teach matters, but *how* we teach it is often the determining factor as to whether our students connect to the material. In the case of this poem, I connected Angelou's ideas to the immediate conditions of Tameka's life and suddenly the same poem she had been asked to engage months before in her English class became so relevant to her life that she "copied it down" so she can re-read it. As a coach, I wanted to come up with something that helped our girls understand that they meant so much more to me than the score they could put on the scoreboard. Tameka's

English teacher could have taught that poem with the same intention and that would have made her a culturally relevant pedagogue. In my mind, that should be our goal with every piece of curriculum we choose; to identify ways to connect it to our students' lives so that they "really get it."

Reviving rites of passage

Most sports teams have rites of passage. Unfortunately, they often result in elitism or exclusion (tryouts and cuts, social cliques). However, many cultures have culturally significant and socially productive rites of passage. Teachers would do well to take up this latter use of this cultural practice in their classrooms. My adaptation of the Definite Dozen from the LWBP into my classroom practice has helped to establish a common language, a basic operating philosophy, and a shared set of experiences. Despite whatever differences they might have when they enter the class, these common bonds allow my classes to see themselves as group with a shared identity. The deliberate design of tools, such as rites of passage, for cultivating collectivity are essential for educators that aim to develop a counter-culture to the socially accepted norms of individualism that are promoted in schools.

Recognizing and winning the war of position

One of the most instructive lessons in this chapter is the conflict that occurred with Adriana. There were a number of ways that I could have handled her disrespectful behavior on that day. I could have ignored it. I could have told her to leave practice. I could have penalized the rest of the team. Each of these would have produced their own temporary solution and long-term outcome, but none of them would have deepened my relationship with Adriana or indicated to the other students that I would be there for them when they were hurting. The real lesson here is that when young people act in disrespectful ways in our classrooms, it is usually an effort to communicate something to us that they lack the words to convey. If we are creative enough to open a space for dialogue where they do not feel they are being punished or judged, we can usually get to the real issue. If we can get there with students, a whole new set of options opens up for our relationship with them. We can become counselors and healers and from these roles, a whole new set of pedagogical options avail themselves to us.

In Chapter 6, I describe this as the war of position. That is, the battle to win the hearts and minds of individual students, particularly influential students like Adriana. In that moment, the whole team was watching to see how I would respond to the young woman that they saw as the heart and soul of the team, even though she rarely contributed on the court during games. My deep concern for Adriana in that moment conveyed a clear message to the other young people on the team that I cared more about them as young people than as basketball players. I was presented with an incredibly inconvenient opportunity to prove that I was willing to live my life by the philosophy I was teaching to them. These are the tests that we have to pass as educators because they lead to larger victories with our students, so that we may win the war of movement for their collective hearts and minds.

NOTES

1   This was made possible through a bookstore in Berkeley, CA that provided me with a significant discount on any book that I was teaching. For the price of a McDonald's value meal, my students could purchase virtually any book that we were reading. This became a very popular practice in my course, and became a very normalized part of the class. By the end of each school year, students had begun building their own libraries and had been introduced to the skill of annotating the texts they were reading. Occasionally, there were a few students that just couldn't afford to purchase their books. In those cases, I just bought the books for them with no questions asked.

2   Summitt is the all-time winningest collegiate basketball coach in the history of the sport (women or men). Our program regularly implemented elements of their offense and defense, as well as some of their team building strategies. Our players were familiar with Summitt and her legend as a coach and motivator, and many of them aspired to play for her one day.

3   At the time, Cooper was consider the "Michael Jordan of women's basketball." The first serious attempt at a professional women's basketball league (WNBA) in the United States had just taken off and Cooper was twice the league MVP and her team had won the championship. Cooper combined exceptional basketball skills with leadership, charisma, and critical intellect to become an integral part of the league's early success and an important role model for young women.

4   The Nor Cal championship game is semi-final game for the state championship. Both Northern and Southern California crown champions and those two meet each other for the State Championship. No Townville High girls' team had ever been in the Nor Cal Championship game before our 2001 team, and no team from the Townville league had been there since the 1980s.

5   These included selections from people such as: Assata Shakur, Gloria Anzaldúa, Harriet Tubman, Dolores Huerta, Audre Lorde, Toni Morrison, Sandra Cisneros, and Alice Walker.

6   I still use the Definite Dozen in my high school classroom. However, they have been radically altered to reflect a more critical and revolutionary spirit. The document is now

a representation of the philosophy that guides the way I live my life, but its origins are here with LWBP. I would like to think that this evolution of my thinking as a person and educator is indicative of a spirit of lasting commitment to critical reflection and growth.

7   After seeing our success with the Definite Dozen, the boys program adopted and adapted the concept for their program as well.

8   Each year, minor modifications were made to the progress reports to increase their effectiveness. The draft included here was the latest version, and was largely modeled off the progress report used in the boys' program at Townville High after they began employing an academic support similar to ours.

CHAPTER TEN

SPRING SEASON (MARCH-LATE JUNE)

As the hype and media attention of the basketball season died down, the Spring season became an especially important period for the program. The intensity of the season, particularly the post-season playoffs, can lead student-athletes into a mental and physical letdown when it's over. To insure we avoided this, we began the Spring by asking students to revisit their goals from the individual meetings, considering their futures through reflection on the past.

Spring individual meetings consisted of students reviewing their performance during the season and then setting goals for improvement during the off-season. They were also asked to evaluate the coaching staff so that we too could chart a course for improvement during the off-season. As with the earlier individual meetings, students were asked to prepare responses to a series of reflective questions. At the time of the meeting, I also had prepared an evaluation of their performance over the season, including areas for their improvement athletically and academically. The following are the four questions that were given out to students to guide this reflection process:

> - What are three strengths you brought to the team this year?
> - What are three areas you feel you need to improve? What is your plan for creating that improvement?
> - What are the strengths of this coaching staff? Be specific.
> - In what areas do we need to improve as a coaching staff? Be specific. Being nice doesn't help us get better!

Each player received a copy of the evaluations we created for them and, in kind, they were asked to provide the coaches with a copy of their evaluations of us. The focus of these meetings was often very different from the pre-season individual meetings.

The individual plans during the Spring often included academic development strategies geared toward strengthening skills we had identified as needing improvement over the first part of the year. For some students, this meant advising them to enroll in summer school courses to replace a low grade in a core academic course. For others, this meant enrolling in a summer math course to get themselves back on pace to be eligible for admission to the University of California (UC) system. Whatever the case, this kind of individualized academic advising is rarely made available to urban youth. For the overwhelming majority of students at Townville High, the UC system is put out of reach as early as their 9th grade year because they are never made aware of the importance of being in advanced math by the beginning of their sophomore year—this is clearly reflected in the enrollment patterns of the higher math courses at the school (see Table 6 and Table 3 for multi-year trend).[1]

Nancy and Mika are both good examples of the importance of combining goal setting and academic advising. Nancy showed tremendous promise in Algebra during her 9th grade year, but would likely not have had access to Calculus in her 12th grade year because she was not programmed into Geometry as a 9th grader. To move her into the highest math track, we advised her to take Geometry during the summer between her 9th and 10th grade year. She did, and when she returned for her 10th grade year, she was enrolled in Advanced Algebra-Trigonometry and she knew the difference immediately.

Nancy: That was a big change for me. Taking Geometry that summer put me into totally different math classes. It was weird because there wasn't that many black kids in there, but I knew I was

in the smart classes and the teachers were harder, but better...
like they knew we'd go to college from that class.

For Mika, the jump was even bigger. She came to Townville High in the more advanced math track. As a 9th grader she had taken Geometry and was on pace to be in Calculus during her 12th grade year. However, she too showed tremendous promise in math and expressed an interest in moving into the highest math track in the school. With the program's advice, she enrolled in an Advanced Algebra-Trigonometry class during the summer between her 9th and 10th grade years and in the Fall of her 10th grade year she enrolled in Math Analysis (Pre-Calculus), one of only two black students in the course, ultimately finishing her high school math courses in Calculus BC.

Structures such as the individual meeting normalized consistent reflection, assessment, and planning that could be tailored to individual student strengths and needs. This goal setting culture allowed for the articulation of long- and short-term goals, along with a collaborative process for planning a course of action to achieve those objectives. Students in their senior year were still expected to go through this process in the spring, focusing on strategies for a successful transition to college in the fall.

K-8 MINI-CAMPS

As a way of developing the students' sense of civic responsibility to the younger members of the community, the program hosted mini-camps in the spring (see Chapter 6 for a more detailed discussion of the mini-camp design and activities). To plan for camp, students signed up to design various basketball stations, a healthy lifestyle station, and a "secrets to high school success" station. Prior to the clinic, students were asked to form groups to collaboratively design lesson plans consisting of drills or discussion topics for the station they would be running. Each group met with me to review their plans and get feedback to fine-tune them.

Camp sign-up sheets were distributed to local elementary and middle school coaches and community centers. The first 60 registrants were invited to spend two days with our students and coaches to receive free basketball instruction and guidance on issues of health and lifestyle choices that are sometimes overlooked in their lives. However, as I reflected in my field notes, the mini-camp in the Spring of 2001 reminded us that our responsibility to the community would not always be convenient.

Field Notes vignette

March 11th, 2001

The commitment of the girls in this program is inspirational and it gives me hope for our community. Just a few short hours after having their season ended with a crushing defeat in the State Championship semifinals at Arco Arena, they came back to the school to run their annual mini-camp for Townville youth. I would have understood if they were just too tired to do it.

On Friday night, they played and won the biggest game in the history of the program. Then one night later, they were playing for the Northern California Division I title in another part of the state and they lost, and didn't get home until after midnight. The next morning they were at the gym at 8:00 a.m. to set up for the youngsters. Not one of them complained. I know they were exhausted... I was and I didn't even play in either one of those games.

The six seniors must have been crushed. Ada cried on the bench during a timeout during the championship game when the game's outcome had become inevitable. Yet, it was the seniors that led the charge to get everything set up for the kids the next morning.

Later that year, Nancy (one of the six seniors from that year's team) helped me better understand where their courage and commitment to the mini-camps came from:

> I loved doing the mini-camps because for us it was a chance to do what you do for us. I liked working with the little kids, and it made me think that I might be a coach one day...sometimes kids from the camp would see me around the neighborhood and they would come up to me. I could never remember their names, but they always remembered me. I really think I could be a coach one day.

The attentiveness of the young participants in the camps quickly heightened our students' awareness about how influential they could be. Requests for autographs at the end of camp became so common that an autograph session became a scheduled part of the event. The relationships built as a result of the mini-camps also led several elementary school teams to start attending some of our home games. Students on these teams, many of whom had attended a mini-camp in the past, would be invited into our team room to listen to our halftime talk and again after the game to talk with the players and to get autographs.

In her interview, Erika expressed how these interactions with younger students affected her sense of responsibility to them:

> I have really started to realize how much those kids hang on my every word. I mean they just stand at my locker and wait for me to talk to them [after games]…they have their mouth open and they are just waiting. And when I talk, they don't even blink, they just listen to everything I say.

These interactions with youth from the community prompted team discussions about the importance of maintaining the program's community of practice outside of the confines of the school. Stories like Nancy's, of our students being approached in public spaces by previous camp participants, mounted over time and helped to solidify the program's attention to civic awareness. Actualizing our students' sense of responsibility to the community, particularly to other young people, was key to the development of the program's counter-culture. It was a strategic response to otherwise low expectations of urban youth to meet their responsibility to the community to be active agents of positive change.

USING SPORTS TO KEEP IT TOGETHER

I was acutely aware that the spring season had the potential to result in emotional and physical letdowns coming off the intensity of the basketball season. To mitigate this, I made sure the cultural hook (participating in a sport) remained intact by maintaining a relatively high level of athletic activity in the program. This is not to say that students were disinterested in doing well in school or improving their communities. Rather, the use of on-going athletic development was recognition of the fact that participation on a sports team was the structure that supported the broader social and academic goals of the program.

The schedule below is what we gave to our students in the spring of 2000 and is typical of the spring schedules they received each year.

> **Monday:** Study table (3:30–5:30 pm)
> **Tuesday:** Weights/conditioning (3:30–5:00 pm)
> Spring league game (see schedule)
> **Wednesday:** Study table (3:30–5:30 pm)
> **Thursday:** Weights/conditioning (3:30–5:00 pm)
> Spring league game (see schedule)
> **Friday:** Study table (3:30–5:30 pm)
> Open gym (5:30–7:00 pm)
> **Saturday:** Conditioning/traveling team practice (2:00–5:30 pm)
> **Sunday:** Conditioning/traveling team practice (2:00–5:30 pm)

The spring league games were typically very similar to the fall league mentioned in Chapter 8. The traveling team practice was preparation for the summer season discussed in Chapter 7, and connected our students to athletes from high schools all over the area.

ACADEMIC SUPPORT

The academic support provided during this part of the school year was similar with respect to the formal tutoring component and the weekly progress reports—tutors from the university still attended study table with regularity and attendance was mandatory for all of our students.[2] Participation in team activities (games, open gyms, conditioning, and travel teams) was dependent on a student's participation in study table.

Ada, like many of her peers, identified the presence of this year-round structure as critical to her continued success after the season ended:

> The structure kept me motivated. I know that I wouldn't have done as good after the season was over if we hadn't kept having study table and if you hadn't stayed on us. Sometimes when the season was over I just wanted to rest, but you kept on pushing us and we knew you expected us to come to everything.

The spring "push" to which Ada refers was even more pronounced for the 11th and 12th graders. Juniors (11th graders) were given support in registering for all three of the college entrance exams (SAT I, SAT II, and ACT), as well as exam tips and preparation materials. Given the dismal proportion of students at Townville High that even took college entrance exams, and their equally meager scores on those exams, it is not surprising that the LWBP was one of the only places at the school where every student was being encouraged to take the tests.

As Shannon commented in her interview, a number of students at the school were either explicitly discouraged from taking the exams or misinformed about them:

> When you told me that I had to take the SAT to go to college, I thought you were joking at first because one of my teachers had said that we didn't need the SAT to go to college. She said that that test was only for the tougher colleges. When I asked her about it after you had talked to us, she said that you guys were just filling our heads with lies. She was really pissed off.

The discouragement Shannon and her classmates received was not always as explicit as what she describes here, but it was not uncommon.

To counter these conditions we made the college entrance exams a normal part of our programmatic culture and also made sure students received test preparation support. Each year, students that were taking the tests were asked to buy the same test preparation book so that they could study together— students sampled different companies over the years and never found much difference between any of them. As was always the case, we supplemented those who did not have enough money to cover the costs. Once they had their books, we gave them a nightly schedule for studying and taking practice exams. When they identified particular sections that they found difficult, they could ask their teammates that were working on that same section, or get help from the tutors, coaches, or supportive teachers. If they still could not master the section, they frequently set up individual tutoring sessions with Wyatt (a deeply committed science and math teacher at the school).[3]

While juniors were prepping for their exams, the seniors were busy finalizing their college selections, completing their Free Application for Federal Student Aid (FAFSA), and completing a video course with me (and Morrell in the earlier years) called "The Secrets to College Success".[4] To help them choose the colleges they wanted to attend we encouraged them to match the schools where they had been accepted to their responses to their college-going questions from the summer component (see Chapter 7). Wherever possible, we connected our current students to former students that attended the schools where they were accepted so that they could get a Townville student's perspective on the school. We also reached out to alumni, professors, and coaches that we knew at those institutions to arrange conversations and/or campus visits. Finally, we maintained a list of important deadlines for housing, financial aid, and selecting their courses so we could remind students and families as those dates neared.

The area where they typically needed the most support was with the Free Application for Federal Student Aid (FAFSA). Parents like Lisa, who was already somewhat familiar with the process of applying to college, commented that this added support helped to share some of the burden and served as a double-check system to make sure nothing was missed.

> **Lisa (Mika's mother):** Although Mika probably could have handled most of the application process on her own, she almost certainly would have missed something. The thoroughness of the program and people like Wyatt helped to close up some of those gaps.

Melinda noted that the system provided a different type support for her because she did not have a working knowledge of the process:

> **Melinda (Ada's mother):** A lot of these things I couldn't have helped Ada with. I think if it was left up to her or the school, those things wouldn't have ever been done and she probably wouldn't get to go to college. But, you (the program) knew the steps and she got important information that she might not have gotten otherwise.

While parents kept up with the college deadlines and prepared to send their children off to college, the program assigned the seniors one final rite of passage. The "secrets to college success" was a 65-minute video was designed to give high school seniors survival and success tips for their freshman year in college. It outlines some of the major hurdles facing new college students and provides strategies for navigating that world. At the conclusion of the video, we gave our seniors their last goal setting assignment in the program. They were asked to draw from the film to identify three things that they knew they would need to improve upon before they entered college in the fall. Then they developed a plan for improving in those areas over the summer and submitted drafts of those plans the week following the video. I reviewed their submissions and gave them feedback on ways to focus and strengthen their summer strategy. After the revisions were completed, we met for our last formal goal setting discussion.

WHAT A COACH CAN TEACH A TEACHER

Maintain—strong and steady

This chapter covers a period of the school year that was always of great concern for me as a teacher. At the end of the Spring semester, when the sun comes out, days are longer, and the school year is winding down – all teachers are susceptible to let downs. Our program avoided this by anticipating this possibility of a letdown and rededicating ourselves to activity and the principles that had brought us success. In our classrooms, we can do the same by acknowledging the fatigue of a long school year and the urge to pack it in early, while recommitting to our collective principles. This is where a collective philosophy like the Definite Dozen and rites of passage are particularly useful because they can be called upon to re-establish commitments made earlier in the school year.

Comprehend comprehensive academic planning

It has taken me years to learn the layers of requirements for university admission, and these regularly change so it is a constant self-education process. This knowledge also allows me to be a better advocate and advisor for my students and a better resource for parents. However, given the importance of the college application process, I often connect my students and their families to Newin Orante, a close friend and tireless youth advocate that has been doing college advising for nearly 20 years.

In under-resourced schools, comprehensive academic counseling is rare. Teachers should therefore equip themselves with an ability to provide these essential services and connect their students to their network of resources, like Newin. In the event that the school does have academic counselors, then it is important that our advising with students is done in collaboration with supportive counselors.

Make it bigger than your class

In the last chapter I explained the importance of creating spaces for our students to be positioned as public intellectuals so that the things they are learning have value beyond our classrooms. In this chapter, you read about the mini-camps that our students hosted for other young people in the community, which adds an additional layer to this idea. The ultimate goal of our pedagogy should be to produce knowledge that students can apply in the service of their community. The more often we can open opportunities for students to apply their learning and reflect on that application, the more relevance and lasting power our lessons will have on our students.

Have a transition plan

This chapter ends with a discussion of our transition plan for our seniors. When students leave our institution, they benefit greatly when we help them develop a plan for adjusting to this change. Whether it is with elementary, middle, or high school students, we often wrongly presume that the next school will effectively usher in our students. Some schools do it better than others, but the best scenario for our students is one where they get support on both sides of the transition. We will not typically have any say about the operations at the places where they are going, but we can control how well we prepare them before they leave us. As they prepare to move on, we can help our students anticipate the new challenges they will face, while also working with them to develop a plan that will allow them to identify the skills and resources they will need to overcome those challenges. Although these transition plans can never fully prepare our students for institutions that might be unsupportive, or even hostile, they are an important additional support we can give to our students.

NOTES

1   Although the UC system only requires that students have 4 years of math, up to Algebra-Trigonometry, it is "recommended" that students take at least up to Pre-Calculus. This requires students to be in Geometry during their 9th grade year, or else, to pick up a year of math during one of the summer sessions. The dearth of college advising at the school often results in students coming upon this information far too late to do anything about it. Issues of access are also at play here, and will be discussed in more detail later.

2   A number of our students participated in other school sports (soccer, volleyball, track, and softball). This was sometimes a source of conflict when we had Fall or Spring league games that conflicted with their school team games. We did our best to defer to the school team's schedule, although our students often asked if they could attend our games instead. We worked to develop collaborative relationships with coaches of other sports that were working with our students, particularly around study table, because no other girls' sports

programs were providing formal academic support. If any of our students involved in other sports fell behind in a class, we would approach their in-season coach and ask that they be excused from practice until they caught up in their classes. This action was usually supported by coaches, albeit sometimes begrudgingly.

3   In spite of these efforts, most of our students still struggled mightily on these exams. There are numerous explanations for these struggles (cultural bias, lack of preparation in their math and English classes, ineffective support on our part), which are supported by research and are almost certainly partially correct. However, in my estimation, this was the weakest component of our program. To this day, I have not found an effective strategy for preparing my students to perform on the SAT in a way that reflects their true ability. I maintain that these tests should be removed from the college admissions process as numerous studies, including extensive research by the National Center for Fair and Open Testing, have shown that they are not meaningful predictors for college success. Until such a time, it will remain a major gatekeeper for college admissions (particularly for entrance into the most prestigious schools) and so I remain open to trying new methods for raising students' scores.

4   (Corry & Rothbard, 1993)

CHAPTER ELEVEN

THE SYSTEM

Virtually any coach that is successful has a system that covers every aspect of the game. Their system is rooted in a set of philosophical beliefs that determines how they teach the game, and it reveals what they feel are the most fundamental aspects of the game and life. There are a number of books[1] that have come out in the last decade that explore the systems of coaches that have earned the respect of their profession and each of them has some lessons for teachers. The overarching lesson though is that successful coaches must be good teachers, and good teachers always have a system.

My success as a coach was no exception to this rule. This book has cataloged the range and depth of the pedagogical system that we used in our program to produce uncommon success. The story I've told here does not document the system I developed to teach the game of basketball, but the program's success in that arena should be an indicator that I had a system for that that was just as developed. I worked hard over the years to apply the lessons we were teaching our students through basketball to their schooling and their lives, and visa versa.

The fact that I can write an entire book on that system should suggest to you that it took years to develop it, that it was a perpetual process of touching up and tweaking, and that the full range of details is ultimately impossible to capture. However, in this final chapter, I'd like to offer you some of my best thinking on the core principles of our system, candor on the failures of our system, and updates on the phenomenal young women whose voices helped write this story.

TOP 10 TEACHER TAKEAWAYS—WHAT A COACH CAN TEACH A TEACHER ABOUT DESIGNING THEIR SYSTEM

Principle #1—Develop your philosophy

Successful coaches have a philosophy about the game they are coaching, the skills that must be taught for success, and the relationship between the lessons of their sport and success in life. Every teacher should be able to articulate a similar philosophy about teaching, learning, and the value of acquiring the skills and content from your course for the development of a more just society. This philosophy should be shared with students and your teaching system should embody its principles. As Howard Zinn puts it:

> I was not going to be one of those teachers that at the end of the semester, at the end of the year, the students wanted to know where does this teacher stand. They were going to know where I stood from the very beginning! That's been my attitude all the way through, and still is (Zinn, 1998).

When you can express your own philosophy, you are much better prepared to teach young people how to use your teachings to develop their own philosophy. As well, you should remain committed to constantly revisiting and revising your philosophy and your system because there is no progress without change.

Principle #2—Establish clear objectives—You can be good at a lot of things or great at a few

I have never forgotten Coach Wooden's advice that I would need to decide whether I wanted my team to be good at a lot of things, or great at a few. Effective coaches know that their teams will not be great at every aspect of the game, so they select the skills and values on which to place their emphasis based on their philosophy. Many of the educators I encounter that aspire to greatness lack this clarity of purpose and this inhibits them from their goals. One remedy for this is to start each school year by turning to your philosophy to identify a set of clear and measurable skills and values that you want your students to develop under your tutelage. Everything you do with them should be contributing to their growth in those areas.

When I do this goal setting for my classroom, I often start by reviewing the state and national standards for my class's grade level and subject area. To Wooden's point, the standards are too numerous, vague, and broad for me to effectively design a teaching plan that prepares my students to be great at all of them. So, I choose the ones that are best suited to allowing students to deepen their understanding of the principles imbedded in my philosophy. Students will still be exposed to standards outside of those selected, but they will not be my focus and they will not factor heavily into my assessments of students' growth. When my students leave my class, I want them to be able to identify with confidence and clarity a very specific set of skills and values that they have learned as a result of their time with me. This process of connecting my philosophy to my intended social and academic outcomes makes that more probable.

Principle #3—Pedagogy (content and delivery)

Coaches that have a clear philosophy and knowledge of the concrete skills their players need to carry it out are not necessarily going to be successful. The planning that we do, as coaches or teachers, is only as useful as our ability to execute that plan with students. Your pedagogy, consisting of *what* you teach (curriculum) and *how* you teach it (delivery), is the most impactful element of your teaching system because it is the interface between you and your students. There is nothing you can invest in as a teacher that will have a greater impact on your time with students than improving your pedagogy.

I would argue that all of the principles in this list are part of pedagogy. My intention in calling out the idea of pedagogy in this list is to emphasize the importance of giving specific attention to our curriculum and the daily practices we use to deliver it to our students. Our ability to successfully link these with our philosophy and purpose will be defined by our capacity to effectively utilize the major pedagogical elements emphasized throughout this book: zone of proximal development, organic intellectualism, critical praxis, critical double consciousness, counter-cultural community of practice, hope, rites of passage, etcetera.

Principle #4—Create structures that develop discipline *and* obtain objectives

When coaches design their practice plans they tend to choose drills that kill the proverbial two birds with one stone—they provide discipline while teaching the values and skills being emphasized. Yang (2009) draws from sports coaching to define the kind of classroom discipline his research identifies as the most effective. He describes discipline in opposition to punishment, arguing that good teachers define discipline as "rigorous mental or physical training through which we may construct new subjectivities and emancipatory practices... part of a rigorous craft that demands intensive work and painstaking creativity towards a common goal" (p. 53). This framework treats discipline as an inclusive framework that busts the binary between entertainment and education by operating a "highly structured apprenticeship, rather than a rule-bound reformatory... not a "safe" space, but rather a community of risk taking, of setbacks, of difficulty... Although collaborative, it is not equalitarian—the teacher exercises authority without becoming authoritarian. In this classroom, everybody swims" (p. 55).

Yang goes on to remind us that effective activity structures that carry out this discipline framework (whether for our classrooms or sports practices) are always "highly context-specific". That is, they prioritize the primary skill and value objectives, while maintaining true to a pedagogical philosophy that is situated in the material conditions and youth cultural practices of the students being taught.

This book identifies a number of structures that we used in the LWBP to take aim at the discipline and objectives targets (e.g. individual meetings, zone of proximal development, rooming assignments during travel). In some of my other work, I discuss structures that I use in my classroom to accomplish the same goal: youth research, film analysis, mock trials, presentations, project-based learning, and debate (see Duncan-Andrade & Morrell, 2008). I will add that I am constantly on the lookout for new activity structures to add to this list. The three most common sources for acquiring these have been student comments about other classrooms, observations of other teachers, and professional conferences.

Principle #5—You have to get buy-in

Successful coaches understand that in order to be consistently successful, they will need to convince their players to follow them down a difficult, and sometimes painful, path. In order for this to happen, the players must trust that the sacrifices required to learn the coach's system will put them in a position where they can experience success under the fire of competition. Effective teachers ask students for the same sacrifices of time and spirit, to endure failures, to cross barriers they believe impassable, and this only happens when students are willing to buy what we are selling. Nowhere is this challenge more pronounced than in communities where this presumed alliance between teacher and student has been continuously violated by schools.

At the end of the day, effective teaching depends most heavily on one thing—deep and caring relationships. Herb Kohl (1995) describes "willed not learning" as the phenomena by which students try *not* to learn from teachers who don't authentically care about them. The adage "students don't care what you know until they know that you care" is supported by numerous studies of effective educators (Akom, 2003; Delpit, 1995; Author, 2007; Ladson-Billings, 1994).

To provide the "authentic care" (Valenzuela, 1999) that students require from us as a precondition for learning from us, we must connect our indignation over all forms of oppression with an "audacious hope" (Duncan-Andrade, 2009) that we can act to change them. The belief that this change will not cost us anything is mendacious; it never acknowledges pain. Audacious hope stares down the painful path, and despite the overwhelming odds against us making it down that path to change, we make the journey, again and again. There is no other choice. Acceptance of this fact allows us to find the courage and the commitment to cajole our students to buy into our system for making these changes. Only then will they join us on that journey. This makes us better people as it makes us better teachers, and it models for our students that the painful path *is* the hopeful path—and that is how we get students to buy into our system and that is how we win the war of movement (see Chapter 6) in our classrooms.

Principle #6—Be dynamic—Learn how to read and react

One of the most admired traits in coaching is the ability to make adjustments. All high level coaches have a system, but the true mark of excellence is the ability to adjust without abandoning your philosophy when the preferred options in your system are not working. Effective teachers must also be able to strike this slippery relationship between staying the course with their students, and recognizing when they need to make adjustments. This begins with having clarity about your philosophy and objectives as a teacher—know what you want to do *and* how you want to do it. We initiate our system with time-tested methods, preferred pathways down which we will send most of our students. Inevitably, this path will become blocked for some students and this is where our ability to adjust makes its impact.

At our highest capacity, we can anticipate or quickly read these blockages and redirect students to a clearer path toward the same objective. These re-directions are not always effective the first time and so we need multiple pathways toward the same goal. The quicker we can make these adjustments, the less frustrated our students become when they feel blocked. It should be added that when adjustments are more common than utilization of the primary path, it is time to re-examine the core objectives and pathways of our system because they are no longer working for the majority of our students.

This ability to adjust operates on two levels: day to day and change over time. On a daily level, Yang (2009) describes the most accomplished teachers as having "quick wits and [being] fluent enough in youth popular cultural codes to win any symbolic confrontation with students, [while detecting and de-escalating] most confrontations between students before they snowball" (p. 56). Effective teachers must also anticipate change over time. Rather than committing to a static set of methods and strategies, our system should anticipate growth in our students' abilities over time. To accommodate this growth, our pedagogy should be adjusting rigor and expectations upward, slowly pushing students toward mastery and polish of the skills we are emphasizing. This ratcheting up of the challenges we place before students is what prepares them for championship level performance. Successful coaches describe this approach by saying that they want their practices to be more challenging than the games so that when game time comes, their players know they can endure whatever they might face. Yang (2009) explains this ability to adjust our pedagogical system over time as the "boundary between the humanization and mechanization of our work"—the difference between teaching as craft and schooling as industry (p. 60).

Principle #7—Classroom as community of practice—Developing generalists *and* specialists

A coach's ability to build a successful team depends on teaching a core set of skills to everyone (known as fundamentals) and developing individual specialized skills (known as a player's role). The fundamentals shape the group values of the team, but to complete the team you must allow individual talents to emerge and find room for them inside your system. This merging of generalist skills and individual specialties is what forms a community of practice: a *joint enterprise* based on *mutual engagement* that develops a *shared repertoire* of resources (Wenger, 1999). Coaches use a process of pre-identifying (recruiting and scouting), testing (tryouts and preseason), developing (practice), and polishing (individual instruction) to cultivate specialized talents into the community.

Throughout the book, I have described this process as possible for educators by using the concept of the zone of proximal development to identify and nurture students' organic intellectualism. Structurally speaking, it can look something like this:

Phase one (recruiting and scouting): Before students join our classroom community, we can actively recruit students whose special talents are a good fit with our system[2]. We can also talk with our colleagues that have worked with our new students in the past to identify their special skills.

Phase two (tryouts and preseason): Once students join our community, our structure should create opportunities for us to further identify students' zone of proximal development for the common skills and values we want to teach to everyone. Our structure should also allow us to better identify their individual organic intellectualism (drawing, orating, leading, arguing, organizing) and open opportunities for them to work these specialized skills into the fabric of our community of practice.

Phase three (practice): As the school year progresses, we should expect that the group values are setting in, which allows us to start ramping up our expectations. Here we should raise the size and scope of the challenges we put to students testing their limits and placing them in situations where they must draw from the "shared repertoire" of resources (general and individual) in order to experience success. It should be clear that the increasing intensity is preparing them for the "playoffs", some set of conditions where they will be expected to execute their skills as a community under the pressure of public scrutiny.

Phase four (individual polish): Instructional methods in this final phase focus on polishing the community so that its shared repertoire of resources can shine. The goal is a smooth flowing exchange of skills and ideas, each person holding up the foundation as a generalist and contributing their specialized skill set so the community is maximizing its talent. Coaches refer to this as championship play and when we get it right, our team is peaking in this phase. Coach Wooden describes his expectation for this phase by saying that if he has done his job correctly, his team should be able to walk onto the court for the national championship game while he sits in the bleachers and watches them execute the system flawlessly.

Principle #8 —Beyond your classroom—colleagues and community

The success of any sports team is made possible by a host of people that most of us never see—families, equipment managers, custodians, tutors, trainers, nutritionists, medical staff, counselors, administrators, fundraisers. Coaches understand that a whole and healthy individual makes for a stronger team—the adage that a chain is only as strong as its weakest link appropriately captures this logic.

It is simply not possible for one person to meet all the needs of all the members of a community of practice. We must work beyond the walls of our classroom to identify resources and form partnerships with colleagues and community to share the load. The alternative is unmet needs which inevitably seep in and weaken the foundation of the community. In our worst moments, we remove this link from our chain, rationalizing that we are not responsible and/or not capable of strengthening every link in the chain. What we fail to recognize is that this ultimately weakens our chain, shortening it and raising questions among our other students about our commitment to seeing them through difficult times.

To meet the inescapable challenge of strengthening every link in our community of practice chain, we need a strategy for eliciting the support of a variety of community partners. This requires us to develop real relationships with families and community partners that we can call on for support with issues that we are not prepared to handle on our own. This may not be possible with all our families, some may not even want it (although I find that to be rare if we are genuine about being a partner), but we need to develop multiple pathways and make a genuine effort. At the very least all parents should receive consistent opportunities to read about, hear about, see what is going on our classroom.

Teachers can also compile a database of community partners that they can call on, or refer students and families to, when they are in need of support in their area of expertise (legal aid, medical aid, academic support, counseling, employment, housing, safety concerns). We can share and build this list in partnership with supportive colleagues, while also forming in-house collaboratives with those colleagues to give students temporary respite when they might just need a change of scenery to collect themselves. It really does take a village to raise our children.

Principle #9—Stay ahead or you are getting behind

One advantage that coaches have over teachers is that if we are winning, we know that our opponents are spending their time figuring out how to prevent us from doing it again. If we are not winning, we also know that our opponents are spending their time making sure that things stay that way. Coaches are provided with a host of sophisticated tools and resources for engaging in the process of critical praxis (coaching clinics, videotaping, websites, videotape exchange with other coaches, coaching books and videos describing effective systems and drills down to minute detail). I describe our use of some of these tools in various parts of this book.

I describe this as an advantage because no matter how you have done in the past as a coach, there is a built in motivator to reflect and revise your system to stay ahead or to catch up. I recognize that some people may feel like they do not want to be competitive as a teacher, but it is my position that this is a stance of convenience that excuses us from the dedication to improvement that our students deserve—I would also argue that teachers working with wealthy and elite children are not afforded this luxury of choosing whether they will continually improve their systems.

A competitive instinct can be useful for teachers if it drives us to improve our teaching without falling prey to corrosive definitions of success that lead us to lose site of the very lessons we are attempt to teach our students. The purest form of this motivation is internal (just as it is with coaches) because its essence is our desire to give our students and communities the type of education they deserve. This is why efforts on the part of policy makers and corporations to "support" classroom teachers by mandating scripted curriculum and obsessive testing, while "motivating" teachers with test score data and school rankings[3], have done little to change achievement patterns.

Oddly enough, these poorly reasoned policies seem to have sparked a revolt of sorts from teachers around the country. A growing number of educators have come to understand our best weapon against these policies is to provide a well-reasoned discussion of the practices and policies that actually produce the results we are looking for in schools. It behooves all of us to participate in these efforts, staying committed to critical reflection on our practice while keeping abreast of the latest innovations in good teaching that are relevant to our context. These activities can include:

- Forming a local teacher reflection group (see Duncan-Andrade, 2004 for a discussion of a critical teaching inquiry group cycle).
- Forming student focal groups from your classes to give you pertinent feedback on your teaching and on youth culture that you can imbed in your pedagogy.
- Choosing some aspect of your teaching that you want to research and then presenting that at a conference—this can also be done as a group process with colleagues or local university faculty.
- Attending local and national research conferences on education: American Educational Research Association (AERA), National

Association of Bilingual Educators (NABE), National Council of the Teachers of English Mid-Winter Conference, National Association for Research in Science Teaching, National Council of Teachers of Mathematics (NCTM) Research Pre-Session.

- Attending local and national conferences for teachers: Teachers for Social Justice (T4SJ), Institute for Transformative Education (Tucson Unified), Free Minds Free People, Association of Raza Educators (ARE), National Council of the Teachers of English (NCTE), National Council of the Teachers of Math, National Science Teachers Association, and National Council for the Social Studies, Radical Math Conference, New York Coalition of Radical Educators (NYCORE).

Principle #10—Battle

Successful coaches and their teams are usually defined by their ability to overcome internal strife and struggle, rather than some external opponent. From the outside, they appear to be without conflict and that is often the image they want to project. When their story is told, however, it is clear that their success was not the result of having been afforded the good fortune of an unencumbered path to greatness. Their paths are often paved with setbacks, defining moments of conflict that border on the potential of destructiveness for their community of practice.

The question for teachers, like coaches, is not whether will we face these moments of stress and strain, but how we will respond when we do. Will we win these wars of position, battles for the hearts and minds of the children we are charged with teaching? I tell my students that I will spend my life battling on their behalf (sometimes with them, mostly for them) because I hate losing more than I love winning, and right now we are losing. Coach Wooden would add that maintaining my spirit in this struggle is made possible by avoiding emotional peeks and valleys—at the end of a struggle, people should not be able determine the outcome based on my demeanor. I find this part of Wooden's advice easier to apply as a coach and athlete than as a teacher. However, I see the value in this advice when I connect it to Sun Tzu's perspective that sometimes we lose battles so that we can learn the lessons that allow us to win the war. For that reason, our victories and losses should both be treated as lessons along our journey, not as destinations.

Our students will also wonder whether they can overcome the difficulties they face in our classroom and in life. Perhaps the most important question students ask us as they gauge whether or not to engage is: "why do I have to do this?" Far too many of us fall back on stock responses like "because I said so" or "because it will give you a better future". Over time, our inability to answer this question meaningfully must take its toll on the faith of most students that what they are learning matters in the larger scheme of things. Successful teachers are able to answer this question in more profound ways. They explain to students that what they offer is part of a path to freedom—if they learn the skills they are being taught, they will be in a better position to think and act critically for themselves and for their community, two essential components of freedom. This does not mean that the teachers ignore the potential of these skills to provide access to college and other opportunities in the future, but they do not rest the relevance of their lessons on the false rhetoric of the bootstrap theory. Neither do they pretend that they have a panacea for ending the litany of stressors that life places in our way. Instead, they build intellectually rigorous lessons that are relevant to the real and immediate conditions of their students' lives so that students can think and respond critically for themselves. They share with students their hope that they will become the agents of change that are too few today. This kind of teaching is hopeful that the battle can be won, but not naïve to the fact that there is another one around the corner. The fortitude required can be found in the Socratic sensibility that all great undertakings are risky and what is worthwhile is always difficult (Duncan-Andrade, 2007). We have to win, there is no other choice—what we do is life and death.

Things I would do differently now

I continue to use the strategies that I have shared with you in this book and each year they look a little different. By the time that this book comes out, I will have begun a new school year with a group of 9th graders. I will put this system back in play and new adjustments will be required to meet the unique needs of my new group of students. This cycle of regenerating my system of pedagogy takes me through a process of reflection where I list out things I would do differently if I had another shot with that same group of students. What follows is a partial list of necessary revisions that I compiled after I left the LWBP in 2002 for improving my work with students and parents. Most of these adjustments have already been incorporated into my teaching system.

Revision for working with students

- Provide more consistency from college tutors so that long-term relationships can be developed between specific students and specific tutors.

- Find more effective means of supporting our students on the college entrance exams.
- Provide more individual support to students to assist them with personal problems. Can I find a solid individual adult advocate for each student?
- Increase non-basketball related group activities to solidify team bonds. More social time, meals together, outings. Maybe do some kind of monthly dinner with the students and their families at the house?
- Provide each new student with a veteran player mentor. Let students select each other.
- Provide "specialty tutors"; individual tutors with expertise in each academic subject area.
- Provide graduating students guidance on managing finances, credit cards, financial aid, renting apartments, getting summer jobs.
- Develop a system to support students after they leave our program so that they complete their degrees.
- Develop a formal pipeline to bring graduates back into the community as teachers and coaches.

Revisions for working with parents

- Increase communication between coaching staff and parents through regularly scheduled meetings or phone calls to provide parents updates on their child.
- Provide more consistent and more productive means of fundraising to off-set the costs of equipment and travel.
- Structure activities for parents to be more directly involved with the program (parent-player games, parents vs. parents games, Booster Club, etcetra).
- Host a parent study tips night (an annual event where parents are given strategies to help their students manage their schedules effectively).
- Host a parent college night (an annual event where parents are given the latest updates on preparing their child for the SAT and ACT, college admissions, financial aid, and athletic recruiting).

Implications—some thoughts for key educator groups

There is not some set of historical glory days that we can return to for some model. There has never been a time in the history of this nation where poor children received equitable and excellent access to a quality public education system. Rather, those who have needed the most help have always received the least—the least adequately funded schools, the least prepared teachers and administrators, the least sufficient facilities, etcetera, etcetera, etcetera. Little has changed in this history and if common knowledge about unequal schooling is not enough to convince us of this fact, there are numerous research studies that document these inequitable conditions.

All of this does not mean that we are short on evidence that, given the proper support, any child can succeed in school. However, the overwhelming majority of the studies of successful practices in urban schools reveal that it is the schools that need to change, not the children. Successful teachers, programs, and institutions are unified around the belief that children are not deficient, but institutions that fail them are. This is not to slander or belittle these institutions or the adults that hold them together in some of our nation's most desperate times. Rather, it is an effort to redirect our focus onto the fact that the students crossing our classroom thresholds are already wonderfully skilled. They are coming to our schools hoping that they will be given the chance to build upon these talents so that they may grow into opportunity. But, as successful educators already know, this does not happen by beating back the culture that students bring with them to school. Nor does it happen by celebrating that culture on an annual holiday, or incorporating it as an afterthought in our pedagogy. Success with students comes from genuinely valuing them and the places where they choose to invest themselves.

We know enough about teaching and learning to do better. We know that to allow a child to stare into a mirror and see herself reflected back as talented leads her down a pathway where she will come to embody those traits in her life. Likewise, if that same child sees herself reflected in a mirror that gives the impression that she is of a lesser God, judged as inadequate in the greater social order, she is almost certainly doomed to failure. Every time a child walks through the doors of a classroom, they look into a mirror. Eventually, they come to believe what we teach them to see.

It is my hope that this book will build on a growing body of work that is investigating effective practices in schools, focusing on discussions of *why* these practices are effective. The implications of these discussions are far-reaching, but speak most closely to four groups: educators (classroom teachers, coaches, program directors, counselors), teacher educators, urban administrators, and educational policy makers. For this research to make its way back into schools as effective practice, these four groups must each make their own account of it.

Implications for urban educators

Conditions in urban schools will not change without this group being on board. As a starting point, educators should consider themselves as ethnographers of their students. By making themselves more aware of the areas where their students are investing themselves, educators can uncover endless pedagogical ideas to impart the social and academic skills they want to teach. Whether it is sports, music, style, or the media, great educators must understand what their students' value in their day to day lives. These are things that young people willingly choose to invest themselves in and there is power in that choice. Rather than dismissing those choices as frivolous, educators can work to understand the value that youth place on these activities.

To engage in this kind of practice, educators can take the approach suggested by Paulo Freire in *Pedagogy of the Oppressed*. Freire (1971) asks teachers to move away from what he calls the "banking concept of education", a model where the teacher has the information that matters and the student is an empty receptacle waiting to have this information deposited. He calls for educational praxis, a system of practice and reflection where the teacher regularly examines their performance and pedagogy. In this approach, educators can be both teacher and student, as can the students in the class. At this point, the lines of expertise are shared and frequently crossed as both parties possess knowledge that matters in the context of the class. However, for this process to take place, teachers must see their students as bearers of knowledge that is worthy of the classroom and they must position the students as the experts in those areas. This requires teachers to have some knowledge of the cultural practices of students and to find ways to effectively incorporate them into the curriculum.

In order for this type of practice to become more common, teachers must be supported in their growth in this direction. Too often, these educators, the ones that have been the pillars and the glue inside the crumbling walls of urban schools, are asked to do it to the tune of institutional dissent and cries of mis-education and malpractice. Our profession must stop making excuses for those that are failing, genuinely support those that are committed to improving, and start holding up those that are already succeeding. The latter of these three groups should be positioned to support those that are struggling to teach our children by giving teachers better structures and more time for collaboration. Teachers should be treated as intellectuals, encouraged and rewarded for pursuing growth opportunities and achieving radical growth in schools.

Implications for urban coaches

Unlike most teachers, coaches have access to students for extended periods of time each day. They also have the advantage of having students engaged in an activity which they willingly invest in. This provides a tremendous window of opportunity for pushing students to see beyond their sport. Coaches have a profound influence over the lives and worldviews of their athletes, but this is too often under utilized beyond the context of sports. Considering the commitments of time, effort, and spirit regularly expected from athletes, sport provides amazing potential for building great students and transformative community members.

Like teachers, coaches can become more reflective on their practice as educators. What are they emphasizing on a daily basis? Are there things happening inside the context of their sport that are transferable into larger social and academic issues?   In order for this movement on the part of coaches to take place, it must become a point of emphasis in the profession. Currently, coaching effectiveness if wrongly judged by wins and losses. This leads to coaching practices that over emphasize winning to the point of excluding anything that would detract from players' focus on that goal. For coaches to be prepared to capitalize on the investment of their athletes in ways that will produce transformative students and community members, more attention must be paid to professional development in coaching.

Although coaches frequently attend coaching clinics hosted by Nike and other corporate giants, those events give little explicit attention to the development of the athletes as young people. The focus of these professional development seminars is on strategy and winning games. Not to be overlooked here is that coaches choose to go to these clinics, often at their own expense, and they turn out in record numbers. They are there to listen to coaches that are winning in the college and professional ranks, and it is at these clinics that they develop their concept of the industry standard. If these teaching sessions were to provide an emphasis on strategies for developing more complete athletes, but not at the exclusion of sport strategy, coaches would likely incorporate more of this into their programs.

These efforts could begin by drawing from the teachings of coaching legends like John Thompson (former Georgetown University basketball coach), Vivian Stringer (women's basketball coach at Rutgers University), Kay Yao (late women's basketball coach from North Carolina State University), John Wooden (the all time winningest coach in NCAA history) and Phil Jackson (winner of the most NBA championships). All of these coaches emphasize the growth of their players as intellectuals and citizens. They did not de-emphasize the growth of their players as athletes, rather they understood that building their players as whole people would result in better athletes (see (Jackson, 1995; Jamison & Wooden, 1997; Johnson, 2000; Wooden & Tobin, 1998)). Certainly all coaches could benefit from learning about how to define success by studying the philosophies of these coaching legends.

Implications for teacher educators

The well-documented changing of the guard in teaching (NCTAF, 2003) will usher in upwards of one million new teachers, mostly into urban schools, within this decade. Either this group of new teachers will receive training that prepares them to perpetuate the cycle of failure in urban schools or they will be prepared to disrupt it. If the first happens, then we will see another 30–40 years of under-performing urban schools and an opportunity to change those schools will have been missed. For the latter of those two outcomes to happen, these new teachers must be prepared to enter the most challenging classrooms in the country with the types of skills that will allow them to engage in dynamic pedagogy.

For teacher educators this means a recognition that the ways in which we prepare teachers to work in urban schools must change. Schools of education must recognize that teachers that plan to work in urban schools need training that is specific to the issues facing those communities—specialized courses of study that provide teachers with the skill sets that research has shown to be effective in urban classrooms. An infusion of courses specifically designed to prepare teachers to develop pedagogies that grapple with the most pressing issues of inequity confronting urban communities are critical to any genuine commitment to changing outcomes in those schools.

This shift in pedagogical practice inside schools of education can be accomplished through a variety of methods. Course readings can better reflect the growing body of classroom-based research where pedagogical theory is tested, modified, and revised. Additionally, courses can emphasize best practices in urban schools, giving teachers in training the opportunity to speak with, and model after, urban educators that are already effective in the schools where they are going to teach. This can be achieved by bringing successful teachers into education classes. Teacher education courses can also have consistent and carefully planned interactive sessions with students, parents, and community members that have experienced effective classrooms. These key informants can provide grounded perspectives on what worked, how it worked, and why it worked. Equally as important is the rethinking of placement practices to insure that teachers in training are only assigned to classrooms where these types of dynamic pedagogical practices are in motion. This will give them practical models on which to model some of their pedagogy. The inclusion of this multitude of voices will also allow future teachers to see the potential for improving their pedagogy by maintaining dialogues with these groups after they enter the classroom.

This work with teachers should also include the continuing development of veteran teachers to encourage their growth as educators. Classes and summer seminars can be provided for veteran teachers to access and contribute to the latest educational research regarding effective practices in urban schools. These types of scholarly collaborations can only help to expand the dialogues around the potential for growth in classrooms and schools. Partnerships between urban school districts and universities can act as powerful tools for the improvement of day-to-day classroom practices, and can create shared knowledge that is currently inaccessible to practitioners.

Implications for administrators

Administrators have significant influence over the climate at their schools. If the professional climate they help create is one that is supportive of new and cutting edge educational practices, these changes are much more likely to manifest themselves. This does not mean a direct critique of those that are not engaged in these types of programs. Rather, the focus should be positive reinforcement of those staff members that are pursuing such endeavors.

The key to producing this type of work environment is the public recognition of outliers. When a staff produces a few teachers that are particularly successful using these types of pedagogical practices it is vital that these stories be made public. The point is not to belittle those who are not, but to identify those that are so that they can be positioned to share a set of practices that are clearly making a difference. Just as a coach will adjust their system to maximize the special talents of individual players, school leaders use teacher successes to open dialogue about how more teachers can find similar success with this same group of students. Because I believe that most teachers want to be successful with their students, an administration that continually reinforces success stories can build hope and peer pressure to replicate these results. This will require a commitment on the part of administrative teams to identifying their most successful staff members (who may not always be in the classroom) and provide time for professional research and collaboration so that their practices can be better understood and shared. Creating this climate of continuous learning, professionalizes and intellectualizes teachers.

Implications for educational policy makers

The testing fetish has delivered a crippling blow to the advancement of improved pedagogical practices in urban schools. Far too many teachers, new and old, find themselves trapped under the stifling demands of teaching to tests that are poor measures of student learning and ability. These teachers' jobs and the monies their school will receive hinge on their ability to raise scores on tests that require less critical thinking skills and subject knowledge than they do knowledge of test taking shortcuts. Little, if any time, can be set aside for meaningful discussions with students about ways to improve the quality of life of in urban communities or our country at large. Rather, success in our classrooms is now being measured by minimal growth on bar graphs and pie charts, which supposedly reflect the knowledge of the scholars we produce despite numerous studies from highly respected scholars that bankrupt this paradigm (Lipman, 2004; Au, 2009).

Educational policy must reflect our goals in schools. If, indeed, our goal in educating the children of this country is to produce young minds that can appropriately fill in the best possible answer within a specified time constraint, then we are on the right track. Testing has never proven to be the truest measure of a student's knowledge or intellectual potential, and yet we are investing billions as a nation to pursue this measurement tool in our schools. This is not to say that we should abolish testing—it has its place. However, educational policy should position schools to provide authentic multi-modal assessments of student learning that are not exclusive to standardized testing.

I would remind policy makers here of Joan Cone's words after over 30 years in the classroom: schools must be better than society if society is ever going to improve. This wisdom should guide the development of policies and standards for education. Our current policy, focusing instruction on basic skill sets, measured by incessant testing for those skills, will not lead to the production of a genuine love for learning, scholarship or critical thinking skills. It does not take a rocket scientist to figure out what this will mean for the future of our society. However, a genuine commitment to developing and assessing students' critical thinking and knowledge creation will naturally result in students developing the same skill sets we currently hope to develop through testing. Schools must be better than society and our educational policy must reflect this goal.

Final reflection

The accomplishments of the young women in this book each stand alone as an amazing story of resiliency. But, collectively they are a story of hope and possibility for all of us that spend our lives fighting for educational justice. They are proof that what we do makes a difference.

Where are they now?

Mika

Mika recently completed her undergraduate degree in — at Dartmouth College. She is currently enrolled in a pre-med post baccalaureate program at the University of California San Francisco and will be applying to medical schools for admission next school year. Her plan is to return to the community as a doctor. I recently signed her up to come and do some tutoring with our next cohort of 9th graders while she is still in the area.

Ada

Ada attended the University of San Francisco for three years but did not complete her degree. She is currently working fulltime for Alameda County Social Services. She continues to play basketball in a highly competitive Pro-Am league. I am actively recruiting her for tutorial and mentorship work with our new cohort and have initiated conversations about getting her back in school to complete her degree.

Nancy

Nancy attended the University of California, Berkeley for one year, but did not complete her degree. Nancy suffered a serious knee injury late in her first season, the details of which she says she "remembers like the back of my hand". The injury, along with some disagreements with her coach, soured her on the school's basketball program and prompted her withdraw. She is currently happily married, just having her third child. She continues to play basketball, on the same Pro-Am team with Ada. She always aspired to open her own business and says that she intends to return to school and set that plan in the motion within the next year.

Erika

Erika graduated from Oregon State University with a degree in _____. She played four years for the basketball team, despite suffering two very serious knee injuries. After graduation, she returned to Townville and took over the girls' basketball program at Townville High. She just finished her first year as head coach and despite a subpar season by her standards, she's hoping to rebuild the program to its former glory. She recently approached me about returning to school to get her teaching credential so that she can teach and coach full time at Townville High.

Adriana

Adriana graduated from the University of California, Berkeley with a degree in Ethnic Studies. She has a son and is engaged to be married. She works with 3rd to 5th graders at a youth development program in Townville. She too recently met with me to discuss returning to school to get an elementary teaching credential so that she can teach fulltime in an urban school.

Sandra

Sandra attended Menlo College, an elite small private school on the San Francisco peninsula. She left school after one-year citing culture shock and feelings of academic struggles as the primary causes. She currently works full time and did some assistant coaching this season with Erika.

Shayna

Shayna, who was the other student in Erika's class in the LWBP, graduated from California State Polytechnic University with a degree in Sociology. She moved back to Northern California and works in an after school program in a surrounding urban district. She recently met with me to discuss her plans to get her special education teaching credential.

Kendra

Kendra graduated from Townville High the year after I left the LWBP and went on to attend junior college in Texas. She will graduate in May 2010 with a degree in Psychology and Sociology from Houston Baptist University. In a recent electronic chat with me, she wrote, "everything I think I want to do comes back to working with kids".

NOTES

1   Some of these coaches meet the standards of success I've defined in this book and some do not. However, every one of the books on their systems has valuable lessons for teachers. Some the coaches whose books I'd recommend include: Tony Dungy, Mike Krychevski, John Wooden, Kay Yow, Morgan Wooten, and Pat Summitt.

2   In my classes, I like to recruit two pools of students. One group that self-selects based on my reputation for preparing students to matriculate to 4-year universities, and a second group that my colleagues and administrators find particularly challenging to work with and are considered highly likely to quit out of school before finishing.

3   This smoke and mirrors "accountability" game is, of course, rigged such that schools (and teachers) are asked to compete on a playing field that everyone knows is unfair and deliberately slanted to favor the wealthy elite—Akom (2008) has called this "Ameritocracy".

APPENDIX A:
THE PYRAMID of SUCCESS

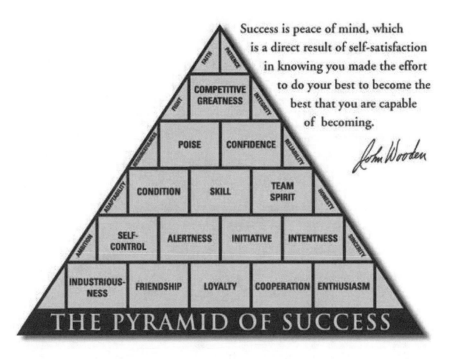

Success is peace of mind, which is a direct result of self-satisfaction in knowing you made the effort to do your best to become the best that you are capable of becoming.

John Wooden

APPENDIX B:
THE DEFINITE DOZEN

THE LWBP DEFINITE DOZEN

"Discipline yourself so that no one else has to."

TO STAY IN THE PROGRAM

1. Be responsible (sit in the front rows);
2. Be respectful (treat people the way you want to be treated; NO MOODY PEOPLE!);
3. Be honest (leaders don't make excuses, they make improvements);
4. Be loyal (handle success like you handle failure);

TO PLAY HERE

5. Work (everyday, everywhere);
6. Play smart (correct your own mistakes);
7. Team before yourself (above all else, character matters);
8. Winning attitude (doubters never win, winners never doubt);

TO BE SUCCESSFUL HERE

9. Communicate (be coachable);
10. Accept your role (know your role and don't try to step out of it);
11. Influence your opponent (make people leave their comfort zone);
12. Be a competitor (never, ever give up).

APPENDIX C: THE DEFINITE DOZEN (2ND EDITION)

THE DEFINITE DOZEN

"Discipline yourself so that no one else has to."

TO ENTER YOUR REVOLUTIONARY STATE OF MIND

1. Be responsible (To yourself, to your family, to your community, to our world.)
2. Be respected, be respectful (Respect yourself. Demand that others respect you. Respect others.)
3. Be honest (Leaders don't make excuses, they make improvements.)
4. Be loyal (Stand alongside those who have the least.)

TO DISCIPLINE YOUR REVOLUTIONARY STATE OF MIND

5. Work (Everyday, everywhere.)
6. Study (To study is a revolutionary duty.)
7. Character over reputation (Character is who you are when no one else is looking. Reputation is who other people say you are.)
8. Believe (Doubters never win, revolutionaries never doubt.)

TO BUILD A SUCCESSFUL REVOLUTION

9. Be self-critical (No revolution is complete without a culture of self-improvement. There is no culture of self-improvement without a culture of self-reflection.)
10. Acknowledge the knowledge (Teach and be teachable.)
11. Build with allies, influence the enemy (Execute the 5 phases: identify, analyze, plan, implement, evaluate.)
12. Be relentless (Never, ever give up.)

APPENDIX D: LA DOCENA DEFINITIVA

LA DOCENA DEFINITIVA

"Disciplínate para que nadie lo haga por ti"
Para entrar en tu estado de mente revolucionaria/o

1. **Se responsable**: (Hacia ti mismo, hacia tu familia, hacia tu comunidad, y hacia nuestro mundo).
2. **Se respetado y se respetuoso**: (Respétate y exige el respeto, respeta a los demás).
3. **Se honesto**: (Un líder no hace excusas, hace mejoramientos).
4. **Se fiel**: (Mantente al lado de los mas necesitados.)

Para disciplinar tu estado de mente revolucionaria/o

5. **Trabaja**: (Todos los días, en todo lugar).
6. **Estudia**: (Estudiar es un deber revolucionario).
7. **Carácter sobre reputación**: (Carácter es quien eres cuando nadie te ve, reputación es lo que otras personas dicen que eres).
8. **Cree**: (Los que dudan nunca ganan y los revolucionarios nunca dudan).

Para construir una revolución exitosa

9. **Se auto critico**: (No hay revolución completa sin una cultura de auto-mejoramiento. No hay cultura de auto-mejoramiento sin una cultura de auto-reflejo).
10. **Reconoce el conocimiento**: (Enseña y acepta la enseñanza).
11. **Edifica con tus aliados e inspira a tus enemigos** : (Ejecuta las cinco fases: identifica, analiza, planea, implementa y evalúa).
12. **Se implacable**: (Nunca, jamás te des por vencido).

APPENDIX E: SUMMER BOOK ANALYSIS GUIDELINES

BOOK ANALYSIS GUIDELINES

Objective: Remember Paulo Freire's advice that "a text to be read is a text to be studied." If it is worth your time to read it, it is equally important that you examine and think deeply about what you have read. DO NOT attempt to prove that you have read the book by summarizing. Instead, your goal should be to examine an issue in the text as it pertains to the characters in the book.

Guidelines: You can choose from any of the following 3 options for your essay:

PSYCHOANALYSIS OF A CHARACTER

In this analysis, you will choose a character from the book and examine their psychology throughout the book. You should map out how the character grows and changes throughout the text. This analysis should focus primarily on what the motivating factors are behind the character's actions. Rather than explaining what happens, or what a certain character does, you should be examining WHY a character does the things they do. Get inside the head of the character and provide a critical analysis of what is motivating the character's actions.

CHARACTER'S INTERNAL OR EXTERNAL STRUGGLE/JOURNEY

In this analysis, you will choose a character that is dealing with issues of personal or external struggle. You will examine the ways in which the character goes through this struggle, focusing on their growth and/or downfall. As with the psychoanalysis, you will need to explore how the character handles the various levels of their struggles and how those struggles impact and influence their actions. However, in this essay, you need to focus explicitly on how *the circumstances* are influencing the character's choices and actions.

COMPARE/CONTRAST OF TWO CHARACTERS

In this analysis, you will need to compare or contrast two characters from the book. The best approach to this essay is to examine the ways in which the two characters respond to similar circumstances or events in the book. If the two characters being compared are similar, you should explain the ways in which their responses to these circumstances are similar. If you feel the characters have contrasting personalities, then use their responses to similar situations to examine how they are different. Your focus should be on an ANALYSIS of the characters' actions and an explanation of what those actions tell us about the characters.

SPECS

- 3-5 pages, type written
- title page w/ your name and date in lower right hand corner and title centered in middle of page
- introductory paragraph must include the book title, the author's name, the character(s) name(s), and your intentions in the essay

DUE DATE: July 26th this is your boarding pass to go to San Diego; No essay, no trip...don't procrastinate!!! Get it done at least a day in advance to avoid any possible catastrophes.

APPENDIX F: WEEKLY PROGRESS REPORT #1

Lady Wildcat Basketball
Teachers' Report of Student Progress

Dear Teachers,

Please fill out this progress report on a weekly basis. This report will allow us to track the student's progress, and to uncover areas where the student might need additional academic support. We provide students with academic tutoring and mentoring, using undergraduates from UC Berkeley on Mondays, Wednesdays, and Fridays from 3:30-5:30 p.m. in Room 324. If you have any questions or concerns about the program, please don't hesitate to call me at home (510)533-6224 or work (510) 435-7233.

-Coach Duncan-Andrade-

Student's Name: _____   Week of _____

	Homework	Tests/Quizzes	Current Overall Grade	Signature	Comments/Missing Work
Period 1	—	Next Week !!	A	Eyn.	go CATS !!!
Period 2	4.8 coming	Find coming JR	OK		Enjoy the break! Ha! Ha
Period 3		8/10	P	KC	ok
Period 4	!!!	!!	A	SXR	!!!
Period 5	N/A	Final Review	A	Eyr	kill the Grapes
Period 6	OK	Passing	Passing		and le Q struggle

Exam on Tues

APPENDIX G: WEEKLY PROGRESS REPORT #2

Lady Wildcat Basketball

Teachers' Report of Student Progress

Dear Teachers,

Please fill out this progress report on a weekly basis. This report will allow us to track the student's progress, and to uncover areas where the student might need additional academic support. We provide students with academic tutoring and mentoring, using undergraduates from UC Berkeley on Mondays, Wednesdays, and Fridays from 3:30-5:30 p.m. in Room 324. If you have any questions or concerns about the program, please don't hesitate to call me at home (510)533-6224 or work (510) 435-7233.

-Coach Duncan-Andrade-

Student's Name: _____   Week of _____

	Homework	Tests/Quizzes	Current Overall Grade	Signature	Comments/Missing Work
Period 1 Reading	begin project for 2nd nine wks - see draft for directions	N/A	B	JW	student should read at home everyday and if possible use
Period 2 Science	review for final	N/A	C+ or B- ?		
Period 3 JROTC	N/A		A		continue to do okay will good participation
Period 4 Computer	good		Passing		
Period 5 Math	much improved	passed	passing ?		
Period 6 English	complete	C-	C	LS	

REFERENCES

Adler, P., & Adler, P. (1985). From idealism to pragmatic detachment: The academic performance of college athletes. *Sociology of Education, 58*, 241–50.

Akom, A. (2003). Reexamining resistance as oppositional behavior: The nation of Islam and the creation of a black achievement ideology. *Sociology of Education, 76*(October), 305–325.

Akom, A. (2008). Ameritocracy and infr-racial racism: Racializing social and cultural reproduction theory in the twenty-first century. *Race, Ethnicity and Education, 11*(3), 205–230.

Alexander, K., Entwisle, D., & Olson, L. (2001) Schools, achievement, anhd inequality: A seasonal perspective. *Education Evaluation and Policy Analysis, 23*(2), 171–191.

American Sports Institute. (1995). *PASS (Promoting achievement in school through sport)*. Video: American Sports Institute.

American Sports Institute. (2008). "The PASS Perspective" taken from http://www.amer-sports.org/progandserv/pass.html on June 22, 2008.

Anyon, J. (1997). *Ghetto schooling: A political economy of urban educational reform*. New York: Teachers College Press.

Apple, M. (1990). *Ideology and curriculum*. (2nd ed.). New York: Routledge.

Apple, M. (1993). *Official knowledge: Democratic education in a conservative age*. New York: Routledge.

Au, W. (2009). Obama, where are thou? Hoping for change in U.S. education policy. *Harvard Educational Review, 79*(2), 309–320.

Banks, J. A. (1994). Ethnicity, class, cognitive, and motivational styles: Research and teaching implications. In J. Kretovicks & E. J. Nussel (Eds.), *Transforming urban education* (pp. 277–290). Boston: Allyn and Bacon.

Berg, B. L. (2001). *Qualitative research methods for the social sciences*. Boston: Allyn and Bacon.

Bourdieu, P. (1973). Cultural reproduction and social reproduction. In R. Brown (Ed.), *Knowledge, education, and cultural change* (pp. 71–112). London: Tavistock.

Bourdieu, P. (1991). Sport and social class. In C. M. A. M. Schudson (Ed.), *Rethinking popular culture*. Berkeley: University of California Press.

Bowles, S., & Gintis, H. (1976). *Schooling in capitalist America: Educational reform and the contradictions of economic life*. New York: Basic Books.

Boyd, T. (1997). *Am I black enough for you?* Bloomington: Indiana University Press.

Braddock, J., Royster, D., Winfield, L., & Hawkins, R. (1991). Bouncing back: Sports and academic resilience among African American males. *Education and Urban Society, 24*(1), 113–131.

California Department of Corrections. (2004). *Facts and figures*. Retrieved December 2004, from http://www.corr.ca.gov/CommunicationsOffice/facts_figures.asp.

California Department of Corrections. (2007). *Pay and benefits*. Retrieved August 2007, from http://www.cdcr.ca.gov/CareerOpportunities/POR/POIndex.html.

California Department of Corrections. (2008). *First quarter 2008, facts and figures.*Retrieved July 3, 2008, from http://www.cdcr.ca.gov/Divisions_Boards/Adult_Operations/Facts_and_Figures.html on.

California Department of Education. (2006). DataQuest. Retrieved October 19, 2006 from http://dq.cde.ca.gov/dataquest.

Cazden, C. (1988). *Classroom discourse: The language of teaching and learning*. Portsmouth, NH: Heinemann.

Coakley, J. J. (1990). *Sport in society: Issues and controversies*. St. Louis: C. V. Mosby Company.

Coleman, J. (1994). Social capital in the creation of human capital. *American Journal of Sociology, 94*(Supplement), S95–S120.

Committee on Public Education. (2001). *Children, adolescents and television* (Policy Statement No. Volume 107, Number 2). Elk Grove Village, IL: American Academy of Pediatrics.

Cone, J. (2003). The construction of low achievement: A study of one detracked senior English class. *Harvard Education Letter, 19*(3), retrieved on December 29, 2008, from http://www.edletter.org/past/issues/2003-mj/teacher.shtml.

Conquergood, D. (1992). On reppin' and rhetoric: Gang representations. Paper presentation at Northwestern University.

Corry, J., & Rothbard, M. (1993). *The secrets to college success* [Video]. Sherman Oaks, CA: Success Films.

Corwin, M. (2000). *And still we rise*. New York: William Morrow & Company.

Cuban, L., & Tyack, D. (n.d.). Mismatch: Historical perspectives on schools and students who don't fit them. Stanford University: unpublished manuscript.

Darling-Hammond, L. (1997). *The right to learn: A blueprint for creating schools that work*. San Francisco: Jossey-Bass.

Darling-Hammond, L. (1998). *New standards, old inequalities: The current challenge for African-American education*. Chicago: National Urban League.

Delpit, L. (1988). The silenced dialogue: Power and pedagogy in educating other people's children. *Harvard Educational Review, 58*(3), 483–502.

Delpit, L. (1995). *Other people's children: Cultural conflict in the classroom.* New York: New Press.

Delpit, L., & Dowdy, J. K. (Eds.). (2002). *The skin that we speak.* New York: New Press.

Dewey, J. (1902). *The child and the curriculum.* Chicago: University of Chicago Press.

Dewey, J. (1938). *Experience and education.* New York: Simon and Schuster.

Du Bois, W. E. B. (1903). *Souls of black folk.* New York: Penguin.

Duncan-Andrade, J. (2004). Toward teacher development for the urban in urban teaching. *Teaching Education Journal, 15*(4), 339–350.

Duncan-Andrade, J. (2005). Your best friend or your worst enemy: Youth Popular culture, pedagogy and curriculum at the dawn of the 21st century. *Review of Education, Pedagogy and Cultural Studies, 26*(4), 313–337.

Duncan-Andrade, J. (2006). Utilizing cariño in the development of research methodologies. In J. Kincheloe, P. Anderson, K. Rose, D. Griffith, & K. Hayes, (Eds.), *Urban education: An encyclopedia* (pp. 451–486). Westport, CT: Greenwood Publishing Group.

Duncan-Andrade, J. (2007). Gangstas, wankstas, and ridas: Defining, developing, and supporting effective teachers in urban schools. *International Journal of Qualitative Studies in Education, 20*(6) (November–December), 617–638.

Duncan-Andrade, J. (2007). Urban youth and the counter-narration of inequality. *Transforming Anthropology, 15*(1), 26–37.

Duncan-Andrade, J., & Morrell, E. (2005). Turn up that radio, teacher: Popular cultural pedagogy in new century urban schools. *Journal of School Leadership, 15*(March), 284–304.

Duncan-Andrade, J., & Morrell, E. (2008). *The art of critical pedagogy.* New York: Peter Lang.

Duncan-Andrade, J. M. R. (2009). Note to educators: Hope required when growing roses in concrete. *Harvard Educational Review, 79*(2), 181–194.

Dunn, K., & S. Villani. (2007). *Mentoring new teachers through collaborative coaching.* San Francisco, CA: WestEd Press.

Durkheim, E. (1933). *The division of labor in society.* New York: Free Press.

Dyson, M. E. (1993). *Reflecting black.* Minneapolis: University of Minnesota Press.

Education Week. (2006). *Quality counts at 10.* Bethesda, MD: Editorial Projects in Education Inc.

Education Week. (2008). *Quality countsreport.* Accessed on July 3, 2008, from http://www.edweek.org/ew/qc/2008/18src.h27.html.

Edwards, H. (1973). *Sociology of sport.* Homewood, IL: Dorsey Press.

Edwards, H. (1983a). Educating black athletes. *The Atlantic Monthly, 252*(2), 31–38.

Edwards, H. (1983b). The exploitation of black athletes. *AGB Reports, 28*, 37–48.

Edwards, H. (1991). Lecture. Berkeley, CA: University of California.

Edwards, H. (1992). Are we putting too much emphasis on sports? *Ebony, 47*(10), 128–130.

Edwards, H. (1994). Black youths' commitment to sports achievement: A virtue-turned tragic-turned-virtue. *Sport, 85*(7), 86.

Edwards, H. (1998). Race, sports and education: African American athletes at a crossroads. *Civil Rights Journal* (Fall), 19–24.

Edwards, H. (2000). The decline of the black athlete. *Color Lines* (Spring), 20–24.

Eitzen, D. S. (1987). The educational experiences of intercollegiate student-athletes. *Journal of Sport and Social Issues, 11*(1 and 2), 15–30.

Eitzen, D. S. (1999). *Fair and foul: Beyond the myths and paradoxes of sport*. Maryland: Rowman and Littlefield.

Entine, J. (2000). *Taboo: Why black athletes dominate sports and why we're afraid to talk about it*. New York: Perseus Book Group.

Fine, M. (1991). *Framing dropouts: Notes on the politics of an urban high school*. New York: State University of New York Press.

Finn, P. (1999). *Literacy with an attitude: Educating working class children in their own self interest*. New York: SUNY Press.

Freire, P. (1970). *Pedagogy of the oppressed*. New York: Continuum.

Freire, P. (1987). *Literacy: Reading the word and the world*. South Hadley, MA: Bergin and Garvey.

Freire, P. (1995). *Pedagogy of hope*. New York: Continuum.

Freire, P. (1998). *Pedagogy of freedom*. Lanham, MD: Rowman and Littlefield.

Gans, H. (1995). *The war against the poor*. New York: Basic Books.

Gay, G. (2000). C*ulturally responsive teaching : Theory, research, and practic*e. New York. Teachers College Press.

Gee, J. (2004). *What video games have to teach us about learning and literacy*. New York: Palgrave.

George, N. (1998). *Hip hop America*. New York: Viking Press.

Ginwright, S., P. Noguera, & J. Cammarota. (2006). *Beyond resistance!: Youth activism and community change*. New York: Routledge.

Giroux, H. (1983). *Theory and resistance in education: A pedagogy for the opposition*. South Hadley, MA: Bergin and Garvey.

Giroux, H. (1992). *Border crossings*. New York: Routledge.

Giroux, H. (1996a). *Fugitive cultures: Race, violence and youth*. New York: Routledge.

Giroux, H. (1996b). Slacking off: Border youth and postmodern education. In C. L. Giroux, Peter McLaren, & Michael Peters (Ed.), *Counter narratives: Cultural studies and critical pedagogies in postmodern spaces*. New York: Routledge.

Giroux, H. (1997). *Channel surfing: Race talk and the destruction of today's youth*. New York: St. Martin's Press.

Giroux, H., & McClaren, P. (Eds.). (1994). *Between borders*. New York: Routledge.

Giroux, H., & Simon, R. (1989). Schooling, popular culture, and a pedagogy of possibility. In H. Giroux & R. Simon (Eds.), *Popular culture, schooling and everyday life*. Granby, MA: Bergin and Garvey.

Giroux, H. A., Lankshear, C., McLaren, P., & Peters, M. (Eds.). (1996). *Counter narratives: Cultural studies and critical pedagogies in postmodern spaces*. New York: Routledge.

Glazer, N. (1995). Scientific truth and the American dilemma. In S. Fraser (Ed.), *The bell curve wars*. New York: Basic Books.

Goldberg, A. D., & Chandler, T. (1995). Sports counseling: Enhancing the development of the high school student-athlete. *Journal of Counseling and Development, 74.*

Goodman, S. (2003). *Teaching youth media: A critical guide to literacy, video production and social change.* New York: Teachers College Press.

Gramsci, A. (1971). *Prison notebooks.* New York: International Publishers.

Grossberg, L. (1994). Bringin' it all back home—Pedagogy and cultural studies. In H. Giroux & P. McLaren (Eds.), *Between borders: pedagogy and the politics of cultural studies.* New York: Routledge.

Haberman, M. (1991). The pedagogy of poverty versus good teaching. In J. Kretovics & E. J. Nussel (Ed.), *Transforming urban education* (pp. 305–314). Boston: Allyn and Bacon.

Hacker, A. (1992). *Two nations: Black and white, separate, hostile, unequal.* New York: Ballantine Books.

Hall, S. (1992). Race, culture and communications: Looking backward and forward at cultural studies. *Rethinking Marxism, 5,* 10–18.

Hall, S. (1996). What is this "black" in black popular culture? In D. K.-H. C. Morley (Ed.), *Critical dialogues in cultural studies* (pp. 465–475). New York: Routledge.

Harris, O., & Hunt, L. (1984). *Race and sports involvement: Some implications of sports for black and white youth.* Paper presented at the American Alliance for Health, Physical Education, Recreation and Dance, Anaheim, CA.

Henry, W. I. (1994). *In defense of elitism.* New York: Doubleday.

Herrnstein, R., & Murray, C. (1994). *The bell curve.* New York: Free Press.

Hill, A. & Wooden, J. (2001). *Be quick but don't hurry.* New York: Simon and Schuster.

Hoberman, J. (1997). *Darwin's athletes.* New York: Houghton Mifflin Company.

Howard, T.C. (2001). Telling their side of the story: African American students' perceptions of culturally relevant pedagogy. *Urban Review, 33*(2), 131–149.

Howard Zinn: History as a political act. (1998). *Revolutionary worker.* Acquired on June 28, 2009, from http://revcom.us/a/v20/980–89/987/zinn.htm.

Hull, G., M. Rose, Fraser, & Castellano. (1991). Remediation as social construct. *College Composition and Communication, 42*(3), 299–329.

Jackson, P. (1995). *Sacred hoops.* New York: Hyperion Books.

James, S. (1994). *Hoop dreams* [Video]. Frederick Marx.

Jamison, S., & Wooden, J. (1997). *Wooden: A lifetime of observations and reflections on and off the court.* Chicago: Contemporary Books.

Jary, D., & Jary, J. (1991). *The HarperCollins dictionary of sociology.* New York: HarperCollins.

Jensen, A. (1969). How much can we boost I. Q. and scholastic achievement. *Harvard Educational Review, 39,* 1–123.

Johnson, N. L. (2000). *The John Wooden pyramid of success.* Los Angeles: Cool Titles.

Katz, M. B. (Ed.). (1993). *The "underclass" debate.* Princeton: Princeton University Press.

Katz, A., & Bender, K. (2002, January 17). Oakland schools rank worst for third year. *Oakland Tribune,* pp. A1 and A9.

Kirsch, J. (2002). *Teaching methodologies: Principles and practices for meaningful educatonal reform.* Marin, CA: American Institute of Sports.

Kirsch, S. (2005). Promoting Achievement in School through Sport (PASS): A Description and Evaluation Study. Paper presented at the roundtable "School Sports: Opportunities and Implications for Teaching and Learning" at the annual meeting of the American Educational Research Association Montreal, Canada.

Kise, J. (2006). *Differentiated coaching.* Thousand Oaks, CA: Corwin Press.

Knowledge is Power Program. (2007). *About KIPP.* Accessed on August 14, 2007, from http://www.kipp.org/01/.

Kohl, H. (1994). *I won't learn from you.* New York: New Press.

Kozol, J. (2005). *Shame of the nation.* New York: Crown Publishers.

Kozol, J. (1991). *Savage inequalities.* New York: Crown Publishers.

Kress, G. (2003). *Literacy in the new media age.* New York: Routledge.

Ladson-Billings, G. (1992). Liberatory consequences of literacy: A culturally relevant instruction for African American students. *Journal of Negro Education, 61*(3), 378–391.

Ladson-Billings, G. (1994). *The dreamkeepers.* San Francisco: Jossey-Bass.

Lee, C. (1993). *Signifying as a scaffold for literary interpretation.* Urbana, IL: NCTE.

Lee, C. (2004). Literacy in the academic disciplines and the needs of adolescent struggling readers. *Adolescent Literacy, Winter/Spring*, 14–25.

Lipman, P. (2004). *High stakes education.* New York: Routledge.

Lochner, L. J., & Moretti, E. (2004). The effect of education on crime: Evidence from prison inmates, arrests and self-reports. *American Economic Review, 94*(1), 155–189.

Lorde, A. (1984). *Sister outsider: Essays and speeches.* Trumansburg, NY: Crossing Press.

Los Angeles Times. (2003, November 24). The guards own the gates. *Los Angeles Times*.

Lucas, T., Henze, R., & Donato, R. (1990). Promoting the success of Latino language minority students: An exploratory study of six high schools. *Harvard Educational Review, 60*(3), 315–340.

Luke, C. (1997). *Technological literacy.* Canaberra: Language Australia Publications.

Luke, C. (1999). What next? Toddler netizens, playstation thumb, techno-literacies. *Contemporary Issues in Early Childhood, 1*(1), 95–100.

Lukes, S. (1973). *Emile Durkheim: His life and work.* London: Allen Lane.

McClendon, Crystal. (1998). Promoting achievement in school through sport (PASS): An Evaluation Study. Unpublished doctoral dissertation, University of Maryland.

McDermott, R., & Varenne, H. (1995). Culture as disability. *Anthropology and Education Quarterly, 26*(3), 324–348.

McLaren, P., & Hammer, R. (1996). Media knowledges, warrior citizenry and postmodern literacies. In H. Giroux, C. Lankshear, P. McLaren, & M. Peters (Eds.), *Counternarratives: Cultural studies and critical pedagogies in postmodern spaces.* New York: Routledge.

MacLeod, J. (1987). *Ain't no makin' it.* Boulder, CO: Westview Press.

Maeroff, G. I. (1988). Withered hopes, stillborn dreams: The dismal panorama of urban schools. *Phi Delta Kappan, 69*, 632–638.

Mahiri, J. (1994). African American males and learning: What discourse in sports offers schooling. *Anthropology and Education Quarterly, 25*(3).

Mahiri, J. (1998). *Shooting for excellence: African American Youth culture in new century schools.* New York: Teachers College Press.

Malkin, M. (2003, January 14, 2003). Hip hop hogwash. *New York Post*.

Marqusse, M. (2000). World games: The U. S. tries to colonize sport. *Color Lines: Race, Culture, Action* (Summer).

Marx, K. (1867). *Capital: A critique of political economy.* (Vol. 1). London: Pelican Books.

Mehan, H. (1996). *Constructing school success.* Boston: Cambridge Press.

Meier, D. (1996). *The power of their ideas: Lessons for America from a small school in harlem.* Boston: Beacon Press.

Meier, D. (1996). *The power of their ideas: Lessons for America from a small school in Harlem.* Boston: Beacon Press.

Melnick, M., & Sabo, D. (1994). Sport and social mobility among African-American and Hispanic athlete. In G. A. W. Eisen (Ed.), *Ethnic experiences in North American sport.* New Jersey: Greenwood Press.

Minton, T. (1999, August 22, 1999). Ahead but already behind. *San Francisco Chronicle*, pp. 4–6.

Moll, L., Amanti, C., Neff, D., & Gonzalez, N. (1992). Funds of knowledge for teaching: Using a qualitative approach to connect homes and classrooms. *Theory into Practice, 31*, 132–141.

Morrell, E. (2004). *Linking literacy and popular culture: Finding connections for lifelong learning.* Norwood, MA: Christopher-Gordon.

Morrell, E., & Duncan-Andrade, J. (2002). Toward a critical classroom discourse: Promoting academic literacy through engaging hip-hop culture with urban youth. *English Journal, 91*(6), 88–92.

Morrell, E., & Duncan-Andrade, J. (2003). What youth do learn in school: Using hip hop as a bridge to canonical poetry. In J. Mahiri (Ed.), *What they don't learn in school: Literacy in the lives of urban youth.* New York: Peter Lang.

Morrow, R., & Torres, C. (1995). *Social theory and education: A critique of theories of social and cultural reproduction.* New York: SUNY Press.

Munoz, C. J. (1989). *Youth, identity, power.* New York: Verso.

NAACP Legal Defense and Educational Fund. (2007). *Dismantling the school-to-prison pipeline.*

National Commission on Teaching and America's Future (NCTAF). (2003). No dream denied: A pledge to America's children (Summary report) (Washington, DC, National Commission on Teaching and America's Future).

Nielson Media Research. (2000). *Report on television.* New York: Nielson Media Research.

Nieto, S. (1992). *Affirming diversity: The sociopolitical context of multicultural education.* New York: Longman.

Noguera, P. (1996). Confronting the Urban in Urban School Reform. *The Urban Review, 28*(1), 1–19.

Noguera, P. (2003). *City schools and the American dream.* New York: Teachers College Press.

Noguera, P., & Akom, A. (2000). Disparities demystified. *The Nation*, June 5, 2000, 29 31.

Oakes, J. (1986). *Keeping track: How schools structure inequality.* New Haven, CT: Yale University Press.

Oakes, J. (1987). Tracking in secondary schools: A contextual perspective. *Educational Psychologist, 22*(2), 129–153.

Oakes, J., & Lipton, M. (2001). *Teaching to change the world.* Boston: McGraw Hill.

Oakland Unified School District. (1997). *Annual report to the community*. Oakland, CA: Oakland Unified Schools.

O'Bryan, S., Braddock, J., & Dawkins, M. (2006). Bringing parents back in: African American parental involvement, extracurricular participation, and educational policy. *Journal of Negro Education, 75*(3) (Summer), 401–414.

Ogbu, J. (1990a). Cross cultural roots of minority child development. In P. Greenfield & Rodney R. Cocking (Eds.). Hillsdale, NJ: L. Erlbaum Associates. [Author Query: Book Title?]

Ogbu, J. (1990b). Minority education in comparative perspective. *Journal of Negro Education, 59*(1), 45–55.

Ogbu, J., & Davis, A. (2003). *Black American students in an affluent suburb*. Mahwah, NJ: Lawrence Erlbaum Associates.

Otto, L., & Alwin, D. (1977). Athletics, aspirations, and attainments. *Sociology of Education, 42*, 102–103.

Parham, W. D. (1993). The intercollegiate athlete: A 1990s profile. *The Counseling Psychologist, 21*(3), 411–429.

Parsons, T. (1951). *The social system*. New York: Free Press.

Payne, R. (2005). *A framework for understanding poverty*. Highlands, TX: Aha Process, Inc.

Pearl, A. (1995). Systemic and institutional factors in chicano school failure. In *Chicano school failure and success: Research and policy agendas for the 1990s*. New York: Falmer Press.

Rist, R. (2002). *The urban school: Factory for failure* (2nd ed.). Edison, NJ: Transaction Publishers.

Rosenthal, R., & L. Jacobson. (1992). *Pygmalion in the classroom: Teacher Expectations and pupils' intellectual development*. Norwalk, CT: Crown House Publishing.

Sacramento Business Journals Inc. (2001, October 16). State touts California as fifth-largest economy in world. *Sacramento Business Journal*.

Schorr, J. (1998, April 7). Custodians clean up in OT. *Oakland Tribune*, pp. 1.

Shulman, J. L., & Bowen, W. G. (2001). *The game of life*. Princeton, NJ: Princeton University Press.

Sizer, T. R. (1992). *Horace's school: Redesigning the American high school*. Boston: Houghton Mifflin.

Snyder, E. (1985). A theoretical analysis of academic and athletic roles. *Sociology of Sport, 2*, 210–217.

Solomon, R. P. (1989). Dropping out of academics. In F. Weis & Petrie (Eds.), *Dropouts from school: Issues, dilemmas and solutions*. New York: SUNY Press.

Solorzano, D., & Delgado-Bernal, D. (2001). Examining transformational resistance through a critical race and latcrit theory framework: Chicana and Chicano students in an urban context. *Urban Education, 36*(3), 308–342.

Stanton-Salazar, R. D. & S. M. Dornbusch. (1995). Social capital and the reproduction of inequality: Information networks among Mexican-origin high school students. *Sociology of Education* 68(2), 116–135.

Steele, S. (1990). *The content of our character: A new vision of race in America*. New York: St. Martin's Press.

Suskind, R. (1999). *A hope in the unseen*. New York: Broadway.

Svare, B. (2003). *Crisis on our playing fields: What everyone should know about our out of control sports culture and what we can do to change it.* Delmar: Sports Reform Press.

Tabb, W. K. (1970). The black ghetto as colony. *The political economy of the black ghetto* (pp. 21–34). New York: W.W. Norton and Company.

Tharp, R., & Gallimore, R. (1976). What a coach can teach a teacher. *Psychology Today*, 75–78.

Thernstrom, A. & Thernstrom, S. (2004). *No excuses: Closing the racial gap in learning.* New York: Simon & Schuster.

U. C. Accord. (2006). Educational opportunity high school report. *Indicators project.* Los Angeles, CA, University of California at Los Angeles: 1–20.

U. S. Department of Labor. (2003). *National occupational employment and wage estimates.* Washington, DC: U. S. Department of Labor.

Valdes, G. (1996). *Con respeto: Bridging the distances between culturally diverse families and schools.* New York: Teachers College Press.

Valencia, R. & D. Solórzano. (1997). Contemporary deficit thinking. In R. Valencia (Ed.) *The evolution of deficit thinking: Educational though and practice* (pp. 160–210). London, UK: Falmer Press.

Valenzuela, A. (1999). *Subtractive schooling: U.S.-Mexican Youth and the politics of caring.* New York: SUNY Press.

Vygotsky, L. S. (1978). *Mind in society.* Cambridge, MA: Harvard University Press.

Wenger, E. (1999). *Communities of practice: Learning, meaning, and identity.* Cambridge: Cambridge University Press.

Wald, J., & Losen, D. J. (Eds.). (2003). *Deconstructing the school-to-prison pipeline: New directions for youth development.* Indianapolis, IN: Jossey-Bass.

Waquant, L. (2000). Whores, slaves and stallions: Language of exploitation and accomodation among prizefighters. *Body and society* (Special issue on commodifying bodies).

Weis, L. (1985). *Between two worlds: Black students in an urban community college.* Boston: Routledge & Kegan Paul.

West, C. (1999). The new cultural politics of difference. In C. West (Ed.), *The new cultural politics of difference* (pp. 119–139). New York: Basic Books.

Wideman, J. E. (2001). *Hoop roots.* Boston: Houghton Mifflin.

Wiggins, D. (1994). The notion of double-consciousness and the involvement of black athletes in American sport. In G. A. D. W. Eisen (Ed.), *Ethnicity and sport in North American history and culture.* London: Praeger.

Williams, R. (1989). *Culture.* London: Fontana.

Williams, R. (1991). Base and superstructure in marxist cultural theory. In C. Mukerji & M. Schudson (Eds.), *Rethinking popular culture: Contemporary Perspectives in Cultural Studies* (pp. 407–423). Berkeley, CA: University of California Press.

Willis, P. (1981). *Learning to labor.* New York: Columbia University Press.

Wilson, W. J. (1996). *When work disappears: The world of the new urban poor.* New York: Vintage Books.

Wooden, J., & Tobin, J. (1998). *They call me coach.* Chicago: Contemporary Books.

Woodson, C. G. (1933). *The miseducation of the Negro.* New Jersey: Associated Publishers.

Zirin, D. (2005). *What's my name fool.* Chicago: Haymarket Books.

INDEX

Studies in the Postmodern Theory of Education

General Editors
Joe L. Kincheloe & Shirley R. Steinberg

Counterpoints publishes the most compelling and imaginative books being written in education today. Grounded on the theoretical advances in criticalism, feminism, and postmodernism in the last two decades of the twentieth century, Counterpoints engages the meaning of these innovations in various forms of educational expression. Committed to the proposition that theoretical literature should be accessible to a variety of audiences, the series insists that its authors avoid esoteric and jargonistic languages that transform educational scholarship into an elite discourse for the initiated. Scholarly work matters only to the degree it affects consciousness and practice at multiple sites. Counterpoints' editorial policy is based on these principles and the ability of scholars to break new ground, to open new conversations, to go where educators have never gone before.

For additional information about this series or for the submission of manuscripts, please contact:

> Joe L. Kincheloe & Shirley R. Steinberg
> c/o Peter Lang Publishing, Inc.
> 29 Broadway, 18th floor
> New York, New York 10006

To order other books in this series, please contact our Customer Service Department:

> (800) 770-LANG (within the U.S.)
> (212) 647-7706 (outside the U.S.)
> (212) 647-7707 FAX

Or browse online by series:
> www.peterlang.com